WRITING ACROSS
THE COLOR LINE

A VOLUME IN THE SERIES
Studies in Print Culture and the History of the Book

EDITED BY
Greg Barnhisel
Robert A. Gross
Joan Shelley Rubin
Michael Winship

WRITING | ACROSS THE COLOR LINE

U.S. PRINT CULTURE AND THE RISE OF ETHNIC LITERATURE, 1877–1920

LUCAS A. DIETRICH

UNIVERSITY OF MASSACHUSETTS PRESS

Amherst and Boston

ISBN 978-1-62534-487-8 (paper); 486-1 (hardcover)

Designed by Sally Nichols
Set in Linotype Palatino
Printed and bound by Maple Press, Inc.
Cover design by Rebecca Neimark, Twenty-Six Letters

Library of Congress Cataloging-in-Publication Data

Names: Dietrich, Lucas A., author.
Title: Writing across the color line : U.S. print culture and the rise of
ethnic literature, 1877–1920 / Lucas A. Dietrich.
Description: Amherst : University of Massachusetts Press, 2020. | Series:
Studies in print culture and the history of the book | Based on the
author's dissertation (doctoral)—University of New Hampshire, 2015. |
Includes bibliographical references and index.
Identifiers: LCCN 2019042839 | ISBN 9781625344861 (hardcover) | ISBN
9781625344878 (paperback) | ISBN 9781613767320 (ebook) | ISBN
9781613767337 (ebook)
Subjects: LCSH: Literature publishing—United States—History—19th
century. | Literature publishing—United States—History—20th century.
| American literature—Minority authors—History and criticism. |
American literature—Minority authors—Publishing. | Authors and
publishers—United States—History. | Authors and readers—United
States—History.
Classification: LCC Z480.L58 D54 2020 | DDC 810.9/8—dc23
LC record available at https://lccn.loc.gov/2019042839

British Library Cataloguing-in-Publication Data
A catalog record for this book is available from the British Library.

A portion of chapter 1 first appeared as "On Commission: María
Amparo Ruiz de Burton and the J. B. Lippincott & Co. Job Printing
Department," *The Papers of the Bibliographical Society of America* 113, no. 4
(December 2019): 395–408. Copyright © 2019 Bibliographical Society of
America. A portion of chapter 2 was previously published as "Charles
W. Chesnutt, Houghton Mifflin, and the Racial Paratext," *MELUS:
Multi-Ethnic Literature of the United States* 41, no. 4 (2016): 166–195.
A portion of chapter 4 first appeared, in an early form, as "'At the
Dawning of the Twentieth Century': W. E. B. Du Bois, A. C. McClurg
& Co. and the Early Circulation of *The Souls of Black Folk*," *Book History*
20 (2017): 307–329. Copyright © 2017 The Society for the History of
Authorship, Reading & Publishing.

For my Mother and Father,
and for Lindsey

CONTENTS

(-uff) : |b|bl|c|handicuff|p|sc|st| (字) ? enough
(-ull) : |c|d|(f)|g|h|n°| (p)f sk| (字) ? { rough
(-uss) |f| tr| (字) ? { tough (字) ?

(a/e/i/o/u) (字) ?

(-cept) | kept | |ac|con|deception|ex|inception) intercept|
|misconcept| per| pre |reception| un-|
(-ject) : |ab| de | e |(in~tion)| ob|pro| re|

(ack) : |æk| |ab|b|bl|cr|h|feed b|L|p|back p|qu|r|
(eck) |s| sh|sm|sn|
(ick)
(ock)
(uck)

(字) ?

ACKNOWLEDGMENTS

It is my pleasure to acknowledge the support I have received during the research and composition of this book, and I would like to begin by thanking some of the many professors who have influenced my work. At the University of New Hampshire, Delia Konzett, Sean Moore, and Reginald Wilburn offered helpful guidance throughout my doctoral program. Their continued encouragement and feedback have been essential for the book's development. I was also fortunate to work with UNH professors Brigitte Bailey, Robin Hackett, Lucy Salyer, Siobhan Senier, Laura Smith, and David Watters. At Boston College, I worked with Robert Kern, Tina Klein, Paul Lewis, James Najarian, Carlo Rotella, Min Song, and Lad Tobin. Special thanks to Christopher Wilson, whose course at BC sparked my interest in nineteenth-century U.S. print culture, and who has remained a model of scholarly generosity ever since. Sarah Way Sherman, my dissertation adviser, has my deepest gratitude. For nearly a decade now, Sarah has found productive ways to challenge my writing and thinking, and she has done so with an almost baffling degree of responsiveness and grace.

Many other people have offered feedback for the project. Through Rare Book School, I have received advice from John Garcia, Juliet Sperling, Blevin Shelnutt, Megan Peiser, E. Haven Hawley, Jack Chen, William Stroebel, Todd Pattison, Steffi Dippold, and David Whitesell. Also at RBS, Michael Winship became a mentor and a crucial source of wisdom and support. At the Futures of American Studies Institute, I workshopped a draft of chapter 2 with Melissa Adams-Campbell, John Burdick, Ivy Schweitzer, and Amanda Stuckey. Through the New England American Studies Association, I have been fortunate to work with M. M. Dawley, Dan Graham, Bonnie Miller, Ben Railton, and Jonathan Silverman. As I published portions of the project in *MELUS, Book History*, and *The Papers of the Bibliographical Society of America,* I received helpful commentary from my anonymous reviewers and from editors Gary Totten, Greg Barnhisel, and David Gants.

For their conversation and perspective, I want to thank so many friends and colleagues: Jeff Noel, Ethan Whittet, Stephen Siperstein, Mike Anderson Campbell, Emma Katherine Atwood, Saman Nouri, Kristin Stelmok, James Finley, Eden Wales-Freedman, Shauna Wight, Beth Sheckler, Catherine Welter, Matthew Cheney, Mike Haselton, Jin Lee, Christopher Dingwall, Michaël Roy, Jonathan Senchyne, Marlowe Daly-Galeano, Xine Yao, Martha Cutter, Lori Harrison-Kahan, Mary Chapman, Stephanie Browner, Desiree Henderson, Jennifer Tuttle, Robert Wauhkonen, Christine Evans, Greg Schnitzspahn, Jeff Diluglio, LaDonna Bridges, Ally Chisholm, Joey Gould, John Sharko, Desmond McCarthy, and Tim Sullivan. I owe a significant debt to countless librarians, archivists, and administrative staff at the universities and libraries where I have worked. And I must also thank my students whose thoughtful discussion and writing are an inspiration.

My scholarship has been funded through a variety of sources. A Dissertation-Year Fellowship from the University of New Hampshire Graduate School provided essential support for an initial draft of this book. A Northeast Modern Language Association Fellowship at the Newberry Library allowed me to perform archival research on A. C. McClurg and Company. A NeMLA Summer Fellowship allowed me to travel to Fisk University to conduct research in the Charles W. Chesnutt and W. E. B. Du Bois papers. An Andrew W. Mellon Foundation Fellowship supported my research on María Amparo Ruiz de Burton at the Library Company of Philadelphia and the Historical Society of Pennsylvania. I am also grateful for scholarships from Rare Book School and for professional development funding from Lesley University.

I would be remiss if I did not thank my editor and the staff at the University of Massachusetts Press. Brian Halley is terrific and has provided sharp editorial guidance as this book made its way toward publication.

The book's anonymous reviewers offered criticism that was generous and constructive. Sally Nichols and Rachael DeShano brought the book through production and design, and Ivo Fravashi helped to polish the final manuscript. I am so pleased to be a part of the Studies in Print Culture and the History of the Book series, and I am grateful to the Editorial Advisory Board and the Press Committee.

Lastly, an acknowledgment of close friends and family: Niles and Mike (among other old friends), Jordan, my grandparents, my aunts and uncles and cousins, my nephews, and my in-laws. There are too many to list individually. My three brothers supported my writing as brothers might—prodding me to work, reminding me of my limits, and celebrating achievements when they came. My son, Ben, arrived not long before this project's completion, and he has given me a new sense of wonder. This book is dedicated to my parents, for all of their love, and to Lindsey, my favorite reader.

WRITING ACROSS
THE COLOR LINE

INTRODUCTION

In its first three issues of the twentieth century, the *Atlantic Monthly* published a trilogy of autobiographical essays by Native American author Zitkala-Ša: "Impressions of an Indian Childhood," "The School Days of an Indian Girl," and "An Indian Teacher among Indians."[1] The series traces Zitkala-Ša's childhood and adolescent life as she moved from the Yankton Sioux reservation, through Quaker boarding school, and on to become a teacher at the Carlisle Indian Industrial School. This was a landmark publication for the *Atlantic Monthly*, recognizing a Native American author's place alongside well-known writers such as William Dean Howells, Henry James, Sarah Orne Jewett, and Edith Wharton. As Dexter Fisher notes in her foreword to the 1985 republication of Zitkala-Ša's *American Indian Stories*, this was also "one of the first attempts by a Native American woman to write her own story without the aid of an editor, an interpreter, or an ethnographer."[2] Published through the *Atlantic*, the series asked a predominantly white audience to consider a Native American writer's experience of cultural hybridity and coerced assimilation.

The extent to which *Atlantic Monthly* readers may have empathized with Zitkala-Ša's life story is a more complicated matter. As with all writing, the essays are open to interpretation. Yet this is particularly true of Zitkala-Ša's autobiographical essays because they are written in the style of literary realism. Even as they describe complex issues of race and nation, the essays depict the author's experience without offering any editorial comment or didactic message. When Zitkala-Ša initially submitted "Impressions of an Indian Childhood" to the *Atlantic Monthly*, editorial assistant William B. Parker reviewed it first. In a letter written on September 20, 1899, Parker responds to the essay and asks that Zitkala-Ša submit additional work for review. In a telling phrase, Parker describes his interest in this "sketch of an Indian convert to white man's ways."[3] For Parker, Zitkala-Ša told a story of ethnic integration, of conversion and assimilation. Yet the Carlisle Indian Industrial School, where Zitkala-Ša worked as "An Indian Teacher among Indians," read the essays rather differently. The trilogy outraged the founder of the school, Richard Henry Pratt, who soon terminated Zitkala-Ša's employment.[4]

Meanwhile, the *Atlantic Monthly*'s editor, Bliss Perry, was aware of these different interpretive possibilities. Reviewing Zitkala-Ša's essays for publication, after his assistant's initial reading, Perry noted that they "will prove to be effective presentations of the cause you have at heart."[5] In contrast to his assistant's interpretation of the essays as a story of assimilation, Perry saw a deeper purpose at the heart of these stories. Yet this "cause" is not clearly identified. With Victorian reserve, Perry recognizes Zitkala-Ša's effective writing but does not paraphrase or translate the essays into his own language. In fact, the *Atlantic Monthly* would draw on this ambiguity when advertising the series (figure 1), describing how Zitkala-Ša "throws a good deal of light upon the vexed problem of Indian education." What type of light will the reader see? Is the "vexed problem of Indian education" the problem of the Indian or the education? A skillful editor, Perry seems to have recognized that the ambiguities of Zitkala-Ša's autobiography could lure a wider audience into the text.

This pattern of circulation was surprisingly common for authors of color as they entered the literary marketplace at the turn of the twentieth century. In fact, it may serve as a template for the ways multiethnic authors entered the literary realm and sought to influence a national, predominantly white audience, despite harsh criticism. Here, a Native American author writes her own life story in a realistic style, open to interpretation. The *Atlantic Monthly*, a prestigious literary magazine, accepted the stories for publication, lending its name and cultural capital to Zitkala-Ša's writing. Indeed, the *Atlantic Monthly* published Zitkala-Ša's work enthusiastically, soliciting additional essays and advertising the trilogy among its top publications for the new century. At the same time, these essays provoked controversy among readers

FIGURE 1. Advertisement for Zitkala-Ša's autobiographical essays. From Houghton Mifflin's Holiday Bulletin 1899, call no. 2003–197, box 7, Houghton Library, Harvard University.

of the *Atlantic Monthly* and effectively ended Zitkala-Ša's employment with the Carlisle Indian Industrial School.[6] Returning to her home reservation to care for her mother, Zitkala-Ša married Raymond Bonnin (also a Yankton Dakota), and moved to the Uintah and Oraye reservation in Utah—immersing herself in the native community as a teacher, mother, and Indian rights activist. Despite appearing in *Atlantic* and *Harper's* in the early years of the twentieth century, she would not return to literary publication for more than a decade.

Writing across the Color Line recovers such arbitrations and exchanges, examining the social dynamics of U.S. ethnic literature within the sphere of commercial trade publication. The book historicizes the late nineteenth century as a period of great possibility for ethnic literature, a period that tested the boundaries of American artistic production and literary culture. At the same time, it sheds light on the tenacity of racist attitudes that dominated the literary marketplace. While select publishers invested in writers of color in hopes that more diverse literature could attract a widespread audience, these efforts were harshly rejected within mainstream literary culture. White readers, guided by racist attitudes, denied twice over the creative potential of emergent multiethnic literature. This is the story of ethnic authors interacting with well-known trade publishers in the decades surrounding the turn of the twentieth century.

U.S. PRINT CULTURE AND THE RISE OF ETHNIC LITERATURE

The late nineteenth century was the first period in U.S. history in which writers of color published literary fiction through commercial trade presses. This is not to say that multiethnic literature appeared for the first time in this era. New for ethnic authors of the late nineteenth century, however, was access to major channels of literary publication and distribution. In contrast to the limited circulations of antebellum periodicals such as the *Anglo-African Review* and the *Cherokee Phoenix,* in the late nineteenth century a wave of ethnic authors were able to address a wider audience, composed predominantly of white readers, with the support of long-established and well-funded publishing houses. These authors sought to achieve national success and literary recognition through the imprimatur of trade publishers. They published in venues that stretched from the *Atlantic Monthly* to Chicago's A. C. McClurg and Company to California's *Land of Sunshine.*

Yet writers of color who entered this literary marketplace were often compelled to take on ambiguous tactics of representation. They deployed styles of literary realism and regionalism in a way that was nonthreatening, satirical, and open to interpretation. Indeed, those who analyze late nineteenth-century ethnic literature have often turned to the aesthetic features of regionalism and realism when describing the emergence of ethnic literature. In his 1993 book *Cultures of Letters,* for instance, Richard Brodhead argues that the vogue for literary regionalism opened up a space for marginalized authors. As Brodhead describes it, regionalism functioned as a form of ethnography, "purporting to grasp an alien cultural system."[7] Regionalist fiction often viewed local cultures as foreign and outmoded, as remnants of history superseded by industrial progress. Regionalism offered readers a tour of a local culture on the verge of disappearance. Yet marginalized authors appropriated this regional fascination for their own purposes, using local color fictions to simultaneously enter and subvert their readers' expectations. In their hands, regional cultures are not merely backward or alien but energetic and dynamic, brimming with life. Numerous immigrant and ethnic authors took advantage of this possibility, including Abraham Cahan, Charles W. Chesnutt, Paul Laurence Dunbar, Finley Peter Dunne, Sui Sin Far, and Zitkala-Ša.

Alongside literary regionalism, writers of color adopted a number of other artistic strategies to accomplish the double maneuver of entry and subversion. The role of the ethnic trickster has particular relevance in this era, and dialect writing and caricature also proliferated. Scholarly critics have often emphasized how writers of color employed these ambiguous strategies to subvert commonplace stereotypes and racist attitudes. Gavin Jones's book *Strange Talk,* for instance, describes the double meanings of dialect. On the one hand, for a predominantly white audience, dialect writing helped to contain and control the possibility of ethnic menace. It made fun of ethnic stereotypes. On the other hand, dialect writing also encoded ethnic resistance, elevating folk culture and minority speech to the level of high art.[8] These ethnic voices were published as literary fiction in some of the most well-regarded and widely distributed publications in America. Elizabeth Ammons and Henry B. Wonham make comparable arguments on the topics of tricksterism and caricature.[9] For Wonham, even as ethnic caricature appeals to its white readers' fantasies of supremacism, the ludicrous form of caricature nevertheless undermines the very idea of racial types, which can exist only as misrepresentations.[10] In other words, authors and artists frequently deployed ethnic caricature in order to critique the absurdity of the depiction itself. Generally, when ethnic authors of the late nineteenth century sought to address a predominantly white audience, they relied on these ambiguous strategies of representation. These artistic strategies, by their very nature, had the potential both to subvert and to reinscribe ethnic stereotypes and racist attitudes.

Yet while critics have paid significant attention to the aesthetic dynamics of regionalism, dialect, and caricature, less is known about the production, distribution, and reception of late nineteenth-century ethnic literature. If writers of color frequently relied on self-caricature and tricksterism in order to influence a white audience, how was their work understood and received? In the case of Zitkala-Ša, for instance, what editorial assistant William B. Parker understood as the story of "an Indian's conversion to white man's ways," the Carlisle Indian Industrial School read, perhaps more accurately, as a sharp critique of forced assimilation—and as grounds for dismissal. Thus while it is important to recognize the subversive potential of this literature, it is also important to recognize the ways in which this work could be misread, and the extent to which such misreadings proliferated.

Consider Bret Harte's 1870 poem "Plain Language from Truthful

James," published in the *Overland Monthly*. The poem depicts a game in which the white narrator, "Truthful James," and his card-dealer companion—with their sleeves stuffed full of "aces and bowers"—cheat against a Chinese player, Ah Sin.[11] In the middle of their con, the narrator accidentally lays down the same right bower as Ah Sin, a card that should appear only once in the deck. Yet the narrator and his dealer companion are not punished for cheating. Rather, they violently wrestle Ah Sin to the ground, laying the blame on "Chinese cheap labor." Harte's poem was meant to satirize the hypocrisy of anti-Chinese attitudes. The title of the poem, with its repeated claim on veracity, calls into question the "plain language" of its "truthful" white narrator. Yet despite Harte's satiric intent, the poem became popular for its caricatured depiction of "the heathen Chinee" and his "ways that are dark." Indeed, proponents of Chinese immigration exclusion adopted this racist language as a popular refrain, and Harte soon regretted having written the poem.[12] In other words, while Harte had intended to use ambiguous caricature to subvert racist hypocrisy, a popular audience understood the poem as reinforcing white supremacist attitudes.

I find myself questioning the subversive impact of dialect writing, caricature, and regionalism in the late nineteenth century. To what extent would readers at the time have interpreted caricatured images with attention and nuance? Would they have sympathized with the forms of ethnic resistance encoded in these texts? What was the political efficacy of these ambiguous literary strategies as they targeted a white audience? While dialect writing and caricature may rely on a self-undermining contradiction (i.e., the caricatured subject can exist only *as* a fictional representation), it does not necessarily follow that readers were aware of this contradiction. The repressed awareness of a white American is quite different from the painful double consciousness of a racialized ethnic minority—even while both derive from the contradictions of racism. And the evil twin of this subversive literary ambiguity, as Amy Kaplan and Matthew Frye Jacobson have described, is the violent hypocrisy of empire.[13] This book shows that it is possible, to a degree, to know how a popular audience reacted to such ambiguous depictions of race. Examining the circulation of literary texts, my project highlights crucial distinctions in how this racial ambiguity was produced and received.

In terms of production, the creators of ethnic literature were attuned to the ways racial ambiguity could target a range of readers with different interpretive sensibilities. The publishers I examine were extraordinarily aware of these possibilities, and worked deliberately to amplify these double meanings. They invested substantial money to help produce, advertise, and distribute multiethnic writing for a literary public. They believed the literary marketplace was opening up in favor of these minority voices. The authors I examine hoped to guide readers into awareness of the ambiguities and contradictions of race. Often times, they approached their audience through strategies of satire, irony, mimicry, and repetition—strategies that go hand in hand with tricksterism, dialect, and caricature. These literary and rhetorical strategies do not directly confront racist attitudes, but do so cunningly, reflecting the contradictions of racism itself. In these efforts, the authors I consider also leverage their own authorial personas; each was attuned to how pen names, portraits, and biographical statements might emphasize their ethnic background or allow them to pass as white. As with caricature and dialect, writers of color deployed these tactics strategically, so that the reader might deal with the ambiguities of the literary text, work through stages of cognitive dissonance, and arrive at more nuanced understandings of ethnic and national identity.

On the other end of this transmission of the text—or what Robert Darnton has called the "communications circuit"[14]—I consider how the work of ethnic authors was received and reviewed by a predominantly white audience. This audience, I argue, was not pulled in two directions by the ambiguities of the text, but rather applied the contradictions of white supremacism like a switch, to cut off the communications circuit. As I will show, a predominantly white audience almost never examined caricature, dialect, or ethnic tricksters for their subversive potential. Rather, white readers decisively rejected this critique through defensive misreading and hostile criticism. On the one hand, they often interpreted hyperbolic use of racial caricature as literary realism, fulfilling and confirming white fantasies of racial domination. On the other hand, they explicitly rejected any text that was critical of U.S. white supremacism in a hostile backlash of reentrenched racist attitudes. In general, then, white readers interpreted the subversions of late nineteenth-century ethnic literature through blind denial or, when these subversive elements could not be ignored, they rejected the literary and cultural merit of the text itself. In this way, readers refused the value and status of writing that they understood to challenge white

supremacism. Moreover, because racism so deeply defined the interpretive outlook of white readers, their reactions shift almost seamlessly
from one form of denial to the next.

Tracing this communications circuit, from author and publisher to
reader, I argue that the turn of the century was an era of great potential
for U.S. ethnic literature, denied by the white literary marketplace, only
to reemerge among niche audiences and counterpublics in future generations.[15] Indeed, it is only by understanding this dynamic—whereby
white readers misread and neglected the ethnic critique—that one can
see the importance of writers such as Zitkala-Ša, María Amparo Ruiz
de Burton, Charles W. Chesnutt, W. E. B. Du Bois, and Sui Sin Far *in
being rejected* within the realm of commercial literature. These authors
brought a latent hypocrisy to the surface and pressured a popular audience to confront the contradictions of racism. Approaching this audience, the authors were certainly aware they might initiate conflict and
disruption: it motivated their writing and the double-voiced literary
tactics they employed. Approaching well-known trade publishers, they
were also mindful of the survival of their books and of more long-term
receptions in posterity. Like so many authors and artists, they hoped
to weather contemporary criticism and achieve influence among the
canon of great authors. Commercial publication, beset with compromise and rejection, nevertheless allowed their work to circulate among
a wider national audience. Indeed, through the publication of their
books, all of the authors I examine exercised long-term influence on
coteries of artists and intellectuals. Their work has been better understood in posterity, even while we should not confuse such readings
with those that predominated historically.

READING PUBLISHERS' ARCHIVES FOR ETHNIC LITERARY HISTORY

Scholarship in book history has not traditionally been applied to the
work of writers of color. Rather, detailed attention to issues of bibliography and editing has often focused on the most canonical texts of
Western civilization. As George Hutchinson and John K. Young note in
their collection, *Publishing Blackness*, "With its philological roots in the
Bible, medieval scrolls, and Shakespeare's folios and quartos, textual
scholarship was slow to come to African American literature."[16] Yet
if critical race studies and book history rarely shared agendas in the
twentieth century, they are increasingly in dialogue in the twenty-first.

For book historians, the rise of digital media has led to an explosion of interest in technologies of texts—efforts to historicize a print culture that is rapidly changing.[17] At the same time, bibliographical scholarship has moved beyond its focus on authorial intentions.[18] Rather than defining the ideal copy-text through authorial intentions, book historians increasingly view textual production as a social process, involving numerous actors and cultural forces.[19]

This shift has particular relevance for analysis of the writing of marginalized people, where authorial agency is often especially limited in relationship to the publisher. Consider, for instance, the white-authored prefaces that surround so many slave narratives, what John Sekora has described as "white envelopes" for the "black message."[20] In such instances, the publisher's framework introduces the text to its audience and can exert a powerful influence on the reader's interpretations.[21] The author's intentions may be in conflict with the process of book production, so that the text is best examined through a lens of social relationships. Moreover, such examples may be seen as particularly salient instances of book production. In recent years, as a result of this shift, numerous scholars have made major contributions to the study of U.S. ethnic print cultures.[22] Indeed, in a 2014 essay, Johanna Drucker conceptualizes the future of book history scholarship as a study of "bibliographical alterities."[23]

My project builds on this scholarship, using the history of books to examine the production, distribution, and reception of U.S. ethnic literature at the turn of the century. I believe that meaning develops at all points where people engage with a textual medium, and I am interested in the process by which authors adjust their artistic techniques, from one project to the next, in response to audience reactions, as the communications circuit spirals through time. My project thus tracks the social relationships that surround the text as it circulates.[24] How was the form of a book influenced by its publishers and editors? How was it marketed, distributed, and sold? How was it understood and criticized by readers? I respond to these questions, in large part, by conducting research in the archives and business records of the publishers with whom authors of color interacted: the *Atlantic Monthly* and its parent company Houghton Mifflin, Philadelphia's J. B. Lippincott and Company, the so-called yellow journalism of the *New York World*, and Chicago publisher A. C. McClurg and Company.

In doing so, my project recovers a number of startling facts about late nineteenth-century ethnic literature. María Amparo Ruiz de Burton's novel *Who Would Have Thought It?*, the earliest-known Mexican American novel in English, was published almost in camouflage, listed in the Lippincott catalog anonymously alongside a number of other sensational novels.[25] It was manufactured to look like any other sensational novel at the time. In the case of Charles W. Chesnutt, a limited edition of *The Conjure Woman* (1899) was produced on large linen paper. It was sold on subscription and bound with unopened pages.[26] This special large-paper version, and not the trade edition, was the first book of African American fiction that Houghton Mifflin published. And notably, Chesnutt satirized such unopened collector's editions in his last short story published in the *Atlantic Monthly*.[27] Yet the large-paper edition of *The Conjure Woman* has received almost no critical attention. Somewhat similarly, the editor for W. E. B. Du Bois's *The Souls of Black Folks*, Francis G. Browne, has been almost universally misidentified by scholars.[28] Browne actively solicited *The Souls of Black Folk*, a collection of essays that Du Bois had not planned to publish in book form. Browne also demonstrated an interest in ethnic literature more broadly and was responsible for publishing the first books of Jewish American and Asian American fiction in English.[29] Overall, then, my project uses the history of books to examine how late nineteenth-century ethnic literature sparked conversations about race, identity, and nation.

AUTHORS OF COLOR

The examples I consider can be viewed as a constellation of multiethnic authors who published literary fiction for a national audience in the late nineteenth century. Born in 1832, María Amparo Ruiz de Burton was raised by an elite landowning family in Baja California, and grew up at the time of the U.S.-Mexican War. In 1848, as the war ended, she and her family traveled as refugees to the town of Monterey in Alta California and became American citizens.[30] Within a year, at the age of seventeen, María Amparo Ruiz married the U.S. Army captain Henry S. Burton. She later moved to the East Coast as her husband served in the Union Army. She wrote and published two novels in her lifetime, *Who Would Have Thought It?* in 1872 and *The Squatter and the Don* in 1885. Charles W. Chesnutt's writing generally "ran along the color line,"[31] and he was himself a light-skinned African American who could be perceived as white. Chesnutt is the first known African American writer to publish fiction under the imprint of Houghton Mifflin, and my analysis traces the path by which he entered and exited this prestigious venue. Finley Peter Dunne was a second-generation Irish American, raised in Chicago. Dunne worked in the city's burgeoning newspaper industry as a teenager, and came of age as Chicago itself rose to prominence. As an Irish American, he occupies a position on the borders of whiteness,[32] and he serves as a sort of "control" case in my overall project, testing the limits of white ethnicity. W. E. B. Du Bois's *The Souls of Black Folk* is now regarded as one of the most important literary texts of the twentieth century, and it is a foundational work for African American belles lettres. Edith Eaton/Sui Sin Far is one of the earliest authors of Asian descent to publish a book of fiction in the United States. She lived in England, Canada, Jamaica, and the United States, working as a journalist, stenographer, and short story writer. Sui Sin Far published only one book in her lifetime, *Mrs. Spring Fragrance,* although she also wrote a novel that was never published and has since disappeared.[33]

Zitkala-Ša was born Gertrude Simmons in 1876 on the Yankton Sioux Agency in South Dakota. She was raised as a traditional Dakota until 1884, when missionaries recruited her and other Dakota children to attend White's Manual Labor Institute, a Quaker boarding school in Wabash, Indiana.[34] She attended White's Institute on and off for eleven years. Later, from 1895 to 1897, Zitkala-Ša enrolled at Earlham College in Richmond, Indiana, before working as a teacher at the Carlisle Indian Industrial School. She would go on to attend the New England Conservatory of Music in Boston, studying violin, at which point she published her autobiographical essays in the *Atlantic Monthly.*

In terms of individual backgrounds, then, these authors can be strikingly different. Chesnutt often expresses the attitudes of a well-to-do businessman; Du Bois, those of a more radical intellectual. For many years, Finley Peter Dunne was one of the highest-paid writers in the United States; Sui Sin Far pieced together a career from one journalistic stint to the next. María Amparo Ruiz de Burton and Zitkala-Ša went long periods of time without publishing any creative writing at all.

Nevertheless, there are also remarkable similarities among these authors as they responded to racial oppression in the late nineteenth-century United States. For African Americans, the post-Reconstruction era was defined by the emergence of Jim Crow violence and segregation.

Southern states increasingly disenfranchised African Americans, and
mob lynchings rose to unprecedented levels.[35] The 1896 Supreme Court
ruling on *Plessy v. Ferguson* codified segregation and racial difference
as federal law. For Native Americans, the progressive era was a period
of coerced assimilation. The 1887 Dawes Act led to the dispossession
of millions of acres of indigenous land, taken by the government and
sold to railroads and other corporations.[36] For Chinese Americans, 1882
witnessed the passage of the Chinese Exclusion Act. This was the first
federal policy to restrict immigration in the United States and would
ultimately serve as a precedent for the racial quotas of the Immigration
Act of 1924.[37] At the same time, U.S. imperialism expanded overseas—
into Cuba, Puerto Rico, and the Philippines—taking on more under-
handed forms of exploitation. The nation broadened its economic
markets in these territories without extending the constitutional rights
and protections of statehood.

Writing in opposition to this culture, and yet from within it, the
authors I examine adopted a set of comparable writing tactics—double
voices that could address both their ideal and actual readers. Ruiz de
Burton paid for her first novel to be published and distributed by a
major U.S. publisher, Lippincott, yet she did so anonymously so that
its Mexican American voice might catch readers unaware.[38] Chesnutt's
fiction mimicked the local color style of Joel Chandler Harris's Uncle
Remus stories to gain entry to the *Atlantic Monthly* and Houghton Mifflin. Dunne's dialect satire is similar to Chesnutt's conjure tales in many
ways; it uses techniques of ethnic caricature and buffoonery to mock
Anglo-American imperialism. Yet where Chesnutt grew skeptical of
this approach rather quickly, Dunne was willing to continue writing his
Mr. Dooley columns for more than two decades. Du Bois's *Souls of Black
Folk* more directly lays bare the double vision of race, yet contemporary
white readers often read the book as a guide to the essential characteristics of blackness. Similarly, Sui Sin Far's *Mrs. Spring Fragrance* resists
the white reader's racial benevolence despite its orientalized cover. In
each case, the authors employ ambiguous tactics of representation, lur-
ing white readers in through racial fantasies in an attempt to produce a
sense of cognitive dissonance.

These writers also adopted similar strategies for authorial self-
presentation, often straddling boundaries of ethnic identification. As a
young man, for example, Dunne took on his mother's maiden name,

Finley, to reflect her influence on his life: literary, feminine, and Irish.[39] Edith Eaton wrote under the name Sui Sin Far to stress similar connections to her mother's Chinese background.[40] Chesnutt would publish all of his writing as "Charles W. Chesnutt." The "W" stood for Waddell, a name inherited from his white, plantation-owning grandfather.[41] At the same time, all three of these authors were able to pass as white, and did so in varying degrees. In other words, all three authors played with the performative aspects of ethnic identification, taking on various authorial personae. They manipulated these possibilities in both their personal lives and in their fiction. Early in his career, Dunne maintained his anonymity in relation to the Mr. Dooley columns. He imagined a better career for himself as a publisher, managing the news and not just writing it. On being identified as the author of the Mr. Dooley columns, Dunne walked a fine line between whiteness and Irish ethnicity. Similarly, Ruiz de Burton published all of her work anonymously, hoping to pass a Mexican American literary voice into the public sphere. Yet there were enough signals in the text of her first novel that a reviewer was able to identify Ruiz de Burton as the author.[42]

Zitkala-Ša was born Gertrude Simmons and adopted her Dakota name later in life. Notably, the *Atlantic Monthly* was happy to advertise this ethnic identity. The 1899 *December Holiday Bulletin* (see figure 1) gives Zitkala-Ša almost top billing; the advertisement for her work is placed above ads for John Muir and Sarah Orne Jewett and just below W. J. Stillman and Walter Hines Page.[43] The advertisement includes a photograph of Zitkala-Ša dressed in traditional Dakota clothing and describes her as "a young Indian girl of the Yankton Sioux tribe of Dakota Indians, who received her education in the East." It goes on to describe the writing itself: "These unique and genuine records of the mind of an Indian child are told precisely in her own words." The advertisement thus emphasizes the significance of Zitkala-Ša's self-presentation, as the biography is neither translated nor written by a white ethnographer. At the same time, it exoticizes Zitkala-Ša's writing for white readers. Her Dakota name is included three times, and the term "Indian" is used eight times in the space of the short advertisement. This is coupled with the image of Zitkala-Ša and a description of the texts as "unique" and "genuine." In a period marked by an "Indian Craze,"[44] the advertisement promotes the writing as an authentic encounter with the Indian other.

One of the goals of my project is to show how the color line is defined not by blackness but by efforts to enforce boundaries around the supposed purity of whiteness. Du Bois was aware of this when he popularized the term, describing the problem of the color line as "the relation of the darker to the lighter races of men in Asia and Africa, in America and the islands of the sea."[45] As Du Bois used it, the term was meant to describe global forces of racial division and colonialism. My title, *Writing across the Color Line,* thus refers to the ways multiethnic authors struck back and challenged their white readers. All of the authors that I examine, including the Irish American Dunne, identified as nonwhite. All of these authors were engaged in antiracist writing. Moreover, in seeking out commercial publishers, all of these authors sought to address a national, predominantly white audience. Needless to say, we cannot draw easy comparisons between Dunne and Du Bois. Nor is it my intention to minimize the differences of these authors when describing them collectively as writers of color. In certain ways, however, as authors who sought to confront racist attitudes among white readers, their work lends itself to comparison.

COMMERCIAL LITERARY PUBLICATION

The authors I examine sought the influence and resources afforded by well-known commercial publishing houses. This type of publication authorized their work and gave it the imprimatur of literature. It allowed their writing to be produced in well-made editions, with moderate print runs, and to be advertised and distributed nationally. Through commercial channels, their message could circulate more widely. The authors I examine were willing to offer ambiguous representations of race in order to achieve literary publication through well-known trade presses and influence a predominantly white audience. In a frequently quoted passage from his journals, Chesnutt described this approach explicitly:

> The object of my writing would not be so much the elevation of the colored people as the elevation of the whites, — for I consider the unjust spirit of caste . . . a barrier to the moral progress of the American people; and I would be one of the first to head a determined, organized crusade against it. Not a fierce indiscriminate onslaught; not an appeal to force, for this is something that force can but slightly affect; but a moral revolution which must be brought about in a different manner. . . . This

work is of a twofold character. The negro's part is to prepare for social recognition and equality; and it is the province of literature to open the way for him to get it—to accustom the public mind to the idea; and while amusing them to lead them on, imperceptibly, unconsciously, step by step to the desired state of feeling.[46]

Here, Chesnutt defines his own role as ethnic trickster, targeting a white audience and pushing that audience to think about racial injustice through literature. His writing will be simultaneously amusing and revolutionary, a crusade that acts imperceptibly on the white reader's feelings. As Chesnutt describes it, his writing would attempt to reach "the American people" through the "province of literature." Like Chesnutt, all of the authors I consider targeted a white audience through the realm of literary culture.

The work of these authors thus differs from work circulated by African American publishers or ethnic presses during the late nineteenth century. As James P. Danky has shown, African American print culture was a diverse and powerful force in the decades after the Civil War, with notable publications such as the *Fort Scott Colored Citizen,* the *New York Globe,* the *Chicago Defender,* and the *New York Age.*[47] Du Bois was deeply involved in these print cultures, as were Frances E. W. Harper and Sutton E. Griggs. Yet such newly established publishers struggled to attain widespread distribution, and it was especially difficult for them to attract white authors or a white audience.[48] A similar argument can be made regarding the circulation and stability of ethnic publications. In the decades surrounding the turn of the century, there were anywhere from eight hundred to thirteen hundred foreign-language newspapers in the United States, including long-standing institutions such as the *Danish Pioneer,* the *Italian American Progress,* and the *Jewish Daily Forward.*[49] Nevertheless, ethnic publications generally "worked at the margins" of U.S. culture, with high failure rates.[50] Of course, I do not wish to belittle these publications nor the significance of ethnic audiences and communities of reception. The authors I consider were involved in such movements, and drew strength from them. However, they also sought a broader, national circulation through the commercial press. Thus, in contrast to the more outspoken radicalism of writers such as Ida B. Wells or Anna Julia Cooper, these authors approached a "gentle reader" through the field of literature. They engaged with white fantasies of racial domination through open-ended artistic representations.

This relationship between authors of color and their commercial publishers is fraught and often complicates the dynamic of authority over the text and its production. The relationship typically involves white editors and other arbiters of literary culture who serve as allies to authors of color. These literary professionals are often willing to support the author but are limited in their ability to do so—both by marketplace demand and by their own imagination and privilege. Walter Hines Page serves this role for Chesnutt, helping to publish *The Conjure Woman* with Houghton Mifflin and supporting Chesnutt's development in the books that follow. Page was a white Southerner who left his home state of North Carolina for work as an editor and publisher in the Northeast. In my fourth chapter, Francis G. Browne of McClurg plays a similar role: a white editor, mindful of the marketplace, with a benevolent interest in publishing writers of color. Browne was responsible for publishing both *The Souls of Black Folk* and *Mrs. Spring Fragrance.*

Likewise, Zitkala-Ša's autobiographical essays were initially sent to the *Atlantic Monthly* through Joseph Edgar Chamberlin, editor of the *Youth's Companion* and a regular columnist with the *Boston Evening Transcript*.[51] In fact, Zitkala-Ša lived in Chamberlin's home in Wrentham, Massachusetts, as she composed the autobiographical essays. The first essay in the series was thus submitted to the *Atlantic* through Chamberlin and read by editorial assistant William B. Parker, who solicited additional essays that Zitkala-Ša forwarded to *Atlantic* editor Bliss Perry.[52] As Ellery Sedgwick describes in her history of the magazine, the newly promoted editor sought to publish a wide range of opinions and perspectives, broadly inclusive and not shielding "white middle-class readers from criticism."[53] Perry sought to remain nonpartisan, moderate, and liberal. From 1901 to 1902, he ran an extensive series of more than fifteen articles on voter disenfranchisement and related racial issues. In editorials, he openly criticized white supremacism (or "Anglo-Saxon domination") as well as U.S. foreign policy in the Philippines. He published poetry by Paul Laurence Dunbar and stories by Chesnutt, and he ran Du Bois's critique of Booker T. Washington as a lead article in the magazine.[54] In this regard, it is significant that one of Perry's first major decisions for the magazine was to publish Zitkala-Ša's essays. Two weeks after his assistant's request for additional materials, on October 4, 1899, Perry wrote to Zitkala-Ša, having received copies of "The School Days of an Indian Girl" and "An Indian

Teacher among Indians."[55] Perry tells Zitkala-Ša that he has read the stories "with a great deal of pleasure," and he arranges to publish the trilogy. In these instances, the extent to which trade publishers supported authors of color, and the ways in which they experimented with the marketability of ethnic literature, are noteworthy.

Yet while editors such as Perry, Page, and Browne supported these texts, their influence also supported publication *for* a predominantly white, middle-class audience. My project thus takes an interest in such literary professionals as mediators. What political, financial, or aesthetic values influenced their decision to publish these texts? How might those values affect editorial decisions and become a part of the book itself?

Publishers also shaped a text's impact through extralinguistic concerns, especially in terms of marketing and distribution. They would determine the design of the book, the size of a book's initial print run, the breadth of its distribution, and the scope and style of its marketing campaign. Here, again, publishers often hedged against the text's subversive elements and against political confrontation with the reader. They designed books so that readers could easily recognize and consume the ethnic experience and even the ethnic body. *Mrs. Spring Fragrance* was published in red and gold, with a cover image of a rising sun and dragonflies; *Mr. Dooley in Peace and in War* was published under a green cover with an image of a shamrock; *The Souls of Black Folk* was black and gold; *The Conjure Woman* was brown. In each of these cases, the book itself was designed in terms of ethnic content. Along these lines, publishers often supported manipulations of authorial identity. This was especially significant because identification of an author as nonwhite could reveal sympathy for the caricatured subject, undermining the book's ambiguous literary strategies. As I will demonstrate, the relatively unknown identities of Ruiz de Burton, Chesnutt, Dunne, and Sui Sin Far would play a significant role in the reception of each text.

WHITE RECEPTIONS AND OTHER READERS

Such maneuvers and adjustments targeted a predominantly white reading public. And while it is not impossible to judge the reception among this audience, doing so poses challenges. Within the communications circuit, as Robert Darnton noted, "Reading remains the most

difficult stage to study."[56] On the one hand, it is often difficult to determine the extent to which a text circulated and the scope of its audience.
This can be especially true for books, in comparison to periodicals,
since each book title is a new commodity with its own distribution
and sales. On the other hand, individual reception is also difficult to
gauge. Interpretations vary, and books can have vastly different meanings over time and from one reader to the next. Moreover, readers may
record, or not record, these interpretations in any number of ways:
in flashes of thought and casual conversations, in marginal notes, in
published reviews and criticism, in autobiographical writing, or in
references and allusions folded into other works of art.[57] Tracing these
receptions, I occasionally refer to biographical essays and memoirs. I
am also attentive to the long-term influence and survival of these texts,
especially within the field academic criticism. My most frequent point
of reference, however, is through reviews published in newspapers
and magazines at the time of initial publication. My approach here is
comparable to Nina Baym's in *Novels, Readers, and Reviewers*, examining
how the reviews themselves express contemporary trends and cultural
attitudes.[58] While this method itself is not groundbreaking, scholars
have rarely examined late nineteenth-century ethnic literature based
on the record of its cross-racial receptions.

Looking at how authors of color were reviewed, the pattern that
emerges is not one of subversive disruption but one that demonstrates the tenacity of racist attitudes within the literary marketplace.
Thus Chesnutt entered the prestigious realm of Houghton Mifflin by
mimicking plantation fiction and allowing his fiction to pass as white-
authored. Readers harshly criticized and rejected his more forceful
critique of white supremacism, aptly titled *The Marrow of Tradition*.
Thus Dunne maintained his successful career by staying in character
as the Irish buffoon; his anticolonial critique was always a joke. Thus
The Souls of Black Folk, with its thorough explication of African American double consciousness, drew astoundingly contradictory reviews.
Readers condemned its message while simultaneously recommending
the book as a depiction of the essential characteristics of the negro race.
Again and again, white readers either overlooked or rejected the subversive potential of this literature. In the case of Zitkala-Ša, this pattern
is readily apparent. On the one hand, Zitkala-Ša's first reader at the
Atlantic Monthly, William B. Parker, was able to mistake her writing as

a story of an Indian's conversion to white man's ways. On the other hand, when the Carlisle Indian Industrial School read these essays as criticizing forced assimilation, it led to a harsh backlash. In response to the subtle ambiguities presented by Zitkala-Ša through Bliss Perry and the *Atlantic Monthly,* white readers undermined the subversive potential of the text.

Scholarship on reception has always recognized the reader's agency in constructing the meaning of the text. As Leah Price points out, some of the most interesting examples of reception study occur when the implied or anticipated audience of a text "differs sharply from what we know about the empirical audience."[59] This is the case in books such as Carlo Ginzburg's *The Cheese and the Worms* and Jonathan Rose's *The Intellectual Life of the British Working Class,* which explore unexpected histories of reading and connect these histories to broader questions of social class and culture.[60] Reception studies also have a tendency to celebrate the agency of readers as they participate in the meaning making of literature. For example, Janice Radway's *Reading the Romance* complicates our understanding of how romance novels have captivated such a massive audience, offering a more sympathetic depiction of why women turn to these books.[61] In *Forgotten Readers*, Elizabeth McHenry recovers the history of African American literary societies in the nineteenth century, showing how middle-class African Americans used literary reading to participate in civic engagement.[62] Whereas these scholarly examples tend to celebrate the agency of the readers they examine, and rightly so, my research focuses primarily on the ways white supremacist attitudes influenced the literary marketplace. I show that these readings did not constitute an occasional harsh review but rather dominated the literary marketplace and exercised a powerful negative response to the emergence of ethnic literature, even when the publishing industry supported authors of color.

Part of what binds my project, then, as it moves from one author and publisher to the next, is its consideration of how whiteness influenced U.S. literary culture at the turn of the century. This approach recognizes U.S. culture for its hostility and violence, as much as its multiculturalism. Drawing on critical whiteness studies,[63] my project turns its gaze onto white publishers and readers, to examine how this culture operates, often by diluting antiracist perspectives to the point that they lose traction or become unrecognizable.

Understanding white receptions of ethnic literature also has implications for our understanding of the text itself. The ambiguities of multiethnic literary realism were not only resistant and subversive. The authors of these texts walked a fine line and risked reinscribing racist attitudes in their work. Understanding the more sinister interpretations of contemporary audiences calls into question any triumphant history of the ethnic trickster. Rather than both entering and subverting the dominant literary order (ambiguity as a type of double power), such tactics were more often ignored and rejected (an ambiguity that was denied as soon as it was recognized). The double vision of the typical white reader of this era did not fluctuate between racial stereotype and a radical undoing of stereotype so much as it fluctuated between racial stereotype and aggressive backlash. In the first instance, the caricature simply reinforces established perceptions, confirming rather than challenging racist norms. If, however, white readers understood the author's ambiguous strategies of representation as a critique of racism, their response generally turned defensive. They responded in a harsh backlash that attempted to delegitimize the text as below the status of literature.

At times, I describe such interpretations as "misreading," and the term deserves some explanation. My research certainly demonstrates how the marketing and advertising of these texts could foster such interpretations. Nevertheless, when an audience fails to notice the subversive potential of a text—a subversive potential that was intended by the authors and discussed with editors, that is available in the text, and that now guides the recovery of this literature among present-day scholars and critics—I think it is fair to say that the interpretation is incomplete and inadequate. The situation might be compared to an encounter in the prologue of Ralph Ellison's *Invisible Man,* when the narrator fights a "sleepwalker." The white reader is a sort of sleepwalker, made blind by a "peculiar disposition of the eyes." Like the invisible man, the ethnic trickster aims to awaken this dreamer, to dispel their fantasies of white supremacism. When confronted with this truth, however, the white reader does not take time for reflection but continues to curse and struggle, even to the point of self-harm. As the invisible man concludes, "There are few things in the world as dangerous as sleepwalkers."[64]

Yet if a white audience rejected emergent multiethnic literature, it was nevertheless significant that authors of color *initiated* such a rejection within the realm of the commercial literary marketplace. These texts not only provoked cross-racial engagement, challenging white readers to reflect on U.S. racial hierarchies, they also laid the groundwork for the rise of ethnic literature in the twentieth century. Publication through well-known trade presses also facilitated influence among ethnic communities. It made these books more widely available among counterpublics, or communities defined by opposition to cultural norms and the dominant public.[65] Chesnutt's brief career with Houghton Mifflin, for example, would influence James Weldon Johnson's *Autobiography of an Ex-Colored Man* in 1912. Chesnutt's writing would then reemerge in the 1920s, when *The House Behind the Cedars* was adapted for the screen by Oscar Micheaux and republished in the *Chicago Defender*.[66] Dunne's writing was hugely popular during his lifetime, and while his compromised writing style was not generally understood as subversive, it did influence Langston Hughes's creation of Jesse B. Semple and Alexander Posey's Fus Fixico.[67] Likewise, while my analysis of *The Souls of Black Folk* emphasizes contemporary white misreadings, African American readers demonstrated a much better understanding of the book. One review, written by John Daniels for *Alexander's Magazine*, hailed the text as "a poem, a thing permanent" and worthy of the "highest place."[68] Sui Sin Far's *Mrs. Spring Fragrance* sold less than seven hundred copies, and was reviewed in only a handful of periodicals. Far's novel manuscript would not be published in her lifetime and, if it still exists, has yet to be discovered. Nevertheless, publication of *Mrs. Spring Fragrance* secured Sui Sin Far's legacy as one of the earliest writers of Asian American literature. In a recent collection, Mary Chapman has recovered Sui Sin Far's early periodical fiction and nonfiction, vastly expanding the author's known body of work.[69] In all of these ways, commercial publication helped ensure what Thomas R. Adams and Nicholas Barker call the "survival" of the literary text.

CASE BY CASE

The chapters of this book are organized as case studies, which progress in roughly chronological order. Each chapter examines interactions between ethnic authors and their commercial trade publishers, and these publishers also move about geographically—with consideration of Philadelphia, Boston, New York, and Chicago. My first chapter examines María Amparo Ruiz de Burton's 1872 book *Who Would Have Thought It?*—the earliest known novel by a Mexican American author in English—which was published by J. B. Lippincott and Company, one of the largest book distributors of the mid-nineteenth century. Referring to Lippincott business records and correspondence, held by the Historical Society of Pennsylvania yet largely unexplored by scholars, my chapter recovers correspondence between the publisher and author and reconstructs the production, sale, and distribution of this major work of Mexican American literature. I show that Ruiz de Burton hired Lippincott to produce the book at her own expense, so that it would be distributed and sold within Lippincott's catalog of other sensational novels. Based on this history, I argue that Ruiz de Burton's novel is best understood within the genre of sensationalism, as opposed to sentimental literature. The chapter also connects this publication history to the novel's narration, which, while written in English to appeal to a white audience, features Spanish interjections and pleas for the reader to empathize with Latino characters. *Who Would Have Thought It?* thus conveys a Mexican American perspective covertly, in the form of an anonymous yet nationally distributed sensational novel.

Charles W. Chesnutt also sought to enter the realm of American literature covertly, masking his African American heritage in early advertisements. Yet Chesnutt's experience diverges from Ruiz de Burton's because Houghton Mifflin more actively marketed his work. My chapter considers Chesnutt's relationship with Houghton Mifflin through the production of materials that framed and promoted Chesnutt's writing at the height of his literary career. In particular, it considers how advertisements and marketing materials were designed as a racialized paratext that would influence the sale and popular reception of Chesnutt's literary work. Within these marketing materials, Chesnutt was advertised first as white, then as mulatto, and finally as the "champion of the colored race." Yet despite substantial investment from Houghton Mifflin, particularly to advertise *The Marrow of Tradition* (1901), Chesnutt's work was poorly received. The chapter concludes with an analysis of Chesnutt's 1904 short story "Baxter's Procrustes," his last to be published in the *Atlantic Monthly*, showing how the text alludes to a special edition of Chesnutt's first book, *The Conjure Woman* (1899), which had been manufactured with uncut pages. Chesnutt thus imagines his own work as being unopened and unread by a procrustean audience that would stretch and amputate its meaning according to racial prejudice.

Like Chesnutt, Irish American author Finley Peter Dunne relied on ethnic caricature and dialect to achieve commercial literary success. Yet while Chesnutt turned away from this dialect midcareer, Dunne traded in ethnic self-caricature for nearly three decades. A journalist born and raised in Chicago, Dunne became hugely popular for his Mr. Dooley columns, a series of fictional pieces that respond to popular news events in the voice of the title bartender. Written in thick dialect, these pieces were initially popular among Dunne's local Chicago community. When Dunne turned his attention to national politics—responding especially to U.S. imperial expansion into the Caribbean and the Philippines—his book collections attracted increasingly widespread attention, making him one of the highest-paid writers of his era. My analysis considers the popularity of Mr. Dooley's dialect voice as it creates an ambiguous political criticism that, depending on a reader's preconceptions, could be read in sharply divergent, even opposing, ways. While critics have described Mr. Dooley's dialect as "ambivalent," I argue that it is better understood as polyvocal, employing a range of styles drawn from journalistic discourse. Because Mr. Dooley spoke in all the voices of the news—objective, editorial, sensationalist, and literary—contemporary readers could easily disregard the anti-imperial aspects of Dunne's humor. Through this compromise of political aims, Mr. Dooley's voice became nearly as popular as the news itself.

Much in the way that Dunne responded to the yellow journalism of New York in order to achieve national popularity, Chicago publisher and wholesale distributor A. C. McClurg and Company sought to compete with Boston and New York publishers to establish their own literary reputation. As part of this effort to promote their brand, McClurg developed a niche list of book titles written by ethnic authors. Among these titles, it published two monumental works of American literature, W. E. B. Du Bois's 1903 *The Souls of Black Folk* and Sui Sin Far's 1912 *Mrs. Spring Fragrance,* one of the first books of fiction by a Chinese North American writer. My chapter examines how this company, which worked primarily as distributors to the expanding American West, came to publish these two books. Using company business records held at the Newberry Library, I show how McClurg actively shaped the content and the production of each book. For example, Du Bois had not considered publishing *The Souls of Black Folk* until the collection was actively solicited by McClurg editor Francis G. Browne. Du Bois corresponded with Browne to make decisions about how the book was designed and how it would be marketed. Browne and Du Bois also made changes to the second printing of *The Souls of Black Folk,* which have been elided in recent Norton and Oxford University Press reprintings of the book. McClurg company records indicate that Browne was also responsible for accepting *Mrs. Spring Fragrance* for publication. Yet despite his involvement in these books, Browne has been almost universally misidentified in scholarly criticism. Comparing the examples of Du Bois and Sui Sin Far, I show that even with the support of a major commercial publisher, and even after significant editorial efforts to target a white audience, both authors encountered harsh criticism and neglect in the literary marketplace.

My epilogue considers the afterlives of these texts. What was the impact of turn-of-the-century ethnic literature, beyond its contemporary audience? Reflecting on scholarly recoveries of ethnic literature, I show how publication through commercial presses facilitated long-term, national circulation. In this way, even as contemporary white readers rejected their writing, the authors under discussion were successful in distributing their work widely and creating new forms of American literature.

CHAPTER 1

SENSATIONAL JOB

María Amparo Ruiz de Burton
in the J. B. Lippincott Catalog

ho Would Have Thought It? (1872)—the first known
novel published in English by a Mexican American
author—was made to look like any other J. B.
Lippincott and Company novel at the time. Bound in blue cloth, the duo-
decimo volume has a simple rectangular pattern on the front cover, with
the book title and publisher name in gold on the spine. The novel was
published anonymously and sold at a retail price of $1.75. In the back of
the copy that is now held by the Library Company of Philadelphia, after
the conclusion of the novel, there are ten pages of advertisements for other
Lippincott titles, including a full page that advertises novels by Ouida, the
Anglo-French sensationalist.[1] *Who Would Have Thought It?* was designed
to fit alongside these novels, and its title echoes others published by Lippincott at the time—such as *Must It Be?* and *How Will It End?*.[2] Because the
novel was published anonymously without reference to its author, María
Amparo Ruiz de Burton, and because it was not advertised with any
description, readers would have purchased and begun reading the novel
in terms of this sensational fiction. Indeed, Ruiz de Burton arranged for
her book to appear in this way.

Yet while *Who Would Have Thought It?* was produced by one of the
world's largest book distributors of the mid-nineteenth century, little
is known about the relationship between Ruiz de Burton and Lippincott. Why was this book selected for publication? Did Ruiz de Burton
correspond and work with particular editors? What might the novel's

publication teach us about Mexican American fiction? In this chapter, I refer to Lippincott business records and correspondence to recon-struct the production and sale of this significant predecessor to Lati-no/a fiction. I show that Ruiz de Burton hired Lippincott because of its specialization in job printing and its ability to produce and distribute books for a commission.[3] Yet while the publication of *Who Would Have Thought It?* was self-financed at a loss, Ruiz de Burton's use of Lippin-cott as job printers nevertheless allowed her to establish a Mexican American literary voice that could be heard across the nation. Indeed, this publication history can be connected to the novel's narrative voice, in which first-person interjections serve as cross-racial pleas to a white reader. *Who Would Have Thought It?* can thus be read as a sensationalist novel, camouflaged to distribute its Mexican American perspective in an anonymous yet impressively durable form.

CALIFORNIANS IN THE NORTHEAST

María Amparo Ruiz de Burton occupies an important place in nineteenth-century American literature, as one of the first Mexican Americans to write novels in English. Born in 1832, she was raised by a wealthy landowning family in Baja California and came of age at the time of the U.S.-Mexican War. In 1848, after the war had ended and the Treaty of Guadalupe Hidalgo was signed, Ruiz de Burton traveled with her mother as a refugee to the town of Monterey in Alta California.[4] There, at the age of seventeen, she became an American citizen and married U.S. Army captain Henry S. Burton, who was later promoted to major and then to brigadier general. In the 1860s, she moved east as her hus-band served in the Union Army—living in Rhode Island, New York, Washington, D.C., Delaware, and Virginia.[5] Ruiz de Burton social-ized in elite circles at this time, but when her husband died in 1869, she returned to California a widow with two children. Ruiz de Bur-ton wrote and published two novels in her lifetime, *Who Would Have Thought It?* (1872) and *The Squatter and the Don* (1885), both offering powerful critiques of the U.S. nation and its expansion into Mexican territories in the mid-nineteenth century. The first novel was published anonymously, and the second under the pseudonym C. Loyal. Ruiz de Burton also wrote a comedic play, *Don Quixote de La Mancha*, staged in San Diego in the 1850s and published in 1876.[6]

Ruiz de Burton's novels and collected letters were recovered and republished from 1992 to 2001 by Rosaura Sánchez and Beatrice Pita through the Recovering the U.S. Hispanic Literary Heritage project, which is managed by Arte Público Press and the University of Houston. As described in its mission statement, this international recovery project aims "to locate, preserve and disseminate Hispanic culture of the United States in its written form since colonial times until 1960."[7] In recent years, Ruiz de Burton's work has received increased scholarly attention from critics such as Jesse Alemán and John Morán González, and in a book collection edited by Amelia María de la Luz Montes and Anne Elizabeth Goldman.[8] As I will describe, however, it was not possible for this scholarship to fully explore the publication history behind Ruiz de Burton's first novel.

As a novel, *Who Would Have Thought It?* centers around the life of a young Mexican girl, Lola Medina, who is born in captivity to Sonoran Indians in California. Lola's mother has been abducted and forced into marriage with the native chief. Both women's skin has been dyed black so that they will not be recognized as kidnapped Mexicans, but they are discovered by a New England archaeologist, Dr. James Norval. Lola's mother explains their situation to Dr. Norval and describes how they have a large fortune of gold, diamonds, and gems hidden nearby. She asks Dr. Norval to serve as Lola's guardian until the girl can be reunited with her father in Mexico. He agrees, and the reader learns throughout the novel that Dr. Norval will honor his word. On returning to his New England home, however, Lola finds that Dr. Norval's family and servants are less trustworthy. While his son Julian (a Union Army officer) is sympathetic, Lola is confronted with harsh racist treatment from Dr. Norval's daughters (Ruth and Mattie), from the family's Irish servants, and especially from Dr. Norval's wife, Jemima Norval.[9] Despite her purported Christian and abolitionist beliefs, Mrs. Norval is disgusted by the presence of Lola and wants nothing to do with the dark-skinned girl. On learning about Lola's inheritance, however, Mrs. Norval is overtaken with jealousy and greed. She begins conversations with a depraved minister, a caricature of Henry Ward Beecher, to find ways to steal Lola's fortune. The two are given even more time and space to collaborate when Dr. Norval must leave for an archeological expedition in Egypt. As his father leaves, Julian is warned to protect Lola and to be wary of Reverend Hackwell and his own mother.

There is a widespread dispersion of characters at this point in the novel, and the narrative focus does not follow Lola exclusively. Mrs. Norval and her daughters proceed to spend as much of Lola's inheritance as possible. It is rumored that Dr. Norval his died in Egypt. Reverend Hackwell leaves the ministry and is secretly engaged to Mrs. Norval. Julian gradually falls in love with Lola, but as a soldier in the Union Army he must respond to Washington, D.C., politics and an increasingly complex war. Ultimately, at the novel's conclusion, Lola is reunited with her father in Mexico and marries Julian, who, disillusioned with his army service, decides he will travel to Mexico to live with her. The novel thus imagines a future defined by interracial marriage and alliances across the U.S.-Mexico border, posing sharp criticisms of the nineteenth-century United States. As Sánchez and Pita describe, the book attacks "idealized constructs of domesticity and nationhood," satirizing the discourse of white womanhood and manifest destiny.[10] Anyone working on Ruiz de Burton owes a debt to Sánchez and Pita for their foundational scholarship.

At the same time, however, it is important to recognize the complexities of Ruiz de Burton's social position. Certainly, Ruiz de Burton did experience firsthand the violence of U.S. imperialism and expansion into Mexican territory. Yet as a relatively elite Spanish Californian, born to a wealthy family that owned large tracts of land, Ruiz de Burton also inherited a legacy of European settler colonialism. As one indication of this attitude, throughout *Who Would Have Thought It?*, representations of Native Americans and African Americans draw on racist stereotypes against people of color. Natives are cast as savages. Lola becomes more beautiful when her skin, dyed black in captivity, becomes lighter in color. At times, such racist judgments are made by villainous characters such as Mrs. Norval and Reverend Hackwell.[11] Frequently, however, Julian and Lola voice this same racism.[12]

In a sense, Ruiz de Burton can be compared to members of the Spanish Texas communities described in Raúl Coronado's *A World Not to Come,* who imagined themselves participating in Western modernity. Like these Hispanic intellectuals in Texas, Ruiz de Burton envisioned herself participating in a *European* culture of letters—not exclusively Anglo-American—that might grow and flourish in the nineteenth century.[13] Yet this world was not to come, and over the course of her lifetime, Ruiz de Burton felt herself being racialized and made into an ethnic American. As a result, the terminology we might use to describe

Ruiz de Burton is itself vexed. Is she Mexican American? Is she Hispanic or Latina? Certainly, she is Californian, but what it meant to be Californian shifted drastically during her lifetime.

Ruiz de Burton's social status—between Mexican and American, colonizer and colonized—has thus become a central tension in critical scholarship and has made her an important figure for historicizing Hispanic subjectivity in the nineteenth century. As Rodrigo Lazo has pointed out, "The multiplicity of contradictory positions inhabited by Ruiz de Burton led to additional critical scholarship that helped to build the archive about her."[14] In contrast with early interpretations of Ruiz de Burton as a marginalized figure, for example, José F. Aranda, Jr., has noted all the ways that Ruiz de Burton was, in fact, at the center of U.S. history.[15] Ruiz de Burton was married to a U.S. Army general; she moved in cosmopolitan circles between San Francisco, Washington, D.C., New York, Mexico City, and Chicago; she even met with Abraham Lincoln in person to secure her husband's military promotion. Notably, while Ruiz de Burton is known today by her full name, María Amparo Ruiz de Burton, she signed her correspondence as "M. A. de Burton," an abbreviated version that recognized her Spanish background (with the preposition "de") but minimizes this heritage in comparison to her husband's name.[16] Ruiz de Burton also published her first novel with the nation's largest book distributor.

In many ways, it can be difficult for a twenty-first-century reader to grapple with the complexities of Ruiz de Burton's life and perspective, and these complexities affect the rhetorical dynamics of her fiction. Who is the target audience for this satirical novel, and what, exactly, is being satirized? Recovering the publication history of *Who Would Have Thought It?* thus expands our understanding of both Ruiz de Burton's social position and of the Latino nineteenth century.[17] Turning to her relationship with Lippincott allows us to better understand Ruiz de Burton's place within U.S. culture.

J. B. LIPPINCOTT COMPANY RECORDS

In the mid-nineteenth century, Lippincott was known for its sheer size and its ability to manufacture all aspects of the book. In an 1852 article from *Godey's Lady's Book,* "A Visit to the Book Bindery of Lippincott, Grambo, and Company," engraver C. T. Hinckley describes the company as "one of the largest publishing houses in the country."[18] The article was part of a series on book production, and was meant to cover only the bookbindery, but, as its introduction describes, the author was so amazed by the "amount of business performed [and] capital invested" that he expanded the article to describe the company more broadly. The piece concludes with further exclamations of the company's massive size, describing the "thousands of books which are sent daily from these rooms to every section of the New World."[19]

As a company, Lippincott dates its origins back to the late eighteenth century and the 1792 establishment of Jacob Johnson's bookstore. Joshua Ballinger Lippincott himself was not born until 1813 in New Jersey and began working in the Philadelphia book trade for David Clark in his teens. When Clark's business failed, Lippincott was put in charge, and the company ran as Clark and Lippincott in the 1830s before becoming J. B. Lippincott and Company, Booksellers and Stationers, in 1837.[20] This company would then purchase Grigg, Elliot, and Company in 1849 and reorganize temporarily as Lippincott, Grambo, and Company, before again establishing itself as J. B. Lippincott and Company in 1855. In the early 1830s, the company occupied the corner of Fourth and Race Street in Philadelphia. But in 1861, the company moved to a large industrial facility at 715–717 Market Street, where it would remain until 1899, when a fire destroyed the building.

The Lippincott catalog was wide-ranging, with a specialization in reference books, medical texts, and bibles. In the *Publishers' Trade List Annual* of 1874 the company's books are listed in almost every category: arts and sciences, educational, guidebooks, history, biography, travel, Sunday school, medical, music, novels, theology and religion, stationery, and so on.[21] Lippincott showed a particular interest in books on the western United States. It published Henry Rowe Schoolcraft's six-volume series on the *History, Condition, and Prospects of the Indian Tribes of the United States* (1851–57) and H. M. Brackenridge's *Recollections of Persons and Places in the West* (1868). In the wake of the Civil War, the company expanded rapidly and in 1868 began publishing *Lippincott's Monthly Magazine.*

In 1871, Lippincott expanded on its 715–717 Market Street location, adding a large factory to the north. This Filbert Street factory was annexed to the Market Street building on its first two floors. The Lippincott offices and factory now covered more than five acres of land, "the largest establishment of its kind in the United States," and the company would remain here until 1899 when a fire destroyed the building.[22] By purchasing paper, type, and ink, the factory could manage all aspects of book production—composing, stereotyping, printing, binding, and shipping. Indeed, *Publishers Weekly* printed a wonderful illustration of the building (figure 2), with a cutaway view of its various departments, including the retail store, shipping rooms, the book bindery, and the magazine department.

Who Would Have Thought It? was made here, just one year after the Filbert Street factory began operation. In terms of the various sections of the building, however, it was not produced through the publication department (that is, selected by editors for publication) but rather through the job printing department. Company records indicate Lippincott received a down payment of $500 for production of the book and that Ruiz de Burton agreed to pay Lippincott a commission on each copy sold.

Scholars have known for some time that Ruiz de Burton self-funded the publication of her second novel, *The Squatter and the Don*. In their introduction to the 1992 Arte Público reprinting of the novel, Sánchez and Pita quote a letter from Ruiz de Burton to her longtime friend George Davidson, in which the author asks for help to fund publication of this later novel:

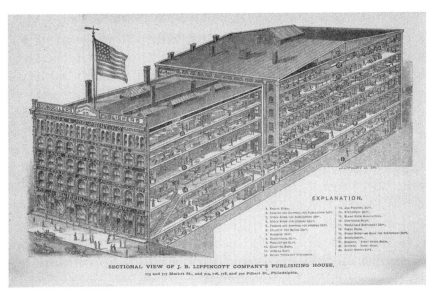

FIGURE 2. "Sectional View of J. B. Lippincott Company's Publishing House," *Publishers Weekly* (April 30, 1887): 583. Image courtesy of the Library of Congress.

I am writing a book, so I hope you won't scold me for being indolent. I don't know whether I shall publish it under my own name, so I want to keep the matter quiet yet. Only two or three friends know I am writing it. I want to publish it this fall, in September. This is an additional reason for my wishing to get my 3 months extra pay, and my pension increased, to have this much to help me with publication. Will you try to help me? Please do so. If I am able to pay for the stenotype [*sic*] plates I will make something; if not, all the profits will go to the pocket of the publishers and book-sellers.[23]

José F. Aranda, Jr., has similarly described how Ruiz de Burton sought to self-publish her second novel, hoping it might allow her to avoid publisher's fees and earn a profit from the book.[24] More recently, Alison E. Fagan has shown that there were two different versions, or states, of *The Squatter and the Don*.[25] Both were printed at Ruiz de Burton's expense, but the second version is revised and includes the name of the publisher Samuel Carson and Company on the title page. Yet despite this interest surrounding the publication of *The Squatter and the Don*, less has been said about Ruiz de Burton's first novel and her interactions with Lippincott. If she hoped to self-finance the publication of her second novel to avoid publishers' fees, what had been her experience with Lippincott?

There are a number of reasons that critics have not looked more closely at Ruiz de Burton's relationship with Lippincott. When Ruiz de Burton asks George Davidson to help fund the publication of her second novel, her letter seems to imply that publication with Lippincott had been a more straightforward affair. Lippincott was a major publisher, and Ruiz de Burton apparently did not earn any money from this first novel. The passage has thus been interpreted as justification for self-publishing her second novel, as a *new* strategy after failed interactions with Lippincott. Even more significantly, there has been a dearth of archival evidence. In her collected correspondence, Ruiz de Burton offers almost no commentary on *Who Would Have Thought It?* Indeed, she rarely discusses her literary work at all, and when she does mention *The Squatter and the Don*, she notes that it is being written in relative secrecy. Meanwhile, it was long believed that the Lippincott company records had been lost in the 1899 fire that destroyed its Market Street offices.[26] If any company records survived the fire, they were not donated to a library or special collections, and it was assumed that they had been destroyed.

However, when the publisher—now known as Lippincott Williams and Wilkins—began preparing to move offices in 1999, it initiated a donation of materials to the Historical Society of Pennsylvania. As it turns out, the company had preserved many of its own business records in storage, and over the span of three years, it donated 144 boxes of materials to the Historical Society.[27] These records are not comprehensive, but they offer valuable information regarding this major nineteenth-century publisher and the titles it produced. The condition of these company records is also noteworthy. Many of the papers have suffered damage from water and mold over the years, and they have not yet been archivally arranged but are held in the cardboard moving boxes in which they were donated. Indeed, it took some time before a preliminary finding aid was created by Michael Winship and Matthew Lyons in 2008 and then finalized and published by the Historical Society in March 2016. Thus while these records are a rich source of information for the study of nineteenth-century literature and publishing, they remain largely unexplored. To my knowledge, one of the only works of scholarship deriving from the materials is an uncensored edition of Oscar Wilde's *The Picture of Dorian Gray,* as the novel was originally published in *Lippincott's Monthly Magazine.*[28]

Among these company records, there are significant materials for understanding the publication of Ruiz de Burton's first novel. There are ledgers that show the cost of production and the sales figures for *Who Would Have Thought It?* There are records of how many copies of the book Lippincott kept in stock. There are pressed letter books that include correspondence sent from Lippincott to Ruiz de Burton over the span of twenty years. These records can tell us a great deal about the production, sale, and distribution of this novel, and about Ruiz de Burton's approach as an author.

PUBLISHING *WHO WOULD HAVE THOUGHT IT?*

J. B. Lippincott and Company took on very little risk to produce Ruiz de Burton's novel. *Who Would Have Thought It?* was neither selected by an editor for publication nor did the company spend money to advertise the book outside of its own catalogs and publications. Yet even while Lippincott ran little risk in publishing Ruiz de Burton's novel, the company offered a number of important services that went beyond merely

466

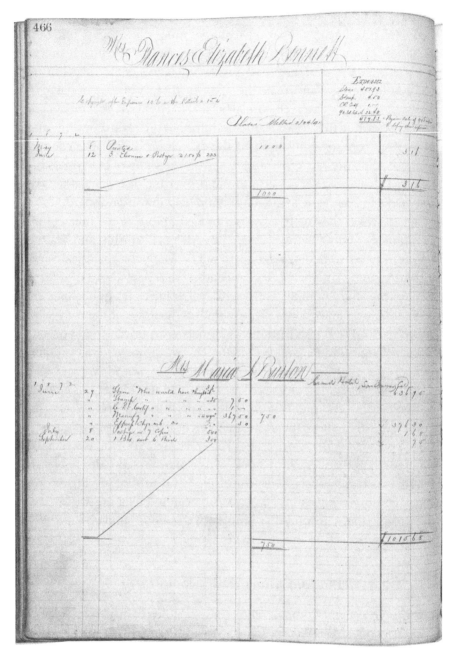

FIGURE 3. J. B. Lippincott and Company ledger detailing costs to produce Ruiz de Burton's *Who Would Have Thought It?* "General & Publication Ledger No. 5, Special No. 1," vol. 71, p. 466, J. B. Lippincott Company Records, Collection 3104, Historical Society of Pennsylvania.

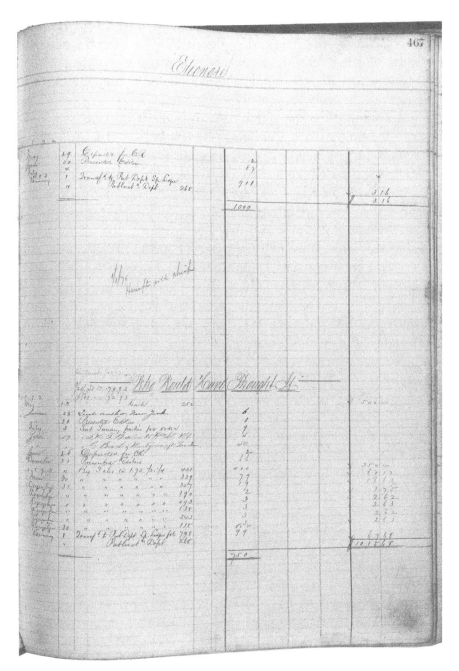

FIGURE 4. J. B. Lippincott and Company ledger detailing sales of Ruiz de Burton's *Who Would Have Thought It?* "General & Publication Ledger No. 5, Special No. 1," vol. 71, p. 467, J. B. Lippincott Company Records, Collection 3104, Historical Society of Pennsylvania.

printing the book. It manufactured the novel in a house style under the Lippincott imprint, shipped copies at Ruiz de Burton's request, listed the book in its catalog, and kept remaining copies of the book in storage, available for sale. It is likely that Ruiz de Burton approached Lippincott deliberately because of these services.

Figures 3 and 4 are from a double-entry accounting book, and they describe the production and sale of *Who Would Have Thought It?* The costs of production are listed on the verso (466), and the revenue generated by the book on the recto (467). These entries show that in June 1872, Lippincott produced 750 copies of the novel at a total cost of $1013.25. The stereotype plates cost $636.95; the stamp for the spine, $7.50; the copyright, $1.00; and manufacturing the book, $367.50 at $0.49 per copy. All copies of the book were bound and none were left as sheets. There were also some shipping charges, bringing the total costs to $1015.68. Ruiz de Burton, perhaps with support from a patron, paid the company $500.00 on May 13 before production began, which was transferred to the Lippincott "cash" account. Production of the novel was somewhat more costly than the average novel, as noted in correspondence between the author and publisher.[29] In a letter from May 20, 1872, Lippincott asked Ruiz de Burton to authorize additional expenses for a copy editor to review proofs of the novel and to revise its "phraseology." The publisher claimed the novel's grammar suffered from lack of practice and that it wanted to be sure the author's first publication was properly edited, and Ruiz de Burton agreed. The novel was also published on a thicker paper stock, so that the company might sell it at retail for $1.75 rather than $1.50.

On December 31, 1872, when Lippincott recorded biannual sales, it had moved four hundred copies of the novel, and Ruiz de Burton was credited $350 for these sales. The round sales figure, precisely four hundred copies, suggests that Lippincott may have sold these books at the publisher's trade auction. Shortly after these initial sales, in a letter from January, Lippincott wrote to Ruiz de Burton asking her to pay the difference between the $1015.68 production costs and the $850 she had been credited for her initial cash payment and for sales of the novel, combined.[30] In other words, Ruiz de Burton was responsible for all costs of publication and owed the company $165.68, even after paying $500 initially and selling four hundred copies of the book. Ruiz de Burton seems to have contested this bill. In the same letter from

January 1873, Lippincott assured Ruiz de Burton that its records were correct. The company reminded Ruiz de Burton that she had "authorized extensive corrections and revisions in the proofs and also added a number of pages of new matter to the volume," and asked her to pay the remaining amount owed. Ruiz de Burton resisted; she did not pay this money but instead allowed additional sales to be credited to her account. When sales are again recorded on June 30, 1873, the book had sold an additional seventy-nine copies, reducing the amount owed by $69.12. In the decade between these sales and January 1883, however, the book sold only thirty-three additional copies. There was never any need to reprint the book, and according to the Lippincott records, Ruiz de Burton still owed the company $67.68.

While "sales" credited to Ruiz de Burton are recorded simply by number, the Lippincott accounts provide more detailed information for special mailings sent out to various people at no cost. At the time of its initial production in June 1872, for instance, six copies were "Sent author, New York," with one other copy "Presented Editors." A few days later, on July 3, 1872, nine copies were mailed out to "sundry parties per order." In September, fifty copies were sent to C. Beach, a bookseller and stationer in San Francisco, free of any charge except shipping. It seems Ruiz de Burton had requested these copies, and Lippincott references them in a letter on November 19, saying, "Please see that the booksellers of your city keep the book on hand. You should charge them $1.17 per copy for the books you supplied to them, which is equal to 1/3rd off."[31] Here, Lippincott worked with Ruiz de Burton to distribute the book at the industry price. The company was willing to ship books per Ruiz de Burton's order but urged her to collect the proper amount for the books, knowing that she still owed money for its production.

Lippincott also sent five copies of the novel to Samuel L. M. Barlow in New York. Barlow was a prominent lawyer who made a fortune at the age of twenty-three by settling land disputes in the Treaty of Guadalupe Hidalgo.[32] He was later involved in a lawsuit that expelled Jay Gould from control of the Erie Railway. Ruiz de Burton sought legal advice from Barlow and corresponded with him sporadically from the late 1860s through the 1880s. One of these letters to Barlow, sent just before Lippincott shipped copies of the novel, mentions the book, asking Barlow to distribute them to New York newspapers for "a puff," or a favorable review.[33] It is unclear whether Barlow forwarded these books to reviewers. Indeed, there were very few reviews of the novel, even while the ledger indicates that Lippincott had "Presented Editors" with sixty-six copies of the book.

In the same way that it distributed copies of the book to editors, Lippincott upheld its end of the publishing contract. The company produced and sold the book for Ruiz de Burton. It kept remaining copies on hand, and for sale, for more than twenty-five years.[34] It kept her account active throughout that time. Although the company did not spend money to advertise Ruiz de Burton's book in outside publications or periodicals, it listed her book in its own catalogs and in some of the advertisements it appended to the back of other Lippincott novels.[35] Moreover, if Ruiz de Burton had paid the remaining amount owed on her account, at any time, she would have owned the stereotype plates and any remaining copies of the novel held in Lippincott storage—and for less than the cost to produce the plates.

Near the end of her life, in 1894, Ruiz de Burton and Lippincott exchanged correspondence once more. The author asked the company to send copies of *Who Would Have Thought It?* to Chicago and also asked about the possibility of Lippincott printing more copies of *The Squatter and the Don*. (Lippincott had not originally published this second novel, but Ruiz de Burton owned the plates.) Responding to the letter, Lippincott said it had sixty-six remaining copies of *Who Would Have Thought It?* on hand, and that it would be happy to ship them to Chicago if Ruiz de Burton would pay the remaining amount owed to the company, $46.02.[36] In other words, more than twenty years after publication, Ruiz de Burton had not yet paid the full cost of the novel's publication. Lippincott advised against reprinting *The Squatter and the Don*, because there was not any demand for the book, but it offered to do so at the author's expense. Ultimately, Ruiz de Burton neither ordered more copies of *The Squatter and the Don* nor paid Lippincott the final $46.02 owed for *Who Would Have Thought It?* The company would hold the remaining copies of her novel until they were destroyed by fire in November 1899. In 1900, Lippincott reimbursed itself for Ruiz de Burton's debt through insurance, or what was labeled a "Contingency Fund" within the records.[37]

More than breaking even on this account, though, Lippincott profited from the novel by selling it on commission. While *Who Would Have*

Thought It? sold at a retail price of $1.75, Ruiz de Burton was credited only $0.875 per copy sold. This is why she earned only $350 for the sale of four hundred copies. The Lippincott ledgers describe its accounting methods: "We a/c sales $1.75 1/3 1/4." In this equation, $1.75 is the retail price of the book, "1/3" is the discount given to booksellers, and "1/4" is the commission fee that Lippincott charges for each sale. On the publisher's end, this commission amounts to $0.295 per copy sold, so that Lippincott would have earned $118.00 from the four hundred copies initially sold, and $158.42 total for the 537 copies sold over the life of the book. Thus while Ruiz de Burton still owed Lippincott $46.02, according to her contract, the company nevertheless made a profit on the book—minimizing its own risk by making Ruiz de Burton responsible for the cost of production. Indeed, it is possible that Lippincott made additional profit in the production of the novel by charging Ruiz de Burton more than its own costs for the stereotype plates and printing of the book.

Within Lippincott, the job printing department played a significant role in terms of publication and revenue. While company records list many titles that paid a royalty to the author, countless others are entered in the same way as Ruiz de Burton's, with a one-third discount to retailers followed by a one-quarter commission for Lippincott. In general, these publications function in the same way as Ruiz de Burton's novel: a down payment is made to cover a good portion of the cost of production; sales are then credited to the author to pay off the remaining cost of production; and the full cost of production must be paid before authors can earn any money. In my review of the records, albeit not a comprehensive examination, I did not find any examples of a book printed by the job department in which the author earned any money from sales beyond the cost of production.

These books also failed to sell because Lippincott did not spend money advertising titles that were printed through the job department. As a major book distributor, it did include these books in shipments to booksellers across the country, and it also listed the books for sale in its catalog. It did not, however, spend money advertising such books in magazines or newspapers. Editors of magazines and periodicals would also have been aware of Lippincott's job printing department, and perhaps this is why the sixty-six editorial copies of *Who Would Have Thought It?* received almost no attention in published reviews or announcements.

Editors must have known that these novels were among countless Lippincott commission publications, printed in small runs at the cost of the author. Indeed, although Lippincott did make an effort to reprint novels by well-known authors and to publish new fiction in its monthly magazine, the company would not have been known as an especially "literary" publisher. It was first and foremost a publishing *giant*, with an established investment in religious and medical texts.

Whether such commission printing was exploitative is open to debate. As mentioned, Ruiz de Burton questioned the amount owed, wondering how she was still indebted to the company after her novel sold more than 475 copies. In a letter soon after publication, Lippincott responded to Ruiz de Burton's worries about sales by saying that the book was neither a "failure, nor a marked success."[38] The company adjusted her bill based on additional sales, and asked her to pay the amount owed. Lippincott also encouraged Ruiz de Burton to consider having another novel published on commission. The company told her, "[We are] afraid that the issue of 'Who would have thought it?' will entail a pecuniary loss—unless, indeed, you make another effort that strikes the popular vein, in which case the present romance would also take a new start."[39] To some extent, Lippincott was preying on authorial vanity, seeking to make a profit from another round of commission printing. Certainly, in this relationship, the publishing house always won.

Yet at the same time, Lippincott records show that a book such as *Who Would Have Thought It?* received all sorts of care and benefits in being published by the company. Ruiz de Burton paid less than half the cost of production for a book that was given the imprimatur and packaging of a major U.S. publisher. That book was distributed and sold throughout the country. It was listed as a Lippincott publication, both within company catalogs and in advertisements included within other Lippincott publications. It was delivered to friends, editors, and booksellers free of charge at Ruiz de Burton's command. Moreover, if the full cost of production had been paid, Ruiz de Burton would have owned the stereotype plates of the novel and the copyright that was understood to accompany them. Perhaps most significantly, Ruiz de Burton was able to express herself in a volume of literary fiction that would not easily disappear from the world.

GOING UNDERCOVER

How might this history of the publication affect our understanding of the novel? While *Who Would Have Thought It?* has often been interpreted as a parody of sentimental writing, its place in the Lippincott catalog shows that it is better understood within the genre of sensationalism. The novel certainly does critique sentimental novels of the era, yet it can be linked more directly to mid-nineteenth-century sensation fiction.

Lippincott published a range of sensational titles at this time, particularly novels by Ouida and translations of the German writer E. Marlitt. Indeed, in the ten-page gathering of advertisements included at the end of the original publication of *Who Would Have Thought It?,* there are full-page advertisements for novels by both Ouida and Marlitt.[40] Likewise, in the Lippincott catalog that is included in the 1873 *Uniform Trade List Annual,* which lists *Who Would Have Thought It?* for sale, the works of Ouida and Marlitt are featured prominently.[41] Lippincott published numerous books by these authors in the 1860s and 1870s. From Ouida, it published *Under Two Flags* (1867), *Tricotrin* (1869), *Puck* (1873), and many others. From Marlitt it published *Countess Gisela* (1869), *The Second Wife* (1874), and more. Marlitt's novels were translated by Anais L. Wister, who lived in Philadelphia, and Lippincott records indicate that Wister translated more than thirty books for the company. Her translations of Marlitt sold anywhere from 4,000 to 23,000 copies per title, and between 1883 and 1897, Wister earned more than $16,000 in royalties from these books.[42]

Who Would Have Thought It? undoubtedly challenges mid-nineteenth-century ideologies of true womanhood, domesticity, and sentiment. This is most evident in the character of Mrs. Norval—a white woman and Northern abolitionist—who despises Lola, steals her money, and enters an illicit marriage with Reverend Hackwell. On the one hand, Mrs. Norval is described as "the best Christian, best mother," an ideal representative of white womanhood.[43] On the other, Mrs. Norval herself exclaims that she "hate[s] foreigners and papists,"[44] and readers see her greed and hatred swell at the sight of Lola. Elsewhere in the novel, it is emphasized that such "good American women" support the Union Army not because of an ethical stance against slavery but because they "believed firmly in 'MANIFEST DESTINY'"[45] (the capitalization is Ruiz de Burton's). In other words, these women support the Union cause in terms of imperialist expansion rather than abolition. In countless instances, the novel offers scathing criticism of the racial, religious, and economic imperialism of these supposedly pure women. Looking at the publication of the novel through Lippincott, however, it is clear that the book participated even more directly in the genre of literary sensationalism.

Sensational fiction itself can be difficult to define, but it is generally marked by provocative plots that involve crime, affairs, and mistaken identity. In a 2012 article, Emily Steinlight describes sensational novels as "notorious for exposing bigamy, adultery, and false identities in the midst of seemingly ordinary and often genteel milieu."[46] Similarly, Andrew Radford defines sensationalism as a genre that employs "psychic disintegration, duplicates, spectres, and transposed identities to erode the seemingly solid and respectable structures of mid-Victorian domesticity."[47] In many ways, then, sensation fiction was already established as a genre that reacted against sentimentalism. As a style of writing, it was wide-ranging and would become influential for crime and adventure fiction of the late nineteenth century. Yet however sensationalism is defined, Ruiz de Burton's novel—with its depraved minister and adulterous women, its vast sums of gold, its lost letters and its mistaken identities—clearly fits within the genre. Published alongside novels by Ouida and E. Marlitt, and manufactured to look like them, customers purchasing *Who Would Have Thought It?* would have recognized it as sensational fiction, if nothing else. Indeed, booksellers would likely have steered customers toward the title in this way.

Discussions of U.S. sensationalism, as opposed to British sensationalism, have noted its particular American inflections. Michael Denning's *Mechanic Accents* argued that U.S. sensation fiction was not a part of middle-class culture but rather "part of the popular culture of the 'producing classes.'"[48] Denning goes on to explore how popular sensationalism became a sort of battlefield between working-class and genteel cultures. More recent discussions of sensationalism have considered how it allowed authors to respond to U.S. imperial expansion. As Jesse Alemán and Shelley Streeby describe, "Sensational literature is more outrageous and less respectable [than sentimental literature], more connected to a lowly world of popular entertainment than the middle-class home, and more concerned with exotic foreign spaces than the domestic sphere, making it an excellent archive of popular fantasies and fears about U.S. imperialism."[49] Beyond its lurid details and even beyond its working-class origins, American sensationalism was a genre particularly engaged in discussions of empire and territorial expansion.

Ruiz de Burton thus recognized an opportunity to adapt sensational fiction for her own purposes. She understood that sensationalism—a genre that had always criticized genteel culture—would serve as a useful vehicle for her own response to white womanhood and manifest destiny. Sensationalism was a tool to reach an audience outside the domestic sphere, to challenge middle-class norms and explore ideas that were otherwise taboo. The genre also allowed Ruiz de Burton to offer metacommentary on depictions of California and the frontier that had typically been represented as sensational. Ruiz de Burton's innovation, then, was not merely to parody the *domestic* novel but to turn the lens of *sensationalism* back on the U.S. nation, so that the nation's own myths of purity and whiteness become illicit material.

Because the book was published anonymously and made to look like so many other Lippincott novels, Ruiz de Burton's critique emerges covertly. Indeed, the material manufacture of Ruiz de Burton's book, camouflaged among Lippincott's other novels in a house style, can help critics better understand the impact Ruiz de Burton hoped the novel might have on a contemporary reader. Her publication strategy aimed to draw unsuspecting American readers into the narrative, in English, and to guide them gradually toward the perspective of an anonymous Mexican American.

This strategy becomes especially apparent in light of the novel's narrative voice. In general, *Who Would Have Thought It?* is written from a third-person omniscient perspective, moving freely between various characters' thoughts and perspectives. At times, however, the narrator steps in to offer more explicit commentary on the events taking place. This technique itself was not new. It might be compared to the narrative interjections that Harriet Beecher Stowe disperses throughout *Uncle Tom's Cabin*, addressing the reader directly to ask for their thoughts on slavery and the separation of enslaved families. But Ruiz de Burton offers a subtle twist on the strategy. In chapter 8 of the novel, for example, the narrator considers what thoughts might be passing through the mind of Mrs. Norval's sister, Lavinia Sprigg. This reflection on Lavinia is then answered with a question: "Quién sabe?"[50] This is the first time in the novel that the narrator breaks the third-person omniscient perspective and interjects by posing a question directly to the reader. And significantly, this interjection is given in Spanish. The narrator is thus introduced to the reader as Spanish-speaking.

The question itself—"Quién sabe?" or "Who knows?"—echoes the novel's title, reiterating its epistemological concerns over the ways identity and knowledge intertwine. Who can offer a different perspective from the ideas that white Americans take for granted? The question, which is later repeated in the novel, is rhetorical, answered by the outsider status of the Spanish-speaking narrator. In other words, as the book parodies American culture, an implied response to the title—*Who Would Have Thought It?*—is proffered through its underlying Mexican American perspective. This is why anonymity was so important to Ruiz de Burton, who never published work under her own name. It is also why she chose to write novels in English. She had hoped to catch her audience unaware, urging readers to question the enclosing boundaries of the U.S. nation and to imagine multiethnic forms of knowledge.

This strategy was not commercially successful, however, and on publication, *Who Would Have Thought It?* was reviewed in only a handful of publications.[51] Among these, reviews in *Godey's Lady's Book* and *Literary World* were deeply negative, recommending that readers avoid the book. The most positive and most frequently cited review was written in San Francisco's *Daily Alta California,* and the article is noteworthy because it interviews Ruiz de Burton as the author.[52] The reporter for the *Daily Alta California* claims to have discovered Ruiz de Burton's identity serendipitously, by mentioning the book to her on a train and witnessing the author's flustered reaction. The reporter decides to make Ruiz de Burton's identity known, despite the author's objections, reviewing the book enthusiastically and noting that it is the first novel published by a native Californian. It seems possible, then, that Ruiz de Burton wrote this review herself, in an effort to claim her authorial identity and advertise the book as a work of Californian literature.

Notably, when this review speaks about the novel, it turns to the language of sensationalism. The subtitle for the review describes *Who Would Have Thought It?* as "A New Sensation for the Public," and the article notes that the book's themes are "developed with sensational effect." This terminology is not merely coincidental. Rather, it indicates how the novel participated in the genre of sensationalism in a way that was easily recognized. For a contemporary audience, *Who Would Have*

Thought It? was meant to be understood as sensationalism and read alongside the novels of Ouida and E. Marlitt.

SENSATIONAL JOB

Ruiz de Burton's publication through Lippincott reflects her liminal relationship to the U.S. nation, neither a participant in Anglo imperialism nor an oppressed minority, and yet both. The border status of the job printing department, at the edges of the Lippincott business model and the edges of the factory itself, is akin to the border status of Ruiz de Burton as an American. Indeed, her relationship with Lippincott's job printing department links her to other ethnic authors from the mid-nineteenth century, particularly Harriet Wilson, who self-financed the printing of *Our Nig* in hopes of making money and spreading her message.[53] Ruiz de Burton's novel tried to imagine a marriage between Mexico and America, a future that would cross national and ethnic boundaries. Camouflaged as popular sensational fiction, the book attempted to align its white readers with a Hispanic way of thinking. Yet rather than marketing herself explicitly as a Californian author, Ruiz de Burton hoped to influence her reader through more ambiguous literary tactics. She deployed sensational fiction as a means of criticizing both white womanhood and manifest destiny, turning the genre against domestic literature and against sensationalized depictions of the western frontier. She then placed this novel, anonymously, alongside other sensational fiction within the Lippincott catalog. While this publication came at a price, and did not garner the reception Ruiz de Burton had hoped, it nevertheless ensured that her book was well-manufactured and distributed across the nation.

CHAPTER 2

ACROSS THE COLOR LINE

Charles W. Chesnutt, Houghton Mifflin,
and the Racial Paratext

érard Genette's concept of the "paratext" has remarkable traction for the study of African American literature. Introduced to describe materials that frame the literary text—prefaces, title pages, book covers, and advertisements—the paratext, in Genette's formulation, remains auxiliary. It is "always subordinate to 'its' text."[1] Yet for U.S. writers of color, especially those hoping to influence a predominantly white audience, the paratext has often become a crucial point of tension. As Beth McCoy argues in a 2006 issue of *PMLA*, the paratext has functioned centrally for African American literature "as a zone transacting ever-changing modes of white domination and resistance to that domination."[2] For example, one might consider the African American slave narrative, in which frontispiece portraits and white-authored prefaces have served to authenticate the text for a mainstream audience.[3] In a reversal that Genette did not anticipate,[4] paratextual materials vie for status over and against the text itself.

Scholarship on African American literature has not traditionally focused on these bibliographical materials. As Leon Jackson argues, "Scholars of slave culture and print culture have rarely shared agendas, nor have, more broadly, African American social, cultural, and literary historians, and those within the community of book historians."[5] Nevertheless, attention to the paratext is informative for the way that literature was framed and presented to its audience. Indeed, because the paratext is an especially fraught space for African American literature, these framing materials can point to important tensions and disconnections in what Robert Darnton has called the "communications circuit" between author, publisher, and reader.[6] As book historians increasingly turn their attention to ethnic literatures, and as critics of U.S. ethnic literature draw on the methods of critical bibliography, they consider what Jerome McGann has called the "bibliographic codes" and the "linguistic codes" of the text, as well as the relationship between the two.[7] This chapter contributes to such scholarly developments by examining Charles W. Chesnutt's interactions with the publisher Houghton, Mifflin and Company and the production of materials that framed and marketed Chesnutt's writing at the height of his literary career.

Chesnutt's relationship to the publishing industry has been a common theme in his critical revival. William L. Andrews's 1980 biography *The Literary Career of Charles W. Chesnutt* pays significant attention both to Chesnutt's popular reception and to his correspondence with publishers. Andrews describes Chesnutt as "the first Afro-American writer to use the white-controlled mass media in the service of serious social fiction on behalf of the black community."[8] Richard Brodhead's work throughout the 1990s—in *Cultures of Letters* and as editor of Chesnutt's journals and conjure stories—not only places Chesnutt in the context of literary regionalism but also emphasizes the cross-racial production of *The Conjure Woman,* as it was solicited by Houghton Mifflin editor Walter Hines Page.[9] In these examinations and others,[10] Chesnutt's literary career and his professional relationship with publishers have remained a central topic of discussion. Indeed, the support of this publishing apparatus is one of the major factors that differentiate Chesnutt from predecessors such as Hannah Crafts, William Wells Brown, and Harriet Wilson, and from contemporaries such as Sutton E. Griggs and Pauline Hopkins.[11]

Yet despite the attention given to Chesnutt's interaction with the commercial publishing industry, few critics have examined the material traces of this relationship in print, which extend beyond the prestige of the Houghton Mifflin name. In addition to this imprimatur, Chesnutt worked with Houghton Mifflin to negotiate how his work would be manufactured and advertised, where it would be distributed, and the extent to which his racial background would be known to readers. Chesnutt's literary career is remarkable not only for the extent that he allowed Houghton Mifflin to direct his own writing but also, conversely, for the influence Chesnutt exercised on his publisher. In the years that he focused almost exclusively on his literary career, taking time away from his stenography business from 1899 to 1901, Chesnutt was exceedingly productive in terms of both literary output and self-promotion. In December 1899, for example, when Houghton Mifflin reported on its advertising campaigns in Boston, Washington, New York, and several other cities, Chesnutt suggested it add Cincinnati, Chicago, and Detroit to its list.[12] Chesnutt also requested and reviewed "circulars" from Houghton Mifflin, so that he might distribute small advertisements to audiences of his readings.[13] In the same way that Cécile Cottenet describes the relationship between ethnic authors and mainstream publishers, Chesnutt was temporarily "able to work from *within,* although [he] continued to embody 'otherness'"[14] Moreover, while Chesnutt's letters to Houghton Mifflin are marked by concerns about the marketing of his work, these advertisements and promotional materials have received little attention among scholars.

In this marketing campaign, depictions of Chesnutt's authorial identity shift across the color line. When Chesnutt's work was initially published by Houghton Mifflin, it was designed to pass as white-authored plantation fiction. This can be seen in fliers and advertisements for *The Conjure Woman,* as well as in the design of the book itself. By the time *The Wife of His Youth* was published, however, Houghton Mifflin had disclosed Chesnutt's mixed-race background, advertising him as a light-complexioned man of color and as the laureate of the color line. Chesnutt's racial ambiguity complemented the open-ended style of the stories themselves. Yet while these advertising strategies were relatively successful within the popular literary marketplace, Houghton Mifflin's subsequent attempt to advertise Chesnutt as the champion of the colored race proved a failure for his 1901 novel *The Marrow of Tradition.* Although the company expended substantial resources to promote the book as the successor to best-selling political novels such as *Uncle Tom's Cabin* and *A Fool's Errand,* its sales disappointed both the author and the publisher.

Houghton Mifflin and Chesnutt thus collaborated in a surprisingly creative yet commercially unsuccessful experiment to pass African American fiction into genteel literary culture.[15] Houghton Mifflin's support in this endeavor, and its experimental nature, is evidenced by the rapid adjustments the company made in its marketing campaign from one book to the next. In the span of two years, the publisher applied its substantial resources to market Chesnutt first as white, then as the laureate of the color line, and finally as a champion of the colored race. These adjustments depended on Chesnutt's own ability to pass as white. The evolution of this marketing campaign also aligned with the literary genres Chesnutt would use to subvert and oppose white supremacist ideologies—from plantation tales to realist stories of the color line to more openly political fiction. Yet despite these efforts, which were particularly substantial for *The Marrow of Tradition,* Chesnutt's writing encountered dual attitudes of resistance and rejection that were deeply entrenched in the popular literary marketplace. On the one hand, when readers interpreted Chesnutt's satirical work in terms of the dominant genres, they tended to see it as reinforcing the racial stereotypes Chesnutt sought to subvert. On the other, when Chesnutt's work was understood as critical or political, it provoked a backlash among the vast majority of his white readers and was harshly rejected. Ultimately, Chesnutt's literary critique of the color line was more successful in gaining support from Houghton Mifflin than from a popular audience.

PASSING THROUGH THE PARATEXT

Charles Chesnutt was born in 1858 in Cleveland, Ohio, the son of free parents with mixed racial backgrounds. Chesnutt's family had migrated to Cleveland from Fayetteville, North Carolina, prior to his birth, and they returned to the South just after the Civil War. Growing up in Fayetteville, Chesnutt excelled in the town's normal school, which had been established by the Freedman's Bureau. He concluded his formal education in 1871, after the death of his mother, and began work as a teacher to help support his father and siblings. Chesnutt taught in several towns in both North and South Carolina before returning to Fayetteville, where he married Susan Perry in 1878 and became principal of the normal school in 1880. By 1883, however, Chesnutt was increasingly troubled by the oppressive conditions of the post-Reconstruction South. He moved to New York City for a brief period, working as a stenographer, and then relocated permanently with his wife and children in Cleveland. There, Chesnutt studied law and passed the bar exam in 1887 before establishing his own stenography business. This court reporting business was Chesnutt's primary occupation and source of income throughout his life, and from the early twentieth century until his death in 1932, Chesnutt remained a relatively affluent businessman. His son, Edwin, attended Harvard University. His daughters, Ethel, Helen, and Dorothy, went to Smith College and Case Western Reserve. (Helen went on to earn a master's of arts from Columbia University, and taught Latin at Central High School in Cleveland. Langston Hughes was one of her students, and the two kept in touch for many years, so that there is a direct lineage between the Chesnutt family and the poet.[16]) Late in life, Chesnutt served on the General Committee of the NAACP, and in 1928 he received its Spingarn Medal. Thus while Chesnutt described his literary career as "Post-Bellum—Pre-Harlem," it is worth noting that his life stretched from the antebellum era into the Harlem Renaissance.[17] Chesnutt lived during the time of slavery, through the Civil War and Reconstruction, to the establishment of Jim Crow segregation, and into the Harlem Renaissance— and his writing responds to these historical shifts.

Before settling on his business career as a stenographer, Chesnutt had hoped for many years to earn his living as a popular author. In one passage from his journals, Chesnutt claimed "It is the dream of my life—to be an author! It is not so much the [fame . . .]. It is not altogether the money. It is a mixture of motives. I want fame; I want money; I want to raise my children in a different rank of life from that I sprang from."[18] The passage aptly conveys the mixed motives that drove Chesnutt's writing. From 1880 through the turn of the century, Chesnutt associated writing with money and fame, hoping he might capitalize on popular literary authorship. Yet Chesnutt also envisioned authorship as a means of enacting social justice. In another journal entry from May 29, 1880, Chesnutt contemplates his future career: "Besides, if I do write, I shall write for a purpose, a high, holy, purpose, and this will inspire me to greater effort. The object of my writings would not be so much the elevation of the colored people as the elevation of the whites."[19] In this passage, Chesnutt envisions himself as a crusader, battling against racial injustice in the United States. Here, as William Andrews notes, Chesnutt accurately predicts "the thematic crux" of his mature work.[20] He hoped to target a white audience through literary fiction and to lift these readers out of ignorance and racism. At this stage in his career, Chesnutt hoped this holy crusade could earn him fame and commercial literary success.

Chesnutt worked toward his literary ambitions deliberately, publishing in S. S. McClure's newspaper syndicates and in magazines such as *Family Fiction* and *Puck* in the mid-1880s.[21] In August 1887, "The Goophered Grapevine" was published in the *Atlantic Monthly*, making Chesnutt the first African American to publish a short story in the prestigious magazine. As Frank Luther Mott notes, the *Atlantic Monthly* "enjoyed a perpetual state of literary grace, so that for a large section of the American public, whatever the *Atlantic* printed was literature."[22] After publishing two additional stories with the magazine in the years that followed, Chesnutt wrote to Houghton Mifflin, the *Atlantic Monthly's* parent company, to pitch his first book—a collection of short fiction called *Rena Walden and Other Stories.*

In this letter from September 8, 1891, Chesnutt also revealed his racial background to Houghton Mifflin, saying the book would be "the first contribution by an American with acknowledged African descent to purely imaginative literature."[23] In the same way that Chesnutt had been open about his racial background with literary acquaintances, including Albion Tourgée and George Washington Cable, he told Houghton Mifflin from the outset that he was African American. Yet Chesnutt was unsure whether this fact should be made known to the public: "I should not want this fact to be stated in the book, nor advertised, unless the publisher advised it; first, because I do not know whether it would affect its reception favorably or unfavorably, or at all; second, because I would not have the book judged by any standard lower than that set for other writers."[24] Even before publishing his first book, then, Chesnutt recognized how his authorial identity, presented through advertisements, would affect the reading and reception of his work. Not knowing how to navigate this dynamic, Chesnutt left the advertisement of his own racial identity to the publisher's discretion. He goes on to address other aspects of the book's publication, asking if it can be "bound in cloth," and requesting "the best terms" Houghton Mifflin can offer. The letter is indicative of Chesnutt's approach throughout his publishing career: the young author is ambitious, direct, and openly self-interested.

Houghton Mifflin rejected the *Rena Walden* manuscript, advising Chesnutt to continue building his reputation with short stories, and Chesnutt took this recommendation. Six years later, the company again rejected a book manuscript submitted by Chesnutt (an expanded version of the Rena Walden story, which would become *The House Behind the Cedars*) but instead solicited a collection of plantation tales in the style of "The Goophered Grapevine." At this point, Chesnutt had actually abandoned the local color style of these conjure stories, explaining to George Washington Cable, "I think I have about used up the old Negro who serves as mouthpiece, and I shall drop him in future stories, as well as much of the dialect."[25] Yet when Walter Hines Page, an editor at Houghton Mifflin, requested additional conjure stories for a book collection, Chesnutt responded enthusiastically. He composed six additional stories in as many weeks, working in spare hours outside of full-time employment.[26]

Chesnutt's conjure stories take on the style of the popular plantation fiction developed by Joel Chandler Harris and Thomas Nelson Page. Where Harris had introduced Uncle Remus, the freedman narrator of the Br'er Rabbit series, Chesnutt introduced Uncle Julius, the freedman narrator of the conjure tales. Chesnutt's stories also follow the standard narrative pattern of local color plantation fiction. As Heather Tirado Gilligan describes, "The 'Uncle Julius' tales conform to the formula of a white frame narrator who prompts an ex-slave for a story of the old plantation; the ex-slave then complies with a story told entirely in dialect; the tales conclude with the reflections of the frame narrator on the tale that he has just heard."[27] In accordance with the genre, the white frame narrator of *The Conjure Woman*, John, provokes Uncle Julius to tell dialect folk tales of the old plantation.

Chesnutt's work differs from the genre established by Harris, however, in the complexity and intelligence of Uncle Julius and the stories he tells.[28] Whereas Harris and Page make the freedman storyteller "testify to his love of the old days and his lack of desire for equal social rights,"[29] Chesnutt's conjure tales are haunted by the trauma of slavery. In "The Goophered Grapevine," for example, Uncle Julius tells the story of an enslaved man named Henry whose body begins to cycle with the seasons of the grape field he is forced to harvest; when the grape vine withers and perishes, Henry also dies. In "Po' Sandy," the title character is magically turned into a pine tree so that rather than being sent as a house servant from one family plantation to another he can remain close to his wife, Tenie. Once transformed into a pine tree, however, Sandy is milled into lumber for the plantation's new kitchen. Uncle Julius tells his white auditors these stories so that they may better understand the traumatic history of the former slave plantation they have come to purchase.

Recent critics have found these stories rich for interpretation, examining a range of topics from reconstruction justice to environmental politics to Chesnutt's use of classical metamorphosis.[30] Critics have been especially drawn to the way Chesnutt adapts the popular plantation genre for his own purposes. In a lengthy chapter from *To Wake the Nations*, Eric Sundquist calls this adaptation Chesnutt's "cakewalk," which mimics the dominant style.[31] Kenneth Price similarly claims, "Because Chesnutt had to penetrate a type of unofficial censorship, he built a duality into his early tales that virtually asked that he be 'misunderstood' by some readers."[32] Even before these critics, David D. Britt had commented on this phenomenon in a 1972 article for *CLA Journal* titled "What You See Is What You Get." Britt argues that the conjure stories are "deliberately structured to allow the reader to be deceived . . . if he chooses, or needs, to be deceived."[33] Needless to say, Chesnutt was intensely aware of this ambiguity when producing the conjure stories. In his journals, he had described how he would approach white readers in an effort to "lead them on imperceptibly, unconsciously step by step to the desired state of feeling."[34]

Yet this potential to be misunderstood within the genre of plantation fiction hinged, as well, on paratextual presentations of the book. Indeed, Houghton Mifflin and Chesnutt collaborated to advertise *The Conjure Woman* in the style of *Uncle Remus* plantation fiction and even, by omission, as a white-authored text. Influenced by this marketing campaign, the vast majority of the book's reviewers resisted its subversive potential, interpreting the conjure stories as following the familiar conventions of plantation fiction. These reviews, in turn, were recycled back into the marketing campaign for the collection, reinforcing the book's meaning within the genre. In other words, efforts to market the book in terms of plantation fiction predisposed readers "to be deceived" by the stories and to misunderstand them. Chesnutt's entry into the prestigious realm of Houghton Mifflin depended on the potential for the conjure tales to pass as white-authored fiction.

Houghton Mifflin's efforts to market *The Conjure Woman* in the style of plantation fiction are most evident in the design of the book, which displays the portrait of an elderly freedman flanked on both sides by rabbits. Because Br'er Rabbit had been introduced through the Uncle Remus series, the cover sets *The Conjure Woman* firmly in the lineage of plantation literature. Indeed, Houston A. Baker, Jr., argues that the book's designers "outdid themselves in suggesting the link between Chesnutt's content and that of the ever popular Joel Chandler Harris's 'Uncle Remus.'"[35] In a 2007 article for the *Papers of the Bibliographic Society of America,* Jean Lee Cole offers further analysis of the cover, comparing it to book designs for Paul Laurence Dunbar and Winnifred Eaton/Onoto Watanna. Cole points out that publishers at this time asked book designers to conventionalize cover art, so that texts could be "easily recognized by genre."[36] In fact, Houghton Mifflin was also the publisher of the Uncle Remus books, which sold consistently well from 1898 to 1907.[37] Its 1892 *Uncle Remus and Friends* had a cover comparable to *The Conjure Woman,* with a landscape image of rabbits and a close-up portrait of the freedman storyteller. Houghton Mifflin company records show that Decorative Designers was hired to produce *The Conjure Woman,*[38] a company that would become the most prolific designer of trade bindings in the early twentieth-century United States.[39] While Decorative Designers would not have produced the earlier Uncle Remus covers for Houghton Mifflin (the company was not established until 1895), it clearly drew on the plantation genre in its design for *The Conjure Woman.*

Like the text itself, it is possible to read this cover as subversive. Henry B. Wonham argues, for instance, that caricatures such as those on the cover of *The Conjure Woman* display not only a nativist impulse against the ethnic other but also a "potential to instigate a radical decentering of identity."[40] From this perspective, the freedman caricature on the book's cover calls into question the very stereotype it inscribes. Indeed, Houghton Mifflin was surprisingly deliberate in its manufacture of the book, producing a cover that mimics the plantation genre in the same way as the text itself. The portraits of the freedman and the rabbits seem to be smirking at the reader, trickster figures that transform into one another. It seems unlikely, however, that such an interpretation was, to borrow a term from Wolfgang Iser, "actualized" by a popular audience.[41] Seen as caricature, the cover more simply animalizes the black male figure, linking the freedman and rabbits in size, facial features, and hair color. The brown cloth cover of the book, which would have been among the first decisions made by Decorative Designers when preparing the binding,[42] also serves as the color of the freedman's skin. The book thus allows the reader to hold and examine the body of the folk storyteller, in the style of plantation literature and ethnographic regionalism.

THE CONJURE
WOMAN 〕〢 〕〢 〕〢
BY CHARLES W. CHESNUTT

HOUGHTON, MIFFLIN & CO., PUBLISHERS
4 Park St. Boston, 11 East 17th St., New York.

Oct. 18, 1899.

FIGURE 5. Promotional leaflet, *The Conjure Woman* (Boston: Houghton Mifflin, 1899). MS Am 2030: (244), p. 8, Houghton Library, Harvard University.

In October 1899, Houghton Mifflin produced a promotional flier for *The Conjure Woman* that similarly allowed the book to pass as a white-authored text (figure 5). This was a small, folded leaflet that could be sent to bookstores or handed out by Chesnutt at readings. In a fascinating maneuver, the pamphlet includes an image of Chesnutt himself. The picture is a medium close-up of Chesnutt's face and shoulders, set between the title of his book and the name of his publisher. Chesnutt's light skin stands out against a dark background; he is dressed in a suit and tie, and his hair is parted at the side.

There is nothing false about the image, but it would allow many readers, especially Houghton Mifflin's target audience, to assume that Chesnutt was a white author. Moreover, Houghton Mifflin was clearly aware of the subtlety of this promotional flier, since Chesnutt had introduced himself as African American in his earliest 1891 letter to the company.[43] The leaflet thus indicates Houghton Mifflin's collaboration with Chesnutt to manipulate the boundaries of the color line. Aware of Chesnutt's African American background, the company was willing to play on its customers' perception of race and whiteness. And while Chesnutt did not choose to pass as white in his own personal or professional life, he was nevertheless willing to allow readers to assume that *The Conjure Woman* was a white-authored text.

Houghton Mifflin also produced a number of catalogs to sell its books, including a catalog of authors, which offered biographical information for each writer. In this paratext, the company discusses Chesnutt's biography in more detail, but nevertheless avoids explicit mention of his African American background. As with the promotional leaflet produced for *The Conjure Woman,* the minibiography calls to mind all the complexities of racial passing. Rather than actively misinforming the reader, it allows Chesnutt to be seen as white through omission and genteel nondisclosure. The biography itself emphasizes Chesnutt's professional accomplishments: a former principal and a law student, Chesnutt "has made court-reporting his business," and "has traveled in Europe."[44] The biographical description also narrates Chesnutt's migrations (from Cleveland to Fayetteville and back to Cleveland), without mentioning the race politics that guided those movements (from the Civil War to Reconstruction and into the post-Reconstruction era). It emphasizes Chesnutt's achievements so that readers would see Chesnutt as a well-traveled teacher, lawyer, and businessman.

The biographical description comes closest to mentioning Chesnutt's African American background when it describes him as the former principal of the "State Normal School at Fayetteville." This school, which remains a historically black university today, was founded by a group of African American men just after the Civil War, and was erected by General Oliver O. Howard, commissioner of the Freedman's Bureau.[45] Readers of the catalog familiar with the Normal School at Fayetteville might therefore question Chesnutt's racial background, but it would have also been possible for a white man to serve as principal. Moreover, while the official title of the school at that time was the State Colored Normal School, the biographical description removes this racial identifier.

The reception of *The Conjure Woman* provides further evidence that, among the majority of readers, the book was understood as white-authored plantation fiction.[46] These reviews considered the stories according to a variety of elements, such as conjuration, dialect, and the character of Uncle Julius, with a tendency to reduce each category to forms of racial caricature. Critics at the turn of the century, for example, commonly praised the stories for their accurate expression of African American spiritual beliefs. An anonymous reviewer in the *Philadelphia Times* summarizes the book as a series of stories "which tell, with delightful accuracy, some of the race superstitions of the negroes in North Carolina."[47] The review sees Uncle Julius as a representative of black superstition, and claims that these stories are accurate reflections of voodoo beliefs. Contrary to this opinion, however, Chesnutt had invented the folk elements of these stories with only a loose connection to actual North Carolina conjuration. In a more outrageous response to the conjure stories, another review argues, "Skepticism cannot rob one of the belief that this [conjuration] was the real religion of the old plantation; the goopher 'mixtry,' not the overseer's lash, the dreaded power."[48] Here, Chesnutt's satire of the plantation genre is entirely misunderstood. Whereas conjuration within the stories functions as a metaphor for the incomprehensible violence of slavery, this review sees conjuration as the "power" behind slavery, in place of the "overseer's lash."

Reviews discussing other aspects of *The Conjure Woman* also miss the book's satiric intent. Several reviews emphasize the pleasure readers will take in Chesnutt's rendering of dialect. One reviewer for the *Springfield Sunday Republican* writes, "The collection of short stories . . .

are really delightful bits of humor couched in a negro dialect as seductive as that of 'Uncle Remus' or Thomas Nelson Page."[49] Rather than noting any of the contrasts with Page or Harris, the review places the conjure stories squarely within the genre. The *Sunday Republican* continues, "The stories are racy, of the soil[,] and the dialect is rich and unctuous." Other reviews conflate Chesnutt with the stories' narrator, John, claiming that the author himself has traveled to North Carolina to open a grape farm. Numerous reviews, such as one in the *New York Times,* describe the fiction as "quaint" and picturesque.[50] In other words, despite the complexities critics see in these stories today, popular reviews at the turn of the century provide little evidence that readers engaged with the more subversive elements of *The Conjure Woman.* If reviewers did see these possibilities within the text, they did not speak of them within the commercial literary marketplace. Much more often, they interpreted the tales as "delightful bits of humor," comparable to the Uncle Remus stories.

Such readings, however, were also enabled by the decisions of Chesnutt and Houghton Mifflin regarding the book's presentation and marketing. *The Conjure Woman* does play on the generic conventions of plantation fiction. The stories' white narrator, John, does express some of Chesnutt's own bourgeois sensibilities. Moreover, Chesnutt and Houghton Mifflin went so far as to recycle contemporary reviews back into their advertising campaign for the book. The flier with Chesnutt's portrait on the front (see figure 5), for example, is a folded leaflet that opens to reveal a set of blurbs copied from contemporary reviews. In line with these reviews, the advertisement emphasizes similarities to plantation fiction, highlighting features of the text such as "Humor" and "Dialect." One quotation from the *Portland Transcript,* praises Uncle Julius for standing "shoulder to shoulder" with Uncle Remus.[51] The book had been designed and manufactured to invoke such comparisons, and the company recycled this popular reception within its own advertising campaign. Another quotation included inside the leaflet, from the *St. Louis Globe Democrat,* commends Chesnutt's use of dialect for showing "an intuitive understanding of the Ethiopian character, with its strange mixtures of American civilization, and barbaric instinct inherited from African ancestors."

Chesnutt approved these fliers. In a letter from October 11, 1899, just one week before the date listed on the archival leaflet, Chesnutt tells

Houghton Mifflin, "I received the package of circulars you sent me, and used some of them for distribution at a reading I gave last night. I may ask you for more of them soon, as there are several ways in which I can use them to advantage."[52] Here, Chesnutt distributes the flier and requests more to be used for promotion of the book. Chesnutt also seems to appreciate the leaflet's ambiguous visual rhetoric, saying that it can be used in "several ways." The design of the flier, like that of *The Conjure Woman*, allowed Chesnutt to pass as white and to be read in terms of popular plantation fiction.

"LAUREATE OF THE COLOR LINE"

Despite this presentation and marketing, Chesnutt was open about his mixed-race background in nearly all of his personal relationships, and because he did not actively commit to passing as a white author, he became increasingly well known as a writer of color. In fact, even as Houghton Mifflin printed fliers and catalogs that allowed Chesnutt to pass as white, it also experimented with advertising Chesnutt as a mixed-race author in targeted locations. By the time Houghton Mifflin published Chesnutt's second book in 1899, *The Wife of His Youth,* the company would not only announce Chesnutt's African American background but would actively use his heritage to promote the collection, aligning Chesnutt's mixed-race identity with the ambiguity of these stories. Whereas Chesnutt had passed as white in the marketing campaign for *The Conjure Woman,* for his second collection of short stories, he became a liminal representative of the color line.

Chesnutt's mixed-race background was first mentioned publicly in August 1898, when an announcement was placed in the *Bookman,* saying, "Mr. Chesnutt . . . has proved himself not only the most cultivated but also the most philosophical story writer that his race has as yet produced; for, strange to relate, he is himself a coloured man of very light complexion."[53] Chesnutt was pleased with the way this announcement was handled, reflecting the language he would use to describe himself at this time, as a person of African descent and a person of color. He wrote to his editor, Walter Hines Page, thanking him for "the graceful and tactful way of alluding to my connection with the colored race."[54] Notably, this initial announcement was made only briefly and did not circulate widely among a popular audience. With a circulation of approximately fifteen thousand copies at the time,[55] the *Bookman* attracted a specialized audience, and it seems Houghton Mifflin used the magazine as a form of niche marketing, or what might today be called narrowcasting. The announcement was made in such a way that it would circulate among a subset of book professionals and literati.

Chesnutt became even better-known following the publication of "The Wife of His Youth," a story that was widely praised by critics. In an 1899 article, for example, the *Boston Evening Transcript* praised the piece as "one of the really fine short stories of last year."[56] The story considers a group of mixed-race socialities, known as the Blue Vein Society since members of the club are all light-skinned. At the outset, a leading member of the Blue Veins, Mr. Ryder, anticipates proposing marriage to Mrs. Molly Dixon, a woman much younger and lighter in color. Ryder intends to give a ball with the Blue Vein Society to make a formal proposal, so that "marriage with Mrs. Dixon would help to further the upward process of absorption."[57] The plot is complicated, however, by the arrival of 'Liza Jane, a "very black" woman who "looked like a bit of the old plantation life."[58] 'Liza appears at Mr. Ryder's house the morning of the ball, seeking a man named Sam Taylor, her husband from more than twenty-five years ago. She shows Mr. Ryder a daguerreotype of her former husband, and he looks at the portrait, agreeing to give the matter some attention. In the final scene of the story, in the ballroom of the Blue Vein Society, Mr. Ryder is asked to give a toast, and it seems he is ready to propose marriage to Molly Dixon. Instead, however, he takes the floor and tells the story of 'Liza Jane, the faithful wife who has searched for her husband for so long. In a string of hypotheticals, Mr. Ryder asks how 'Liza Jane's husband should respond to his wife's return, if he had lost contact during the war and continued on to a successful life without her. In rapt attention, Molly Dixon and the crowd answer that the husband "should have acknowledged" the old black woman.[59] Mr. Ryder promptly thanks them for their response, and announces himself as the husband in the story. 'Liza Jane is the wife of his youth.

The story is often read by scholars in terms of Mr. Ryder's declaration of his African American identity, acknowledging his own blackness in association with 'Liza Jane. In this interpretation, the mixed-race protagonist chooses to identify with his black history rather than assimilating into whiteness, and convinces an entire mixed-race society to do the same. Indeed, Lorne Fienberg has argued that the story can be read to affirm Chesnutt's "own process of creating a positive entity for himself as a black author."[60] As Mr. Ryder acknowledges the wife of his youth, Fienberg sees Chesnutt acknowledging his own African American identity. In another work of recent criticism, Anne Fleischmann interprets this acceptance of black identity with skepticism, as dramatizing the ideology of the one-drop rule in the era of *Plessy v. Ferguson*. Fleischmann argues, The Wife of His Youth' is not so much a racial romance, as it is an allegory for the disappearance of the biracial person as a social and legal entity during the darkest days of Jim Crow."[61] In other words, Mr. Ryder's acknowledgement of 'Liza Jane can be read as an acceptance of second-class negro citizenship, confirming and reifying the impenetrable boundary between black and white.

At the same time, however, the story can be read as even more ambiguous and open-ended than such criticism allows. While Mr. Ryder ultimately acknowledges 'Liza Jane as the wife of his youth, the story stops short of revealing the future of Mr. Ryder and 'Liza Jane or, for that matter, of Molly Dixon and the Blue Vein Society. The story simply allows its mixed-race protagonist to make a choice between 'Liza Jane and Molly Dixon without revealing the outcome of this decision.

Among Chesnutt's contemporary audience, this ambiguous ending was recognized and widely praised as exemplary of literary realism. In May 1900, for example, Chesnutt would win both the attention and the approval of William Dean Howells in a review for the *Atlantic Monthly*. Howells praised *The Wife of His Youth and Other Stories of the Color Line* as "realistic fiction," and called Chesnutt a member of the "good school, the only school," alongside "Maupassant, or Tourguénief, or Mr. James, or Miss Jewett."[62] Howells admired the ambiguity of these stories in particular, mentioning Chesnutt's "artistic reticence" and his "passionless handling of a phase of our common life which is tense with potential tragedy." Indeed, as other scholars have noted, Howells's positive review simultaneously served as a warning that Chesnutt should tread lightly with his popular audience, avoiding polemical fiction.[63] The review opened by describing Chesnutt's "self-restraint" and concluded that he had "sounded a fresh note, boldly, not blatantly."[64] This praise had thus depended on Chesnutt's artistic distance and ambiguity, which aligned with Howells's definition of literary realism. In June 1900, the *New York Times Review of Books* echoed this assessment, including *The Wife of His Youth and Other Stories of the Color Line* on a list of the "Year's Best Books." The recognition included a very brief description of the book, describing it as "nine stories, all touching the color line. Situations forcefully put, without attempts at solution."[65] The ambiguity of the stories—forceful without attempting any solution— was one of their distinguishing features.

Howells's May 1900 review in the *Atlantic* is also notable because it announced Chesnutt's mixed-race background for a more general audience than ever before. In doing so, Howells grappled with the proper language to describe Chesnutt, calling him a writer "of negro blood—diluted, indeed, in such measure that if he did not admit this descent few would imagine it, but still quite of that middle world which lies next, though wholly outside, our own." The review thus placed Chesnutt in a middle position between pure negro blood and an imagined white reader. In the review, Howells also considered how Chesnutt's mixed-race background affects the writing itself, describing Chesnutt's "unerring knowledge" of the story's "peculiar racial characteristics."[66] Howells's review thus bolstered Chesnutt's literary reputation while simultaneously revealing his racial background to a widespread audience. It praised Chesnutt for his ability to dwell in a middle world of literary and racial ambiguity.

Houghton Mifflin's promotional fliers for *The Wife of His Youth* would function similarly, recognizing Chesnutt as a person of color without foreclosing possibilities of interpretation. In this way, readers could view Chesnutt's mixed-race background according to their own politics and preconceptions. The leaflet advertising *The Wife of His Youth* was structured much like that for *The Conjure Woman;* it included the same image of Chesnutt on the front and incorporated quotations from popular reviews on the interior.[67] In a crucial shift, however, reviews for *The Wife of His Youth* made frequent mention of Chesnutt's mixed-race background. One blurb, quoted from New York's *Mail and Express,* calls Chesnutt "the Laureate of the Color Line." Another review drawn from the *Watchman* notes, "The stories all have the trace and pathos of the 'color line,' and give one an insight into experiences through some of which doubtless the author has passed." Here, the advertisement complements the central theme of the book collection with a description of Chesnutt himself as having "passed" through different racial experiences, offering his readers a vicarious description of the complexities of the color line.[68]

The extent to which Houghton Mifflin supported Chesnutt in this campaign is remarkable. As Chesnutt adapted his writing style from the conventions of plantation fiction to those of realist short stories, Houghton Mifflin likewise adjusted its advertising. This is somewhat in contrast to the norms for marketing African American literature that would emerge in the twentieth century. As John K. Young describes, in the early decades of the 1900s, the predominantly white U.S. publishing industry would typically represent blackness as "a one-dimensional cultural experience," grafting "a mythologized version of the 'black experience' onto all works marked by race."[69] In Chesnutt's case, however, Houghton Mifflin was surprisingly flexible in adapting its marketing from one title to the next, working collaboratively with Chesnutt to manipulate and respond to the color line. As the first work of African American literature published by the company, Chesnutt's writing allowed Houghton Mifflin to experiment and test the marketability of various dimensions of African American experience.

Revealing Chesnutt's mixed-race identity also lent authenticity to Mr. Ryder's dilemma. As a representative of the problem of the color line, Chesnutt's authorial identity served to make the writing itself more vivid and real. His image on the Houghton Mifflin flier, understood by white readers as being not-quite-white, could now stand in for the experience of the mulatto. Augusta Rohrbach describes how a similar dynamic operated in the author portraiture of mid-nineteenth-century slave narratives: "Locating the author as a physical body helps foster the reader's empathy. . . . In order to be successful, these texts must identify the author as a subject whose suffering is not just plausible (as in the fictional setting) but *real*."[70] The marketing leaflet for *The Wife of His Youth* functions in the same way, except with reference to the tragic mulatto figure rather than the slave. The flier establishes the realism of the text with reference to Chesnutt's biographical experience. It appeals to the reader's sympathies by describing Chesnutt as a mixed-race author who has endured the "trace and pathos" of the color line.

Critics reviewing "The Wife of His Youth" often expressed feelings of empathy for the suffering of the story's mixed-race protagonist, or for an experience of nonwhiteness that they understood as suffering. Indeed, Chesnutt pointed to this interpretation from Richard Watson Gilder, editor of the *Century*. In a letter to Walter Hines Page, Chesnutt quotes Gilder as saying, "It seems as though that poor fellow [Mr.

Ryder] was entitled to a compromise of sorts. I don't know just what it would be, but the precise outcome hardly seems humanly right."[71] Here, Gilder resists the outcome of the story whereby Mr. Ryder acknowledges the wife of his youth. In a way, Gilder recognizes the unjust force of race that pressures Mr. Ryder to choose between social justice for 'Liza Jane and the economic opportunity of marrying Molly Dixon. He reads with a sense of dismay for "that poor fellow" caught on the boundary of the color line with no recourse for compromise. Yet Gilder is not able to resolve the dilemma posed by the story; he neither condones Mr. Ryder's acknowledgment of 'Liza Jane nor criticizes a system that values whiteness. Lamenting Mr. Ryder's decision thus allows Gilder to express an emotional attachment to the mixed-race protagonist without responding to the force of white supremacism that underlies the entire story.

Chesnutt's letter responds to Gilder's interpretation by defending the rights of 'Liza Jane. As Chesnutt says, "It is surprising what a number of people . . . do not seem to imagine that the old woman was entitled to any consideration whatever, and yet I don't know that it is so astonishing, in the light of history."[72] In other words, Chesnutt views Gilder's interpretation as part of a trend in the story's popular reception, whereby readers felt sympathetic toward Mr. Ryder while ignoring the figure of 'Liza Jane. Chesnutt's response links this interpretation to a long-standing history of such attitudes, indicating that he had intended for his readers to give their consideration and sympathies to the story's title character. Gilder's reading, on the contrary, focuses almost exclusively on Mr. Ryder. He is drawn to sympathize with the difficult situation of the light-skinned protagonist, who stands in for the author.

Among other critics, the story's ambiguous ending was also open to the interpretation Anne Fleischmann describes, in which Mr. Ryder does not make a difficult ethical decision to acknowledge 'Liza Jane but merely accepts second-class citizenship according to the one-drop rule. Indeed, a review written by Hamilton Wright Mabie for the *Outlook* offers precisely this interpretation, describing Mr. Ryder's decision in terms of scientific racism. In the review, Mabie admires Chesnutt's writing according to dominant patterns of reception: it offers a window into the tragic circumstances of the light-skinned mulatto author, without dictating how this situation should be interpreted. Mabie responds to the story biographically, admiring Chesnutt's "restraint and balance," much in the same way as Howells.[73] Mabie even describes "The Wife of His Youth" as one of the best short stories in American literature. However, the review goes on to offer Mabie's interpretation of these ambiguous stories and does so in terms of scientific racism. Mabie argues that the tragedy of "The Wife of His Youth" is driven by a situation in which the negro must reach "a higher stage of evolution" and work on "his journey toward a higher self-development." Mabie thus reads Mr. Ryder's acknowledgment of 'Liza Jane not as resistance to white supremacist norms but as an additional step that is required of Mr. Ryder to advance the negro race. His interpretation places the burden of social justice on negro self-development. Perhaps most importantly, this interpretation shows how the story could be admired even while it was interpreted according to white supremacist attitudes. Mabie reads the story as both a great work of American literature and a justification for the one-drop rule of racial segregation.

Overall, then, during this middle stage of his career with Houghton Mifflin, Chesnutt continued to adapt his authorial identity to align with his literary strategies and style. He collaborated with his publishers to announce his mixed-race identity, and *The Wife of His Youth* likewise straddled the boundary of the color line. For Howells and many other critics, this approach met the qualifications of realist fiction, to be praised alongside the work of Henry James and Sarah Orne Jewett. It was balanced and restrained, and left the onus of interpretation on the reader. Yet even within the relatively sophisticated audience represented by the *Atlantic,* the *Century,* and the *Outlook,* few readers interpreted "The Wife of His Youth" as resistant to the forces of white supremacism. For a critic such as Richard Watson Gilder, the story represented the dilemma of the color line, a seemingly irresolvable conflict. Howells had expressed a similar view, saying that Chesnutt had acquainted his reader with "those regions where the paler shades dwell as hopelessly, with relation to ourselves, as the blackest negro."[74] Yet as Chesnutt's response to Gilder demonstrates, the author did not view the negro's situation as irresolvable or hopeless but as a product of history. As Chesnutt's career continued, he would push beyond the elegant ambiguities and open-ended conclusions of literary realism. Openly invoking his identification as African American, and not merely a light-skinned mulatto, he would offer an explicit critique of racial prejudice and a direct response to the supposedly hopeless tragedy of the color line.

SELLING *THE MARROW OF TRADITION*

By the time Chesnutt began work on *The Marrow of Tradition,* in December 1900, competing publishers were actively soliciting his fiction. Chesnutt had established himself as a leading author of literary fiction, prepared to write "a race problem novel of the present day."[75] He anticipated that his next novel might propel him to wealth and renown, telling Houghton Mifflin, "If *The Marrow of Tradition* can become lodged in the popular mind as the legitimate successor of *Uncle Tom's Cabin* and *A Fool's Errand* as depicting an epoch in our national history, it will make the fortune of the book and incidentally of the author."[76] Here, Chesnutt envisions *The Marrow of Tradition* in the lineage of major nineteenth-century political fictions, as a novel that would confront racial prejudice directly to achieve mass popularity and sales. Whereas Harriet Beecher Stowe and Tourgée had depicted the "national history" of the antebellum and Reconstruction eras, *The Marrow of Tradition* would be the definitive representation of the *Plessy v. Ferguson* "epoch."

Houghton Mifflin sought to market *The Marrow of Tradition* within this lineage of best-selling political novels, ranking the book highly among its own catalog of fiction and expending significant effort to promote it. While critics have frequently commented on the commercial failure of the novel—which marked a turning point in Chesnutt's literary career—the failed campaign nevertheless gauges Houghton Mifflin's willingness to experiment in a more radical literary critique of racism. Indeed, the company predicted a large audience for Chesnutt's more explicitly political fiction, and it invested substantial funds to advertise the book. When this campaign proved a commercial failure, with underperforming sales and harshly critical reviews, the company chose to deemphasize the novel's political message and distance itself from Chesnutt's subsequent work.

The *Marrow of Tradition* offers a fictionalized retelling of the Wilmington insurrection of 1898, in which a group of Democratic white supremacists overthrew the legitimately elected, biracial government of Wilmington, North Carolina. White insurrectionists killed dozens of African Americans and destroyed black-owned neighborhoods and property, including the city's African American newspaper, the *Daily Record.* In the wake of the riots, thousands of African Americans fled Wilmington, turning it from a black-majority into a white-majority city. White supremacists thus succeeded in overthrowing the elected government, ushering in a violent era of segregationist politics. Chesnutt's fictionalized account of the insurrection, set in the town of "Wellington," interweaves several plot structures. As many critics have described, the plot turns on issues of racial masquerade, property theft, and mob violence.[77] Yet *The Marrow of Tradition* also centered around issues of family and domesticity, which Chesnutt would emphasize in his own description, saying the book considers "the fate of the child of a proud old family [Dodie] related by an unacknowledged tie to the family of a colored doctor [Dr. Miller]. The father of the child leads a reactionary political movement against the Negro, while the doctor is at the head of an enterprise for the education and uplifting of his people."[78] The story thus begins and ends by considering the fate of the child, Dodie, positioned between white supremacist parents and unacknowledged familial ties to the black doctor. It concludes with a scene of potential reconciliation, in which Dr. Miller and his wife decide they will attempt to save the life of Dodie, despite the death of their own son during the insurrection. In this way, Chesnutt would take a sentimental approach to the politics of racial injustice.

Chesnutt's correspondence with Houghton Mifflin indicates that he was satisfied with the publisher's efforts to sell the book, and that he worked collaboratively to promote it. In the same letter cited above to discuss *Uncle Tom's Cabin*, Chesnutt told Houghton Mifflin he was "very much pleased with the interest that has so far been manifested by the house and the enterprise displayed in the preliminary advertising."[79] In a letter from November 4, 1901, he similarly pointed out, "I notice the book advertised much more extensively so far as I can see, than any of my former books."[80] Houghton Mifflin's company records confirm Chesnutt's observation, showing that the company made significant investment to advertise the novel. Whereas it had spent $386.50 advertising *The Wife of His Youth* and $831.01 on *The House Behind the Cedars* (Chesnutt's 1900 novel that dealt with the tragedy of the color line in a restrained realist style), the company spent $1,466.13 advertising *The Marrow of Tradition*.[81]

Initially, this campaign materialized in advertisements that emphasized the book as a forceful narrative comparable to *Uncle Tom's Cabin*. The promotional leaflet that Houghton Mifflin produced for *Marrow*, for instance, differs significantly from advertisements for his previous work (figure 6). Whereas those are folded pages with interiors quoting from popular reviews, the flier for *The Marrow of Tradition* is a single flat leaf, devoting its entire recto to the new novel, with brief descriptions of previous books on the reverse.[82] The advertisement offers a synopsis of the novel, describing it as a story of "contemporary Southern life," and as a "strong, virile, and exciting novel." The flier openly describes the novel's white supremacist characters as "a reactionary political movement" (the same language Chesnutt would use in his own summary of the novel) and claims that the main facts of the story's climactic riot are "true to recent history." The flier closes by noting, "At many points the story will recall 'Uncle Tom's Cabin,' so great is its dramatic intensity and so strong its appeal to popular sympathies." The advertisement, in other words, presents *The Marrow of Tradition* as a strong political novel based on the facts of the Wilmington insurrection. More than ever before, Houghton Mifflin thus lent its imprimatur to the more radical potential of Chesnutt's writing. The flier itself is printed in green ink

FIGURE 6. Promotional leaflet, *The Marrow of Tradition* (Boston: Houghton Mifflin, 1901), MS Am 2030 (245), p. 72, Houghton Library, Harvard University.

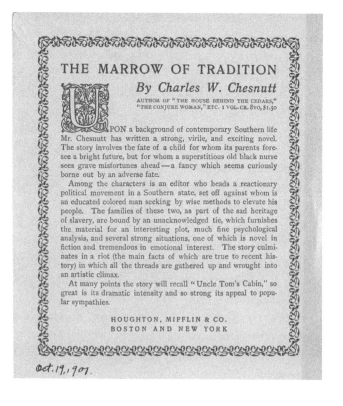

and framed with a border of leaves, creating a sort of laurel wreath that marks *The Marrow of Tradition* as both a classic and a triumphant work of literature.

Advertisements in other venues also highlighted the comparison to *Uncle Tom's Cabin*. The December 1901 *Atlantic Monthly Advertiser*, a supplement to the magazine, contains two large advertisements for *The Marrow of Tradition*.[83] The first of these, on page fifty-six, advertises Chesnutt's novel with Sarah Orne Jewett's *The Tory Lover* and Ellen Olney Kirk's *Our Lady Vanity*, establishing a sentimental connection between the three novels.[84] The ad lists all books for sale at $1.50, denoting their equal value. *The Marrow of Tradition* is given top billing, however, occupying the full upper half of the page while the other two books share the lower half. As with advertisements for *The Conjure Woman*, this announcement includes blurbs excerpted from contemporary reviews. The *N.Y. Commercial Advertiser* claims, "No novel since the days of 'Uncle Tom's Cabin' is more visibly the outburst of long pent-up feeling." The *Chicago Record-Herald* praises *Marrow*: "Ably told, without exaggeration, it is a strong, convincing, and convicting picture of negro wrongs." The *Boston Herald* claims, "The colored race is to be congratulated on having found so able a champion as Mr. Chesnutt." In these descriptions Chesnutt is depicted neither as an unmarked white man nor as a mixed-race figure who can navigate both sides of the color line but as the champion of the colored race. Houghton Mifflin more explicitly advertises *The Marrow of Tradition* as African American fiction, invoking the type of "black literature" that would, as George Hutchinson describes it, become increasingly marketable throughout the course of the twentieth century.[85]

Yet even while these December advertisements hailed Chesnutt as a champion of the colored race, they also took steps away from the strong language of the October flier. The second announcement in this *Atlantic Monthly Advertiser*, for example, sets *Marrow* within a list of Houghton Mifflin's holiday books and offers a paragraph-length summary of the novel.[86] The advertisement draws on the language of the leaf-bordered flier, and concludes with the same sentence, comparing *Marrow* to *Uncle Tom's Cabin* in its "dramatic intensity." In comparison to the October flier, however, this later advertisement deemphasizes the political nature of the book. It begins, "This is a novel of character rather than of politics." The synopsis then goes on to say that the novel is set "in

a Southern City" during "the exciting movement for negro disfranchisement." Here, Houghton Mifflin further distances the novel from
its political critique of the white supremacist movement. Whereas the
initial flier for the novel had described the insurrection as a "reactionary political movement," the *Atlantic* advertisement denies the political
nature of the book and makes ambiguous the "exciting movement for
negro disfranchisement." By December 1901, then, Houghton Mifflin
already sensed the potential controversy the book would cause among
its white readership, and hedged its marketing strategy accordingly. It
sought to represent the book as *both* the successor to *Uncle Tom's Cabin*
and as moderately apolitical.

Not surprisingly, many critics reviewed *The Marrow of Tradition* in
comparison to Stowe's novel. The *Argonaut* describes it quite favorably,
claiming *Marrow* will be "a great revelation of conditions existing as
was 'Uncle Tom's Cabin' at the time that was written."[87] In *World's
Work,* the book is called "a contemporary 'Uncle Tom's Cabin.'"[88] The
review goes on to criticize the book, however, saying that the book is
not convincing because the negroes are all "blameless" and the whites
are "unrelievedly bad." A review in the *Outlook* counters this opinion,
noting that "good and evil are recognized on both sides of the color
line."[89] It then compares the novel to *Uncle Tom's Cabin,* saying, "It is
less exuberant, less overflowing with vitality, than the earlier novel;
but it is more thoroughly balanced, more carefully constructed, more
condensed and restrained." Chesnutt initially looked on these reviews
favorably and considered a polarized reception of the book to be
advantageous. In an earlier letter to Houghton Mifflin, Chesnutt had
responded to his harsher critics: "I anticipated such criticism and imagine it is a healthy sign. . . . It is quite likely that people will buy a book
they disapprove of, if the disapproval is strong enough."[90]

In general, however, reviews of *The Marrow of Tradition* were not
only critical but also negatively affected sales. The *Independent,* a magazine that Chesnutt admired, reviewed the novel as "vindictive to a
remarkable degree . . . indignant . . . and rash."[91] Upset by this unfair
critique, Chesnutt contacted the *Independent* through Houghton Mifflin,
but the magazine's editor defended the review and would not rescind
it.[92] Among these criticisms, the most significant negative response
came from William Dean Howells himself, who in the December 1901
North American Review reversed his previously favorable assessment

of Chesnutt's work. Howells opens this review claiming that Chesnutt is better than the average novelist, but quickly goes on to criticize the novel as "bitter, bitter."[93] (Notably, advertisements for *The House Behind the Cedars* had hedged against this interpretation, describing the novel as having "no touch of bitterness."[94]) With *Marrow*, Chesnutt's writing style had moved beyond the "self-restraint" that Howells admired in his earlier 1900 review. Rather than maintaining artistic distance and the ambiguous style of literary realism, Chesnutt had turned to more explicitly political fiction. Despite the positive outlook expressed at the conclusion of *The Marrow of Tradition*, which offered a hopeful prospect for cross-racial recognition and reconciliation, Howells understood the novel as a bitter response to the problem of the color line.

By December 1901, just two months after the book was published, Chesnutt began to recognize its relative failure and declining sales. On December 30, he wrote to Houghton Mifflin asking about his chances of producing a book on the subject of the color line that might sell "20,000–30,000 copies."[95] Chesnutt went on to lament, "I am beginning to suspect that the public as a rule does not care for books in which the principal characters are colored people, or with a striking sympathy with that race as contrasted with the white race." While Chesnutt had been optimistic about producing a commercially successful novel, writing and promoting his books at a frenetic pace from 1899 to 1901, this letter marks a turning point, as his hopes for *Marrow of Tradition* were not realized.

Houghton Mifflin's records indicate that the company was also expecting stronger sales from *The Marrow of Tradition*. Its publishing costs show three initial printings in October 1901, for a total of 4,500 copies.[96] While this is not an extraordinary print run, it is two to three times the number of copies the company had produced for any of Chesnutt's previous books. Similarly, while the company had given out 256 editorial copies of *The Conjure Woman* and 299 copies of *The House Behind the Cedars*, it distributed 421 editorial copies of *Marrow*. These levels of production and distribution indicate that Houghton Mifflin anticipated much better sales. The company hoped the moderate success of Chesnutt's earlier books might signal better commercial sales for *The Marrow of Tradition*.

On the contrary, Houghton's records of book sales detail the novel's poor performance, which follows a sharp trajectory. While the novel sold 3,276 copies in November and December 1901, it sold only 111 copies in all of the following year.[97] This sudden drop in sales aligns with the pattern of the book's reception: it was marketed as a major novel from a "champion" of the colored race but was quickly reviewed as a vilification of white America. Between November and December 1901, such an interpretation became dominant, and sales of the book ceased abruptly. In fact, in January 1902, booksellers returned 173 copies of the book to Houghton Mifflin. While the company had initially paid Chesnutt for the sale of 3,335 copies of the book, it charged back his royalties for these 173 returned copies.[98] In the next three years—from 1903 to 1905—the novel sold zero copies, and Houghton Mifflin put the book on clearance in 1906, in an effort to sell the initial print run. Comparatively, *The House Behind the Cedars* was a much more consistent title. After selling 2,994 copies in its first two years, the book sold 140 copies in 1902, and continued to sell between 40 and 70 copies annually through 1907. Indeed, throughout his later life Chesnutt would call *The House Behind the Cedars* his best work and his best-selling work. It was made into a movie by Oscar Micheaux in 1921 and was republished serially by the *Chicago Defender* in 1922.[99]

These marketing and sales figures might also be compared to texts outside Chesnutt's oeuvre. In 1898 Houghton Mifflin published *Caleb West: Master Diver,* a romance novel with a story that centers on the construction of a New England lighthouse. While the company spent only $1188.91 advertising the book,[100] nearly $300 less than it had spent promoting *Marrow of Tradition,* the novel sold 23,632 copies in its first year and 5,324 copies in its second.[101] *Caleb West* thus falls into the range of sales that Chesnutt had described as a popular success, and with less money spent on advertising. Other titles had even more extraordinary sales figures. In 1900, for instance, Houghton Mifflin produced the best-selling book of the year with Mary Johnston's *To Have and to Hold,* a romance novel that sold 258,684 copies. Or to give another sense of the popular literary marketplace at the time, the first novel in Thomas Dixon's Ku Klux Klan trilogy, *The Leopard's Spots,* sold over 100,000 copies in 1902 and was succeeded by his even more popular *The Clansman* in 1905.[102] Meanwhile, as Claire Parfait has described, *Uncle Tom's Cabin* was being printed by numerous publishers with introductions that generally recontextualized the novel, "without paying particular attention to the present conditions of African Americans."[103]

In light of these examples, the "nadir" of U.S. race relations becomes strikingly apparent.[104] For while Albion Tourgée had nearly replicated

Stowe's commercial publishing success in the Reconstruction era, there simply was not a popular market for such writing at the turn of the century. As the tide of popular reception turned against Chesnutt and *The Marrow of Tradition,* sales of the book came to an abrupt halt. Responsive to this market, Houghton Mifflin adjusted its campaign to advertise *Marrow* as a "novel of character rather than politics," and to emphasize the book's portrayal of the "exciting movement for negro disfranchisement." With the failure of *The Marrow of Tradition,* Houghton Mifflin came to recognize that its investment in Chesnutt offered only modest returns and may actually have been a liability for its reputation among white readers. Chesnutt's next novel manuscript, *Evelyn's Husband*, was rejected by the company in October 1903, and would not be published in his lifetime. Another novel manuscript, *The Colonel's Dream,* would eventually be published by Doubleday, Page, and Company, but only after Houghton Mifflin rejected it.

CHESNUTT'S PROCRUSTES

In June 1904, Chesnutt published "Baxter's Procrustes" in the *Atlantic Monthly*. It was his last short story for the magazine and his last publication within the prestigious realm of Houghton Mifflin. The story centers on its title character's involvement with the Bodleian Club, a gentlemen's club interested in books and book collecting. When the club asks Baxter if he will manufacture a book of his own poetry for auction, he tricks members of the Bodleian into paying exorbitant sums of money for a sealed edition of his book, the *Procrustes*, the pages of which are blank. The story can thus be read as a depiction of a communications circuit gone wrong. The elitist culture of the club, the sale of books based only on outward appearances, the club members' ignorant reviews and accolades—all have parallels in Chesnutt's own interactions with the publishing industry. In what follows, I outline a number of previously unknown autobiographical elements of the story (even as I would caution against a purely biographical interpretation). I show that "Baxter's Procrustes" is both a satire of literary culture at the turn of the century and an allegory for how white supremacism circulates and gains currency. Baxter's *Procrustes* thus merges Chesnutt's experiences as an author with his analysis of the color line to offer a sharp critique of white reading.

The story is narrated by a member of the Bodleian Club, identified only as Jones, who describes the club's activities as it collects literary objects and holds annual auctions. In addition to collecting, the club has also begun producing books, and encourages Baxter to publish his poem, the *Procrustes*, as one of these special editions. Although reluctant to do so at first, Baxter agrees on the condition that he "supervise the printing, binding, and delivery of the books."[105] As the *Procrustes* moves through these stages, members of the club praise the poetry for its quality and style. However, it becomes unclear whether they have actually read the poem, since each copy of the book has been wrapped in paper and sealed with wax. On a night set aside for review of the book, an English visitor in attendance unties the ribbon around one copy, cuts the pages, and finds that the book is blank and contains no text. Outraged by the discovery, members of the Bodleian Club ask for Baxter's resignation, and he flees the scene. In the denouement, however, after most members of the group have burned or destroyed their copies of the book, the president tells the club that Baxter was wiser than they realized: "To the true collector, a book is a work of art, of which the contents are no more important than the words of an opera."[106] At auction, with only a few sealed copies remaining, the *Procrustes* sells for $250, the highest price of any volume produced by the club.

The short story functions as a sort of indictment of the Bodleian Club and its devotion to the material book without reference to content or meaning. From the opening paragraphs, the Bodleian is shown to fetishize book objects—"a lead pencil used by Emerson, an autograph letter of Matthew Arnold"—that are obliquely connected with authorial identity and celebrity. In describing and praising Baxter's poem, the contents become insignificant in comparison to its material manufacture. Trusting its artistic merits to Baxter, the club's literary committee evaluates the text strictly on details of bookmaking: "The paper was to be of handmade linen, from the Kelmscott Mills; the type black-letter, with rubricated initials. The cover, which was Baxter's own selection, was to be of dark green morocco, with a cap-and-bells border in red inlays, and doublures of maroon morocco, with a blind-tooled design. . . . The whole edition of fifty numbered copies was to be disposed of at auction."[107] As Jerome McGann would describe it, the club is concerned with the book's bibliographic codes rather than its linguistic ones.[108] When asked about Baxter's *Procrustes*, the narrator and other members of the Bodleian Club turn to these paratextual elements. For example, the narrator tells fellow club members that the book's "cap-and-bells border was significant of the shams by which the optimist sought to delude himself into the view that life was a desirable thing."[109] Here, Jones decides on the poem's meaning based on the design of its exterior cover. He not only fabricates his reference to the "optimist" of the text but invents a cynical philosophy for this character based on the book's cover. Notably, this "cap-and-bells" design for the *Procrustes* might be compared to the cover of *The Conjure Woman*, in which the rabbits' ears resemble a jester's cap. Like Chesnutt and Uncle Julius, Baxter plays the role of trickster. Moreover, as in *The Conjure Woman*'s popular reception, the cap-and-bells cover of the *Procrustes* is interpreted according to Jones's preconceptions, without reference to the text itself.

The character of Baxter can likewise be seen as standing in for Chesnutt. In a 1977 article, William Andrews elaborates on this comparison. He describes "Baxter's *Procrustes*" as a "hoax narrative" in which a central character tricks a group of "self-assured but self-deluded gentlemen," exposing the biases and prejudices of these supposed superiors.[110] While Chesnutt had always relied on such narrative forms, this story pays special attention to the trickster himself, making strong connections to Chesnutt's own career. For example, the narrator points out that "perhaps Baxter might be an unsuccessful author."[111] He goes on to say that Baxter had "always spoken in terms of such unmeasured pity for the slaves of the pen, who were dependent upon the whim of an undiscriminating public for recognition and livelihood." Here, the narrator depicts Baxter in terms we might apply to Chesnutt at the time of composition: a commercially unsuccessful author, disillusioned with his dependence on public opinion. And while Jones is an unreliable narrator, Chesnutt is nevertheless deliberate in establishing this link between himself and the title character. William Andrews goes so far as to call Baxter "the most transparent of the many masks [Chesnutt] wore in his fiction."[112]

The story is also autobiographical because of Chesnutt's relationship to the Rowfant Club, a group of bibliophiles based in Cleveland, Ohio. In a 1974 article in the *CLA Journal,* Robert Hemenway reads the story as a response to Chesnutt's own interactions with this bibliographical society. Like the Bodleian Club in the story, the Rowfant Club was an exclusive group of book lovers and book collectors, "famous for its limited editions in superb bindings" and "made up largely of the monied aristocracy that tended to rule the Cleveland bar."[113] Chesnutt had been invited to meetings with the Rowfant Club as early as 1899. But his application for full membership with the club was refused in 1902, on grounds that the time had not yet come for "a gentleman of his race to be proposed."[114] He was rejected from club membership in terms that were explicitly racist. Later, in 1910, Chesnutt was admitted to the club and became an active member. He presented speeches for the club over the course of many years, and Chesnutt's papers, now held in special collections at Fisk University, include many Rowfant Club publications and pamphlets. However, at the time that he published "Baxter's Procrustes" in 1904, rejection from the Rowfant Club coincided with rejection of his later novels.

The connections between Chesnutt and Baxter, between Cleveland's Rowfant Club and the fictional Bodleian Club, extend even further to include Chesnutt's work with Houghton Mifflin. Indeed, in another striking similarity, Houghton Mifflin had actually worked with the Rowfant Club in 1899 to produce a special issue of Chesnutt's *The Conjure Woman*. Chesnutt would describe this version of the text in his essay "Post-Bellum—Pre-Harlem," writing, "A limited edition . . . appeared in advance of the trade edition in an issue of one hundred and fifty numbered copies and was subscribed for almost entirely by members of the Rowfant Club. . . . It was printed by the Riverside Press on large hand-made linen paper, bound in yellow buckram, with the name on the back in black letters on a white label, a very handsome and dignified volume."[115] Here, Chesnutt describes the special issue of *The Conjure Woman* in language almost identical to his fictitious description of the *Procrustes*. Both books were printed on "hand-made linen" paper in limited editions. Both were sold in advance, in numbered copies, to subscribers from the club.[116]

This special issue of *The Conjure Woman* differs significantly from the trade edition with the freedman caricature on the cover (figure 7). In Houghton Mifflin's company records, it is described as a large-paper, or "LP," edition; it is printed from the same plates but in a larger octavo volume. While the trade version of *The Conjure Woman* cost only $0.08 to print, this special issue cost $0.706 per copy.[117] Moreover, the linen paper is watermarked with the Houghton Mifflin publisher's device—an image

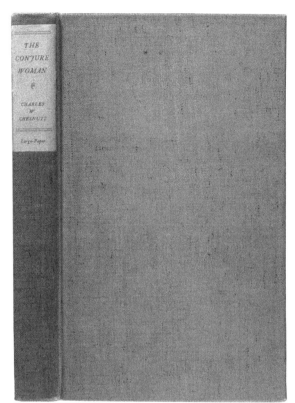

FIGURE 7. Large paper edition, *The Conjure Woman* (Boston: Houghton Mifflin, 1899). Call no. 84HM-38, Houghton Library, Harvard University.

of a man playing a pipe, sitting beneath a tree. with an inscription of the company's motto, "Tout bien ou rien." The motto translates roughly as "All or Nothing," or "Anything worth doing is worth doing well."

In one sense, this book is a better representative of what Chesnutt hoped to write, a more "dignified volume," as he describes it. Because the book was printed on larger paper with the same plates as the trade edition, it has wide margins, which would encourage reflection and note taking. The special issue's unmarked buckram cover weaves together a variety of flesh-toned threads—beige, tan, and brown. It is a sharp contrast from the caricatured freedman illustration on the trade edition.

And yet, in the copy at the Houghton Library, the book's hand-made linen pages remain not only uncut, with a deckle edge, but also unopened.[118] That is, the sheets stitched together in the bound book remain folded in octavo format, preventing the text from being read. Like the books in Jay Gatsby's library, and like Baxter's *Procrustes,* this edition is less a source of knowledge than it is a symbol of status and ownership.

Chesnutt thus uses the story of "Baxter's Procrustes" to satirize Houghton Mifflin and a culture industry devoted more to exterior surfaces than to substance. The story is wonderfully metatextual in this critique of the publishing industry. It is not only a publication about publication but also a story titled after a story. In a maneuver that is almost postmodern, the very first line tells us, "Baxter's *Procrustes* is one of the publications of the Bodleian Club." Here, in addition to his critique of Houghton Mifflin and the Rowfant Club, Chesnutt seems also to mock the *Atlantic Monthly.* By repeating the story's title in its first line, Chesnutt essentially tells his readers that "Baxter's Procrustes," as a short story, is being published by a group comparable to the Bodleian Club. He then elaborates on some of the more peculiar features of this club. Bodleian members Thompson and Davis, for example, apply erudite philosophical interpretations to the *Procrustes,* admiring its "Hegelianism" and its "Spencerian view."[119] Thompson and Davis have not read Baxter's book, the text of which does not exist, yet they still manage to find an application for Western philosophy. Notably, this "Spencerian" interpretation assumes that the book participates in social Darwinism.

Indeed, throughout his career, Chesnutt's writing offered metacriticism of the ways literature circulates and is read. In the conjure stories, the white auditors John and Annie embody realistic and sentimental modes of reading, respectively. Uncle Julius embodies yet another mode of literacy, in his mythological folk style, so that the stories depict a range of hermeneutic possibilities. In *The House Behind the Cedars,* John Warwick's decision to pass as white and follow "the blood of his white fathers" is made after reading from the canon of Western literature.[120] His library includes Fielding's complete works, Walter Scott, *Tristram Shandy, The Pilgrim's Progress, The Spectator, Robinson Crusoe,* Milton, Shakespeare, and the Bible. As one other example, in Chesnutt's posthumously published novel, *The Quarry,* the mixed-race protagonist Donald Glover visits the Bascombe family in England, whose private library includes a first folio of Shakespeare and a Gutenberg Bible.[121] Donald considers marrying into this wealth through Lady Blanche Bascombe, but refuses the temptation, which would require he pass as white. In all these ways, Chesnutt's writing offers a metatextual reflection on the act of reading and writing itself. Indeed, Chesnutt's career as an author is marked by rapid generic shifts that respond to dominant modes of reading and writing.

"Baxter's Procrustes" builds on Chesnutt's ongoing critique of Anglo literary culture through the allusion of its title. In the classical myth, Procrustes is a highway robber who would lure guests to his home and stretch or amputate them to fit his iron bed. According to the legend, Procrustes kept two beds, one very short and one very tall, manipulating the standard so that no guest could escape torture. In "Baxter's Procrustes" this allusion is applied only loosely, as the narrator, Jones, gathers Baxter's philosophy and poetic style through conversations and not from the text itself. According to Jones, "Society was the Procrustes which, like the Greek Bandit of old, caught every man born into the world, and endeavored to fit him to some preconceived standard, generally to the one for which he was least adapted. The world was full of men and women who were merely square pegs in round holes, and vice versa. Most marriages were unhappy because the contracting parties were not properly mated. Religion was mostly superstition, science for the most part sciolism, popular education merely a means of forcing the stupid and repressing the bright."[122] In this passage, the narrator interprets Baxter's book as expressing a cynical view of "society" at large. The book mocks all forms of social exchange and value, including marriage, religion, science, and public education. The myth of Procrustes is thus applied in a vague and wide-ranging critique.

In a passage from *The Marrow of Tradition*, however, Chesnutt had relied on the procrustean myth to offer a much more direct criticism of the ways Jim Crow segregation stretched and confined African Americans. The passage takes place in chapter 5, "A Journey Southward," in which the novel's mixed-race protagonist, Dr. Miller, talks with his white friend, a former medical instructor, on a train headed south. As the train crosses the Mason-Dixon line into Virginia, the conductor asks, and ultimately forces, the two friends to separate into "White" and "Colored" cars. When Dr. Miller is physically pushed into the Jim Crow car, he thinks to himself,

> Surely if a classification of passengers on trains was at all desirable, it might be made upon some more logical and considerate basis than a mere arbitrary, tactless, and, by the very nature of things, brutal drawing of the color line. It was a veritable bed of Procrustes, this standard which

the whites had set for the negroes. Those who grew above it must have their heads cut off, figuratively speaking, —must be forced back to the level assigned to their race; those who fell beneath the standard set had their necks stretched, literally enough, as the ghastly record in the daily papers gave conclusive evidence.[123]

The passage is an important one within Chesnutt's writing. In what was meant to become his best-selling book, Chesnutt offers his protagonist's thoughts on the Jim Crow car. He argues that the color line is an "arbitrary" and "brutal" mode of classification, and he does so in terms of the procrustean myth. Like the torturous methods of Procrustes, the laws of Jim Crow stretch and amputate African Americans to impossible standards.

By alluding to this passage in the title of "Baxter's Procrustes," Chesnutt indicates that Baxter's empty book is related to Jim Crow violence and segregation. But how so? In the passage from *The Marrow of Tradition*, Chesnutt describes the racial "standard" as the bed of Procrustes. At the same time, the passage indicates that Procrustes occupies the position of white people: the procrustean bed is the "standard which the whites had set." Here, Chesnutt uses both a passive linguistic construction and a classical allusion to soften his critique of white supremacist violence. Yet the passage nevertheless indicates that whites are enacting torture. Adapting this reference for his short story, Chesnutt thus depicts white supremacism in the form of an elaborately produced book whose pages are blank. It is a pristine object, devoid of content.

Throughout the story, Jones focuses on the book as an object, concerned with its economic value, or what Cheryl L. Harris might call "whiteness as property."[124] Early in the story, for example, the club realizes the value of its limited editions when an unopened *Essay on Pipes* sells for seventy-five dollars: "Since every member of the club possessed one or more of these valuable editions, they were all manifestly interested in keeping up the price."[125] In this instance, the value of the book is increased because it is kept inviolate and unexamined. Members of the club take notice, and further invest in elaborately produced books. Later, when Jones is expected to review the *Procrustes,* he hears that an unopened copy of the book has sold for one hundred and fifty dollars. Consequently, Jones tells us, "A proper regard for my own interests would not permit me to spoil my copy by opening it."[126] The narrator is meant to review the contents of the *Procrustes*, and has the opportunity to realize that it is empty. Instead, he is financially invested in leaving the book unopened and unexamined.

As he creates the book, Baxter anticipates this response. He understands the desire for pristine exteriors and he produces the *Procrustes* accordingly. Indeed, when the club gathers to review the book, it is received enthusiastically. The club begins chanting—"Baxter! Baxter! Author! Author!"[127]—a passage that calls to mind Chesnutt's own youthful ambition "to be an Author!" In an ironic critique of authorship, and what it might mean to be hailed as such, Baxter gives the audience what they desire without producing any literary content. Baxter recognizes the biases of his audience and how these biases skew their perception of the text. The reception of his book shows that, indeed, the Bodleian Club is happy to own and consume books as commodities, regardless of content.

This is why, in the final irony, the book sells for "two hundred and fifty dollars, the highest price ever brought by a single volume published by the club."[128] After the hoax is initially exposed, members of the club are so upset that they destroy the book. They cannot bear to have its empty contents exposed, and so they cut their copies, burn them, and mail them to Baxter with angry notes. Ultimately, Baxter reimburses the Bodleian Club for the cost of producing the book. The president of the club, however, retains his copy, announcing that Baxter's *Procrustes*, "from the collector's point of view, is entirely logical, and might be considered as the acme of bookmaking."[129] Here, the president of the Bodleian Club doubles down on the "logic" of the *Procrustes*, arguing that the book is in fact *more* valuable for its fulfillment of the club's belief system. Rather than deny the club's focus on appearances, the book is interpreted as the ideal realization of its beliefs.

In this regard, the parallel with Chesnutt's career becomes especially striking. Like Baxter, Chesnutt had attempted to expose the hypocritical beliefs of his readers, to persuade his audience to examine the "logical" foundations of segregation. Yet he conducted this critique through literary fiction that ambiguously reflected the views of white supremacism itself. If this critique of race was exposed and became explicit, Chesnutt's work could fuel harsh and destructive reactions—in the same way that members of the Bodleian Club denounced and burned copies of the book. Indeed, much like the *Procrustes,* unsold copies of *The Marrow of Tradition* were returned to the publisher, and the profits were deducted from the author's royalties. However, the text could also be judged entirely by its exterior, as when *The Conjure Woman* was praised for its caricatured depictions. Whereas Baxter had hoped to both enter the Bodleian Club and expose its unexamined biases, his work was instead harshly criticized and interpreted as fulfilling the very ideologies it aimed to critique.

THE RACIAL PARATEXT AND THE COMMERCIAL LITERARY MARKETPLACE

Chesnutt has long been understood as one of the first major African American novelists and as a precursor to the Harlem Renaissance. His work has also been recognized for its strained relationship to the genteel publishing industry. In looking at these paratextual materials, Chesnutt's career becomes an even more significant example within the development of African American literature. Framing Chesnutt's work, these paratexts mediate between the author's predominantly white audience and his increasingly political fiction. These paratexts also served as a cover by which the African American text would initially be judged. As I have shown, such materials are not merely supplementary but become deeply imbricated with interpretations of the text itself.

Looking at Houghton Mifflin's catalogs, advertisements, cost books, and sales figures, it becomes clear that the company invested substantial time and resources to support Chesnutt's literary career. The company developed a surprisingly creative marketing campaign that was sensitive to Chesnutt's writing strategies: *The Conjure Woman* passed as plantation fiction; *The Wife of His Youth* depicted the problem of the color line ambiguously; *The Marrow of Tradition* aimed to build on the success of explicitly political novels such as *Uncle Tom's Cabin.* These rapid adjustments, made from 1899 to 1901, indicate the experimental nature of the collaboration between Chesnutt and Houghton Mifflin as they sought to produce a literature that was both genteel *and* critical of U.S. racial injustice. Perhaps, as Mr. Ryder had won over the Blue Vein Society, Chesnutt could convince his white readers to acknowledge the rights of their black counterparts. Indeed, Houghton Mifflin's substantial investment in *The Marrow of Tradition* demonstrates the company's belief that African American literature might find a popular audience among white readers. On the contrary, however, the vast majority of these readers were not converted or intrigued by Chesnutt's critique of white supremacism; they were incensed by it. As Chesnutt's own views on race became more well known, the dominant reaction was to denounce his work as bitter and vindictive. Ultimately, Houghton Mifflin bowed to this audience's judgment. True to its motto, "Tout bien ou rien," the company had marketed Chesnutt to the best of its ability, then ceased publication of his work entirely.

CHAPTER 3

SATIRE OF WHITENESS

Finley Peter Dunne's Newspaper Fictions

T he turn of the twentieth century witnessed substantial shifts and expansions in the definitions of white identity. As Matthew Frye Jacobson has described, massive waves of European immigration influenced a "fracturing of whiteness into a hierarchy of plural and scientifically determined white races," which were later reconsolidated with the Immigration Act of 1924.[1] European immigrants to the United States at this time encountered a range of options for participating in American culture. They might choose to live in relatively segregated ethnic communities and enclaves; they might choose to more actively assimilate and Americanize; or they might be compelled to Americanize by social, legal, and economic pressure. This chapter examines the work of Finley Peter Dunne, a second-generation Irish American newspaper columnist and political satirist. It considers how Dunne employed the double-voiced ironies of political satire to critique Anglo supremacism and imperialism from within the boundaries of Irish American whiteness. As with Charles W. Chesnutt's conjure tales, the work of Dunne's satire is twofold. Ostensibly, by adopting strategies of dialect and caricature, Dunne's writing can be understood as reinforcing racist attitudes and stereotypes. At the same time, Dunne's columns can be read as profoundly antiracist, offering a subversive critique of the boundaries of whiteness, ethnicity, and nation. Dunne's own Irish American background further complicates this dynamic, since revelations of his white ethnic identity

would not necessarily predetermine the politics for his audience's textual interpretations. Rather, by assuming an off-white status, Dunne
walked a fine line between subverting and supporting normative racist
attitudes. In what follows, I consider both of these aspects of Dunne's
writing, examining how his work *can be* read and how it *was read* by
contemporaries.

In the early twentieth century, Finley Peter Dunne was one of the
most popular writers in the United States. He was born in 1867 and
schooled in Chicago journalism alongside writers such as Eugene
Field and Theodore Dreiser. Throughout his life, Dunne aspired to
manage his own newspaper publication, but he became most famous
for his Mr. Dooley columns, a series of fictional sketches narrated from
the perspective of the title bartender, Martin Dooley. In articles of six
hundred to eight hundred words, written in comedic Irish vernacular,
Mr. Dooley offered everyday advice and political opinions to the cli-
ents of his South Side Chicago saloon. These weekly articles, initially
popular among a local audience in Chicago, became widely syndicated
and extraordinarily popular when Dunne turned to national politics,
satirizing the Spanish-American War. Dunne's first book collection, *Mr.
Dooley in Peace and in War* (1899), sold 10,000 copies per month for its
first year.[2] His second book, *Mr. Dooley in the Hearts of His Countrymen*
(1899), sold nearly as well, with booksellers ordering more than 25,000
copies before it was even published.[3] As Dunne's newspaper columns
continued to be syndicated nationwide, he became one of the highest-
paid writers of his era, and soon moved in elite literary circles. He
was friends with Mark Twain, and Edith Wharton introduced him to
Henry James.[4] As Wharton describes the interaction in her memoir, a
quick-witted Dunne was frustrated by James's slow, deliberate speech.
Dunne's work was also influential for Alexander Posey and Langston
Hughes when they created Fus Fixico and Jesse B. Semple.[5]

Examining the popularity of Mr. Dooley's voice, this chapter moves
through three distinct sections. I begin by considering how Dunne's
upbringing, as an Irish American journalist in Chicago at the turn of
the century, located him both inside and outside of mainstream U.S.
culture. Here, I consider how Dunne's position—not only racially but
also geographically and professionally—allowed him to develop his
popular satirical style. In a second section, I then examine how Dunne's
satirical voice can be read through a variety of interpretive lenses.

While his writing has been discussed in terms of literary realism and modernism, I consider how the Mr. Dooley columns participate in a more radical form of anticolonial mimicry. Finally, I complicate this interpretation further by examining Mr. Dooley within the context of newspaper syndication. In this section, I examine how Mr. Dooley's voice is not only subversive but also draws on the writing styles of sensationalism and yellow journalism. I show that Dunne's writing was often read as supporting yellow journalism and jingoism, rather than as a critique of U.S. imperialism. Such interpretations, in turn, hinge on audience assumptions regarding Dunne's outlook and identity as a white author. Ultimately, the enormous popularity of Dunne's satirical columns was driven by his ability to mimic a range of generic voices without explicitly committing to any one. At a time when the newspaper was the most widely read medium in the United States, Mr. Dooley spoke in all the voices of the news.

FINLEY PETER DUNNE AND IRISH AMERICANIZATION AT THE TURN OF THE CENTURY

Growing up in an Irish American family in Chicago at the turn of the century, Dunne was uniquely positioned as both an insider and an outsider to American popular culture. As many historians have argued, Irish Americans were the "classic ethnics" of the nineteenth century,[6] and served as models for the religious and urban communities of the so-called new immigrants who arrived at the turn of the century.[7] As such, the Irish were the targets of social discrimination. They were labeled as "colored" and were often forced to take on jobs as laborers or servants.[8] While stereotypical depictions of the Irish are perhaps best known in the political cartoons of *Puck, Punch,* and *Harper's Weekly,* comparable stereotypes can also be found in the literature of Thoreau, Emerson, and Hawthorne.[9] These negative depictions persisted toward the turn of the century. In 1896, for example, the *Atlantic Monthly* published an article, "The Irish in American Life," which claims, "A Celt is a notoriously passionate, impulsive, kindly, unreflecting, brave, nimble-witted man; but he lacks the solidity, the balance, the judgment of the Anglo-Saxon."[10] This type of racist classification was commonplace, whereby Irish Americans such as Dunne were viewed as less than the Anglo-American. To draw on Matthew Frye Jacobson again, the Irish were granted "probationary" status as white, alongside Italian, Polish, and Jewish immigrants.[11] As an Irish American author of an Irish American character, Dunne's authorial persona was understood in this way. A 1907 newspaper article, which included an illustrated portrait of Dunne, noted, "Mr. Dunne's physiognomy . . . is worthy of the companionship of Mr. Dooley."[12] Here, the author is described as recognizably Irish and comparable in appearance to the caricature he invented.

Along these lines, it is worth noting Dunne's deliberate affiliation with his Irish American background through the name "Finley." This was not Dunne's given name from birth but was rather his mother's maiden name, which Dunne adopted—first as "P. F. Dunne" in 1886, and then, more permanently, as "F. P. Dunne" in 1888.[13] According to his biographer, Elmer Ellis, Dunne's mother had been the primary influence on his intellectual development, and Dunne took on the name "Finley" as a tribute to her.[14] The name has strong associations with Ireland; it may remind us of the Fenian Brotherhood or, after Dunne's lifetime, of *Finnegan's Wake*. Dunne's assumed name might also be considered alongside the name of Huckleberry Finn. For while Shelley Fisher Fishkin has said that the voice of Huck Finn was modeled after a black child,[15] other critics have argued that Twain's character was stereotypically *Irish*. Hugh J. Dawson claims, for instance, that Huck's last name would have identified him to readers as Irish, and that his vocabulary and speech would have been recognized as the dialect of the working-class Irish. Moreover, Huck's social status, as the son of a drunken Irishman, was a contributing factor in the character's sympathetic identification with Jim. As Dawson argues, identifying Huck Finn as Irish meant that the character shared "his ethnic group's special kinship with American blacks."[16] By assuming the name "Finley," Dunne claimed this type of affiliation, and he did so just two years after *The Adventures of Huckleberry Finn* (1884) was published.

Yet despite any slippage between the terminology of "Irish" and "colored" in the nineteenth century, there were unquestionable differences in the forms of discrimination applied to the Irish and to African Americans. As Noel Ignatiev points out, the Irish were always granted essential rights as citizens. They could "compete for jobs in all spheres. . . . They were citizens of a democratic republic, with the right to elect and be elected, to be tried by a jury of their peers, to live anywhere they could afford."[17] Thomas Guglielmo has made a similar argument regarding Italian immigrants in his book *White on Arrival.* There, Guglielmo shows that Italian Americans in Chicago were never subject to legal oppression, and that "challenges to Italian immigrants' color status were never sustained or systematic."[18] In his book *White by Law,* Ian Haney-Lopez agrees with this assessment, showing how race at the turn of the century was defined through legal rulings that codified whiteness as European.[19] While discrimination against Irish Americans persisted throughout the nineteenth century and into the twentieth, it did so through social and economic spheres, rather than the political and legal system.

The turn of the twentieth century was a defining period for Irish Americanization and assimilation. As William Shannon argued in his 1963 book *The American Irish,* the turn of the century era witnessed a transition for many Irish immigrants from proletarian poverty to bourgeois respectability.[20] Subsequent critics have generally echoed Shannon's claim, which is worth emphasizing: Dunne wrote the Mr. Dooley columns during a transitory phase of Irish American identity. He was on the verge of assimilation into the American bourgeois, while still in the realm of probationary whiteness.

The fact that Dunne grew up in the Midwest and in an urban environment also played a role in his embourgeoisement. On the Eastern Seaboard, established communities of Anglo-Americans set limits on economic opportunity for the Irish, and there was more potential for growth for Irish Americans who migrated westward. As Kerby Miller points out, "The Irish were most prosperous and influential in urban centers that were relatively new (San Francisco), rapidly expanding (Chicago) and multiethnic and/or Catholic in origin (St. Louis), much less so even by the early 1900's in cities with old industrial economies and entrenched Yankee elites."[21] Timothy Meagher reiterates this idea, claiming that areas in the Midwest offered Irish Americans growth economies and more fluid social structures.[22] Land itself was sold cheaply in the Midwest and would appreciate quickly. Overall, Irish Americans who settled in emergent western cities were well positioned for economic and social advantage.

Within Chicago, a sprawling city composed of distinct neighborhoods, the Irish occupied two ethnic enclaves. The first, the working-class community of Bridgeport, was originally settled in the 1840s to build the Illinois and Michigan Canals.[23] Located above the stockyards and below the Chicago River's south branch, Bridgeport remained well populated throughout the late nineteenth century as a working-class neighborhood. As David Noel Doyle points out, "Everywhere, the Irish-born from 1850 to 1880 are dis-proportionately laborers, servants and semi-skilled workers, enjoying modest social and occupational advance."[24] In contrast to Bridgeport, however, in the 1860s a middle-class Irish neighborhood had also sprung up in Chicago's Near West Side, just outside of the Loop district, and Dunne was raised here.[25] By the late nineteenth century, the path out of immigrant labor and toward the American middle class was reflected in the physical environment of the city. To live in the Near West Side meant that an Irish American had moved beyond the railroad and canal labor of the Bridgeport neighborhood and had settled in a middle-class area of a city with incredible potential for growth.

Dunne's biography thus follows an almost ideal model for Irish American assimilation and professional success. Growing up in Chicago after the Great Fire of 1871, Dunne was positioned to take advantage of the city's exponential growth. Moreover, Dunne did not arrive in Chicago straight from New York City, desperate for work as a day laborer. Rather, as a second-generation Irish American, his parents had immigrated to New Brunswick before moving to Chicago. Once there, Dunne's father worked as a carpenter and boat builder, and his uncle served as priest at Saint Patrick's Church.[26] Thus while Mr. Dooley's saloon is set in the working-class neighborhood of Bridgeport, Dunne grew up in the middle-class Near West Side. Coming of age alongside a rapidly expanding metropolis, Dunne was well situated to enter the American mainstream.

Dunne began work for the *Chicago Telegram* at the age of seventeen and soon transferred to the *Chicago News*, where he worked alongside Eugene Field.[27] There, Dunne was assigned to report on baseball, traveling with the Chicago White Stockings during the 1887 season. On the road with the team, Dunne and fellow writer Charles Seymour reported on the games in narrative form, retelling them in dramatic fashion. Elmer Ellis says that Dunne and Seymour are "correctly credited" with having invented this type of reporting, which has been foundational for modern sports journalism. Dunne moved to the *Chicago Times* soon afterward and was promoted to city editor of the newspaper, directing a staff of reporters. His knowledge of the city made him an asset to the paper, and at the age of twenty-one he was the youngest city editor in Chicago.

By 1892, Dunne moved to the *Evening Post,* where he was given control of the editorial page. In conjunction with his managing editor, Dunne transformed the page to offer short satirical paragraphs, similar to the Dooley columns but without the dramatic form and dialect. When the *Evening Post* began to run a Sunday edition of sixteen pages, rather than the standard eight, Dunne experimented with dialect for the first time. These dialect pieces went through several iterations, beginning with a character named Colonel Dolan, and then Colonel McNarry. Throughout the summer of 1893, for example, Colonel McNarry visited the Chicago World's Fair on a weekly basis. McNarry mocked the Buffalo Bill show and the two Irish exhibits in the Chicago Fair's midway.[28] Later that same year, in the fall of 1893, Martin Dooley permanently replaced Colonel McNarry.

Dunne experimented with this dialect voice as a means for a political critique he could not make as easily in nonfiction journalism. Describing the creation of Mr. Dooley, Dunne himself said, "It occurred to me that while it might be dangerous to call an alderman a thief in English, no one could sue if a comic Irishman denounced the statesman."[29] Here, Dunne distinguishes between Mr. Dooley's perspective and an "English" one, describing the bartender's comic Irish approach as a covert means of denunciation. He also indicates that this perspective is angled against corrupt politics and the state, in order "to call an alderman a thief." The caricature serves as a cover for this underlying political critique. The typical Mr. Dooley column accomplishes this critique through indirect satire, in conversational exchanges between the saloonkeeper and his customers—sometimes a German neighbor, sometimes the white-collar Mr. McKenna, and, most frequently, Dooley's jingoistic adversary, Mr. Hennessy.

In one early example of the column from the summer of 1894, Dunne responded to the Pullman Strike. Led by Eugene Debs in the wake of the financial Panic of 1893, this was a strike of more than 100,000 American Railway Union workers against decreased wages and increased costs of living in Pullman company towns. Ultimately, federal courts ruled against the union boycott, and federal troops were deployed to break the strike. In a column from August 24, 1894, titled "What Does He Care?," Mr. Dooley responds to the situation. Focusing his attention on George Pullman himself, Dooley tells a customer that Pullman must be the happiest man alive since he "can go his way with his nose in th' air an' pay no attintion to th' sufferin' iv women an' childher."[30] Dooley goes on to describe how he himself can barely walk the streets of Chicago without seeing all of the women and children made destitute by Pullman's labor policies. But God must have quarried George Pullman's heart differently: "'Ah, what th' 'ell,' says George, 'What th' 'ell,' he says. 'What th' 'ell,' he says."

The piece is a good example of how these columns function. Mr. Dooley addresses relevant news and politics in conversation with one of his customers. While the humor targets corruption and greed, that criticism is masked in dialect and hyperbole, with Mr. Dooley ostensibly admiring George Pullman. Dooley places himself on familial terms with Pullman, calling him "George," and mocking him as a personal acquaintance. The dialect also allows Dunne freedom to speak explicitly and to curse. He drops the "h" from "hell," so that it can appear in print. And yet the "h" is provided by the abbreviated article that precedes it: "th' 'ell.'" Notably, in this same era, Stephen Crane's *Maggie: A Girl of the Streets* would be censored for its use of the word "hell." The novel, which had originally been self-published in 1893, was viewed as obscene and was republished by D. Appleton and Company in 1896 with substantial deletions.[31] Dunne's use of dialect helped him bypass such censorship, allowing him to curse Pullman to hell. According to Elmer Ellis, this article was memorized and reread all over Chicago and "became a highly important factor in rousing public sentiment to the reality of suffering in Pullman, and in bringing into being a relief fund that aided the worst cases."[32] Dunne's satirical columns thus had an immediate and real political impact.

The earliest Mr. Dooley columns dealt primarily with local issues regarding Chicago and its Irish community. Yet Dunne occasionally turned to national issues as well. In 1895, he compared the threat of war with Spain to a barroom brawl.[33] In 1896, he used the column to comment on the Bryan–McKinley presidential campaign. By 1898, Dunne commented regularly on American expansion into the Philippines and Cuba. One piece in particular, on admiral George Dewey's victory in the Battle of Manila Bay, made Mr. Dooley a national sensation almost overnight.[34] At the time, May 1, 1898, the American public awaited the outcome of Admiral Dewey's engagement against the Spanish fleet in

Manila. Yet because of a cut cable, there was no news of the battle's result. Dunne responded to the situation with a column titled "On His Cousin George," speaking this time about admiral George Dewey (as opposed to George Pullman). In the column, Dooley claims he is closely related to the admiral, saying of their last names, "Dewey or Dooley, 'tis all th' same."[35] He goes on to predict American victory, joking that Admiral Dewey was in no rush to wire back news of the battle because he had "ilicted himself king iv the' F'lipine Islands." This prediction for American victory was correct, and in fact Admiral Dewey *had* ordered the cable to be cut. As Ellis describes it, the column was reprinted in more than one hundred newspapers across the country, propelling Mr. Dooley to national fame. When subsequent columns were just as popular, Dunne and his publisher, now the *Chicago Journal,* had the pieces copyrighted for publication.

Up to this point, Dunne had not wanted to reveal himself as the author of Mr. Dooley, and the columns had been published anonymously. Dunne had also been reluctant to collect the columns in book form. On his national success, however, Dunne released *Mr. Dooley in Peace and in War* in December 1898, a book that gave a national audience access to previously unknown Mr. Dooley columns dating back several years. The book sold incredibly well and remained on the best-seller list for a full year,[36] until it was displaced by Dunne's second book collection, *Mr. Dooley in the Hearts of His Countrymen.*[37] Dunne's name was not included on the title page of either of these books, but he did sign his initials to the introduction and preface. As a result, although the books were published anonymously, Dunne was soon known as the author of the Mr. Dooley columns.

DIALECT REALISM, MODERNIST WORDPLAY, AND CRITICISM OF U.S. EMPIRE

In terms of scholarly criticism, Dunne's writing was initially recovered by Charles Fanning in a 1978 book that won the Frederick Jackson Turner Award from the Organization of American Historians.[38] After Fanning's book, a burst of criticism responded to various aspects of the Mr. Dooley columns, interpreting them as both realist immigrant fiction and as metalinguistic modernist wordplay. In this section, I consider how critics have interpreted Dunne and how a postcolonial apparatus might also be applied to his dialect critique of U.S. imperialism. Even beyond styles of literary realism and modernism, I argue that Mr. Dooley's ambiguous speech can be read as radically antiracist and anti-imperialist. Yet these different interpretations of Mr. Dooley are not mutually exclusive. Indeed, Dunne's style of writing allows them to exist alongside one another simultaneously.

Charles Fanning's initial recovery of Dunne focused on the early years of the column, from 1893 to 1899, which were more devoted to life in Chicago than to national politics. Fanning promoted the recovery of Dunne's writing as realist literature, and would later go so far as to claim, "The Chicago Dooley pieces constitute the most solidly realized ethnic neighborhood in nineteenth-century American literature. . . . With the full faith of the literary realist, Dunne embraced the common man as proper subject and created sympathetic, dignified even heroic characters."[39] Here, Fanning describes the Mr. Dooley columns in terms of the dominant literary style at the time, dealing with common and everyday subjects. And in fact, William Dean Howells had similarly praised Dunne in a 1903 review of Chicago writers.[40] Fanning's book considers more than three hundred of the Dooley columns from the 1890s, as they describe Chicago's Bridgeport community.

Dunne himself, however, expressed disdain for realism and realist novels. In a 1912 issue of the *Metropolitan* magazine, for instance, Dunne offered some advice about writing and art. He says that the first maxim for writing fiction is a simple one: "Don't tell the truth." Dunne soon elaborates on this view, saying that art is not at all true to life, and that artists simply create representations, or an "illusion of probability."[41] For Dunne, then, realist writers are not defined by having a better grasp on reality but by the style with which they create artistic representations. In the article, Dunne goes on to criticize realist writers for their pessimism, saying they tell only "small, ugly, mean, distorted, and disproportioned fragments of the truth."[42] Although Dunne may have participated in certain features of literary realism, he did not consider himself a realist writer.

Decades earlier, Dunne had expressed a similar skepticism in regard to dialect literature. In fact, just weeks before he first experimented with the genre, Dunne described dialect writing as "a very bad thing. . . . It has filled the magazines so full that we sometimes wonder why they do not explode; it has flooded the bookstands with its pink and yellow covers and its horrid drawings of Dakota farmers and Tennessee moun-taineers."[43] Based on this description, it seems clear that Dunne did not turn to dialect writing out of affection for the popular style. Rather, he decided to write in dialect as a metacritique of the genre, shortly after publishing this article. Along these same lines, if Dunne wrote in the style of literary realism, it was not because he aspired to be a realist author but rather because the Mr. Dooley columns respond to popular trends in realist writing. Dunne's criticism of these literary styles may explain his reluctance to be known as the author of the Dooley columns. As someone who always wanted to work in journalism, Dunne seems to have viewed fiction writing as a lower and less truthful pursuit.[44]

Critics have also posed a number of other possibilities for the generic classification of the Mr. Dooley columns. Arthur Power Dudden, for example, argues that Dunne was less influenced by contemporary realists than by mid-nineteenth-century comic figures such as Artemus Ward, Hosea Biglow, and Major Jack Downing.[45] Dunne's chief innova-tion was adapting this style to an urban environment. Dunne's extreme use of dialect, to the point of caricature, also complicates the realism of these columns. In an article on "Mr. Dooley's Brogue," John Rees points out that the dialect in these tales not only produces ostensibly authentic speech but also creates complex wordplay and puns. For example, when Mr. Dooley discusses "pollyticks," he evokes the many ("poly") blood-sucking parasites involved in the political system.[46] The joke, in this case, is extradiagetic; it is made in the space between Dool-ey's realistic speech and Dunne's transcription of that speech.[47] Such wordplay occurs throughout the columns. In the piece on the Battle of Manila Bay, cited earlier, Admiral Dewey "ilicted himself king." Here, the dialect misspelling points to the illicit nature of U.S. military power, claiming sovereignty through self-election. The column goes on to offer another great example of linguistic wordplay, when it speaks in the voice of Admiral Dewey to describe the battle: "At 8 o'clock I begun a peaceful blockade iv this town. Ye can see th' pieces ivrywhere. I hope ye're injyin' the same great blessin'."[48] In this excerpt, the pun on "peaceful" and "pieces" reveals the double-talk of U.S. diplomatic pol-icy, which offers peace and delivers violence. When Dewey hopes that Americans are "injyin" this same peacefulness, the criticism is pushed even further. The spelling implies that U.S. peace and blessings are enjoyed only through the conquest of Indian lands.[49]

These disconnections, between sign and signified, indicate Mr. Dooley's place among literary modernists. Indeed, Grace Eckley points out that several of Dunne's puns, which included multilingual wordplay, are borrowed directly by James Joyce in *Ulysses* and *Finnegan's Wake*.[50] Likewise, in a poem he wrote in 1916, Joyce envisioned Mr. Dooley as a model for responding to the violence of World War I. The poem is titled "Dooleysprudence" and it begins,

> Who is the man when all the gallant nations run to war
> Goes home to have his dinner by the very first cablecar
> And as he eats his cantelope contorts himself in mirth
> To read the blatant bulletins of the rulers of the earth?
> It's Mr. Dooley,
> Mr. Dooley,
> The coolest chap our country ever knew.[51]

The poem imagines Mr. Dooley as a modernist hero, along the lines of Leopold Bloom. Despite the ever-present clashes of warfare and empire, Dooley carves out his own interpretation of the newspapers, "contort[ing] himself in mirth / To read the blatant bulletins of the rulers of the earth."[52] Then, when Joyce describes Dooley as "the coolest chap our country ever knew," it is unclear to which nation he is referring. The claim on citizenship poses a question more than it defines Mr. Dooley's nationality. And, notably, Dunne played with the same idea in the title of his second book, *Mr. Dooley in the Hearts of His Countrymen.*

The Mr. Dooley columns were thus composed so that they could be read as both dialect realism and literary modernism. On the one hand, the columns become an encounter with the ethnic other, which is authentic and real. The reader enjoys the Dooley columns for their depiction of the Irish community in Chicago. On the other hand, understanding Dunne as a modernist, the columns become more playful. Mr. Dooley might remain a caricature to some extent, but he becomes more self-aware in this role. He is an urban businessman, and his perspective is thoroughly modern. This is especially evident in Mr. Dooley's use of multilingual puns, which make a joke of his transnational identity. Indeed, if the techniques of literary modernism can be defined by disjunctions of the urban center and the colonial periphery—as argued by Terry Eagleton, Fredric Jameson, and Edward Said[53]—Mr. Dooley anticipates those techniques in his humorous sense of dislocation.

The Mr. Dooley columns can thus be situated in a more wide-ranging discussion of dialect literature and ethnic mimicry at the turn of the century. As discussed in my introduction, numerous scholars have examined dialect writing as it responds to issues of race and national identity. In terms of the early twentieth century, Michael North's *The Dialect of Modernism* is perhaps the best known, showing how modernist writers such as T. S. Eliot and Gertrude Stein expropriated the black voice for its "insurrectionary opposition to the known and familiar language."[54] Other critics, including Henry Wonham and Gavin Jones, have argued that late nineteenth-century texts shared similar strategies of linguistic mimicry. Gavin Jones's *Strange Talk* attempts to move beyond judgments of authentic/inauthentic dialect to examine the anxieties and motivations surrounding the use of vernacular speech. Jones offers a sympathetic interpretation of Paul Laurence Dunbar, for instance, describing how the author was in "the classic situation of blacks donning the white-defined mask of blackness, using the racial conventions of mainstream entertainment to gain public recognition."[55] The same description might be applied to Charles Chesnutt's early conjure tales.

Dunne similarly adopts what I have called ambiguous tactics of representation to mimic stereotypes of the Irish American. He does not take on the black voice, as T. S. Eliot and Gertrude Stein attempt, but wears the mask of Irish American stereotypes. In this way, Dunne's work can be compared to Chesnutt's or Dunbar's because it plays on stereotypes that had been applied to his own ethnic background and identity. Indeed, in the mid-nineteenth century, the forms of blackface and whiteface minstrelsy were quite similar. As James P. Byrne has argued, the overlap of "Irish and black minstrel shows would lead to a syncretism and even suffusion of stereotypical tropes between both styles," so that the "two theatrical styles would become almost synonymous."[56] Thus, even while the rights accorded to Irish Americans and African Americans were incomparable, minstrel shows of the "paddy" and the "darkie" were quite similar in the 1850s and 1860s. Within these whiteface minstrel performances, the Irishman was typically caricatured as "a hirsute, muscular laborer, with cheek whiskers, a broad lip, a button nose, and prognathous jaws. Sometimes the features were distorted to give a simian aspect."[57] The caricature is similar to blackface in many ways, and, in fact, one of the chief proponents of

Irish theatrical caricature, Edward Harrigan, had begun his career as a blackface minstrel performer.[58] Dunne drew on this tradition, taking on the persona of the caricatured Irishman. Like Chesnutt and Dunbar, he adopts this persona in a complex form of mimicry that responds to the process of racialization itself. Rather than addressing Jim Crow segregation and violence, however, Dunne's caricature takes aim at notions of whiteness, white ethnicity, and Anglo-American supremacy.

Throughout the Dooley columns, we find this type of ambiguous caricature, which both reinforces and criticizes ideologies of race and white supremacism. Consider, for instance, Dunne's column "On the Anglo-Saxon." In this example, Mr. Dooley addresses the development of a political alliance between the United States and England in opposition to Spain, Germany, Russia, and other world powers. Dooley tells Hennessy of their new duties in partnership with England: "You an' me, Hinissey, has got to bring on this here Anglo-Saxon 'lieance."[59] As with so many of the columns, this political critique functions at the level of spelling and dialect. When Dooley describes the Anglo-Saxon "'lieance," the spelling quite literally puts the "lie" in contemporary Anglo-Saxon political ideologies. Yet even more than he ridicules the political formation of the Anglo-Saxon Alliance, Dooley criticizes the very concept of the Anglo-Saxon, as indicated by the title of the column, "On the Anglo-Saxon." He tells Hennessey, for example, that an Anglo-Saxon is "a German that's forgot who was his parents." Dooley then claims that he is himself an Anglo-Saxon and adds his neighbor Schwartzmeister to the list. He notes that one of his acquaintances is forming "th' Circle Francaize for the Anglo-Saxon club" and that his friend Domingo will head the "Dago Anglo-Saxons whin the time comes."[60] Toward the end of the column, "Afro-Americans" join the Alliance as well and raise a battle cry. At this point, Dooley concludes, "it'll be all day with th' eight or nine people in th' wurruld that has the misfortune of not being brought up Anglo-Saxons."

Dooley's satire of the Anglo-Saxon is layered. By noting the German origins of a term applied to the English, Dooley points to the hypocrisy of Anglo-Saxon claims on racial purity. To claim Anglo-Saxon identity requires the erasure of historical migrations and race mixing. The progression of the column from beginning to end is also important, as the scope of the Anglo-Saxon community expands in a way that mirrors racist hierarchies in the United States. Anglo-Saxon identity first absorbs the Germans and the French. Domingo and the "Dago Anglo-Saxons," however, must wait until "the time comes" before Italians can attain whiteness. Similarly, "th' Bohemian an' Pole Anglo-Saxons" will be slower to assimilate.[61] This postponement recognizes the "probationary whiteness" described by Jacobson, as the era's new immigrants from Eastern Europe wait to attain social status alongside Anglo-Americans. The expansion of whiteness is then taken to its extreme when African Americans become a part of the Alliance and "raise their Anglo-Saxon battle cry." The column thus pushes the idea of racial absorption to its furthest end, so that the colonized subject becomes the colonizer. It takes on precisely the aesthetic forms of "irony, mimicry, and repetition" that Homi K. Bhabha describes as responses to colonialism.[62] Dunne's writing employs these styles in a mockery of white empire. While claiming to take on the duties and responsibilities of the Anglo-Saxon alliance, it exposes the impossibility of Anglo purity.

In her book *The Anarchy of Empire in the Making of U.S. Culture*, Amy Kaplan further elaborates on this double-movement of American empire. As she puts it, "The idea of the nation as home . . . is inextricable from the political, economic, and cultural movements of empire."[63] Kaplan uses this interpretive lens to consider how a variety of seemingly mundane cultural phenomena—from domestic magazines to romance novels to early cinema—supported American imperial expansion at the turn of the century.[64] Especially relevant to Mr. Dooley, Kaplan devotes one chapter to journalistic descriptions of the United States' role in the Cuban war for independence.[65] She considers how domestic attitudes regarding race relations within the United States were applied to the international setting of the Spanish-American War.

Kaplan's chapter focuses especially on the iconic Battle of San Juan Hill, as narrated in Theodore Roosevelt's *The Rough Riders*. Here, Roosevelt not only dismisses the Cuban fight for independence, describing Cuban soldiers as incompetent and unmanly, but also narrates the story as one that conveys his own mastery of African American soldiers. As Kaplan points out, African Americans played a central role in the battle. Accounts of their heroism were published shortly after the war, circulating through the black press "to bolster the case of black commissioned officers."[66] Roosevelt, however, applies minstrel stereotypes to dismiss any African American contribution, claiming that these soldiers deplete the strength of the U.S. military. He even threatens to kill any soldiers who behave with cowardice. In Roosevelt's narrative, the black soldiers promptly obey, "flash[ing] their white teeth at one another, as they broke into broad grins."[67] By describing these soldiers with the stereotypes of minstrelsy, Roosevelt transports racist attitudes from a domestic U.S. setting into Cuba: the Cubans are incapable of fighting and claiming their own independence; they require American intervention; yet this intervention is threatened by the inferiority of African American citizens. In Roosevelt's telling, it is not until these African American soldiers submit to his superiority that the troops can unite and claim victory.

I describe Kaplan's analysis of *The Rough Riders* in some detail because this criticism of Roosevelt originated with Dunne. In a column that offers a review of *The Rough Riders*, Dooley describes Roosevelt's book as a great work of "litherachoor," renaming it "Th' Account iv th' Desthruction iv Spanish Power in th' Ant Hills,' as it fell fr'm th' lips iv Tiddy Rosenfelt an' was took down be his own hands."[68] Dooley's review then focuses on the same scene that Amy Kaplan analyzes, in which Roosevelt threatens violence against his own troops and takes full command. Speaking as Roosevelt, Mr. Dooley tells us, "I r-ran into th' entire military force iv th' United States lying on its stomach. 'If ye won't fight,' says I, 'let me go through.' . . . This showed me 'twud be impossible f'r to carry th' war to a successful con-clusion unless I was free, so I sint th' ar-rmy home an' attackted San Juon hill. Ar-rmed on'y with a small thirty-two which I used in th' West."[69] The column is not as explicit as Kaplan in recognizing the multiracial composition of American troops. It does, however, draw attention to the construction of Roosevelt's narrative, which places the author himself in the role of hero. Roosevelt's autobiography devalues and mocks the very military force it claims to uphold, criticizing the U.S. army for "lying on its stomach." The column thus exposes how Roosevelt claims his own status as national hero by denying the role of fellow soldiers. Roosevelt must remain "free" to command the military and attack foreign lands. The reference to the same gun "used in th' West" also points to the continuity of American empire. Roosevelt's Rough Riders were a group of militant American expansionists who helped overtake western territories in the United States before continuing on to international territories such as Cuba, Hawaii, and the Philippines. Dooley concludes the column by describing Roosevelt's *Rough Riders* as a fantasy of individual conquest: "If I was [Roosevelt] I'd call th' book 'Alone in Cubia.'" It's a phrase Kaplan borrows as the title for this section of her critique of American imperial expansion, "Alone in Cuba."

The Mr. Dooley columns have been read in all of these ways. The dialect lends authenticity to stories of Chicago's working-class Irish community. And yet, constant misspellings simultaneously disrupt this authenticity with metalinguistic and extradiagetic puns. This doubling—between realistic representation and modernist wordplay—might in turn be read as a product of colonialism. It is an ambiguous strategy of representation that both fulfills and critiques fantasies of Anglo-Saxon purity and dominance. With close attention, Dunne can be interpreted as realist, as modernist, and as radically postcolonial. This is not, however, the way Dunne's work was generally interpreted by a contemporary audience, reading the columns as they were syndicated in newspapers nationwide. As I will show, Mr. Dooley's popularity was sustained by its potential to be read much less carefully.

NEWSPAPER CIRCULATIONS

One of the challenges for analyzing Dunne's work is its unique form: weekly newspaper fiction from Chicago that was nationally syndicated and then published in book collections. Indeed, a basic impediment to sustained criticism of Dunne is the short, serialized form of his prose. The dialect of the pieces is also difficult, of course. Yet the challenges of reading dialect fiction have not prevented the work of Chesnutt and Dunbar from receiving more widespread critical attention in recent decades. In contrast to the fiction and poetry of Chesnutt and Dunbar, however, the Mr. Dooley columns are brief sketches, filled with references to the daily political minutiae of his era. The columns mimic the news, posing a sarcastic critique of yellow journalism and sensationalized front-page stories. In this way, Dunne is not only positioned between Irish and Anglo-American, and between realism and modernism, he is also positioned between journalism and literature. This newspaper context can help us understand why the Mr. Dooley columns were often interpreted as supporting, rather than criticizing, U.S. imperialism.

The turn of the twentieth century marked the height of newspaper production and consumption in the United States, and the rise of the medium supported Dunne's massive popularity. Throughout the nineteenth century, the expansion of U.S. infrastructure and the development of industrial print technologies laid the groundwork for a national print culture. Publishers were able to bind their books in stylized cloth covers, to set retail prices, and to distribute across the United States. By the turn of the century, newspapers and periodicals reached even wider audiences because of increased advertising revenue. In a process described by Richard Ohmann, newspaper and magazine publishers at the turn of the century sold more advertisements than ever before. This allowed publishers to lower their retail prices in order to attract more readers.[70] These expanded readerships could then attract more advertisers, so that newspapers and magazines could be sold for lower and lower prices, and even below the cost of production. In this way, periodicals achieved unprecedented mass readerships.

This process, in turn, was indicative of a major structural shift in the publication of books and periodicals. Throughout the mid- and late nineteenth century, monthly magazines had generally supported the book trade. Major publishers created "house magazines" to advertise their catalog, to serve as a testing ground for new authors, and to stir up interest in serialized fiction.[71] These magazines were often published at a loss to support the book trade. As they emerged at the turn of the century, however, mass magazines and periodicals were fundamentally different. As Ohmann puts it, "Their main 'product' was not the physical magazine itself, but the interested attention of readers, sold en bloc through ad agencies to manufacturers, who were now the main customers."[72] These new periodicals did not sell content to readers but sold the reader's attention to advertisers.

Studies on this shift toward mass culture have focused especially on the transition from genteel subscription magazines (*Harper's Monthly,* the *Atlantic,* and *Scribner's*) toward ten-cent magazines funded by advertisements (*Munsey's, McClure's,* and *Cosmopolitan*).[73] In this same era, however, newspapers underwent a similar process. As Charles Johanningsmeier has shown, in the late 1880s and 1890s the emergence of syndication allowed newspapers to be read by mass audiences across the country. This syndication occurred through a system of local, regional, and metropolitan newspapers, so that the newspaper was the medium that most cut across boundaries of gender, geography, and socioeconomic status.[74] In fact, the strategies of mass magazine publishers were influenced by the commercial form of the newspaper; they sought to make genteel literary interests amenable to a wider population of middle-class readers. Johanningsmeier has thus argued that mass literary culture developed in newspapers prior to its emergence in middle-class magazines.[75] Richard L. Kaplan similarly notes, "The near-universal reading of newspapers contrasted greatly with the consumption of magazines and books, which varied by education and social class."[76] In this way, Dunne's columns would have achieved as wide a circulation throughout the United States as had ever been possible.

During the peak of Dunne's career, syndication in newspapers also became a lucrative outlet for literary prose. Syndicate companies such as Tillotson's Fiction Bureau and S. S. McClure's Associated Literary Press worked as brokers between authors and the newspaper publications of the time, attracting writers such as Henry James, Stephen Crane, Sarah Orne Jewett, Robert Louis Stevenson, Joseph Conrad, and Arthur Conan Doyle.[77] All of these writers published literary fiction in syndicated newspapers. Indeed, throughout the 1890s, the Mr. Dooley columns would have been printed alongside the major literary authors of his era.

The expansion of venues for literary publication in this era—across newspapers, magazines, and books—thus takes part in a broader commodification of literary writing, which increasingly served to attract the reader's attention and consumer interests. Genteel magazines struggled to retain celebrity authors in competition with mass magazines. Magazine editors chased after well-known authors, often creating assignments or suggesting ideas for their writing.[78] Less-well-known writers were pressured to produce dependable, generic content. While Dunne entered this milieu as a journalist, such changes in periodical literature guided and constrained his career. Much in the way that advertisers of this period invented brands to market their products across mass platforms, Mr. Dooley became a familiar name and a sort of brand. Mr. Dooley's persona reflected the concerns of his middle-class readership. By responding to well-known national news stories, and yet doing so in colloquial speech, Mr. Dooley attracted a massive nationwide audience.

Syndication also required that Mr. Dooley keep up with the news on a regular basis, because the column was published once a week.

In the preface to the first book collection, for instance, the character of Mr. Dooley is defined in relation to current events: "He reads the newspapers with solemn care, heartily hates them, and accepts all they print for the purpose of drowning Hennessy's rising protests against his logic."[79] Here, we have a description of Dooley as an avid, albeit conflicted, reader.[80] Indeed, Dooley frequently explains to his customers how the newspaper *should* be read, referencing the "news" or the "paper" more than twenty-five times in *Mr. Dooley in Peace and in War*. The Dooley columns thus allow Dunne to comment not only on the news as current events but also on how that news is represented and how it should be interpreted. When Dooley claims he has information from "th' paper" or "th' newspaper," the stories create an awareness of the process of reading itself, as if Mr. Dooley is commenting on the very paper in which he is printed.

In a sense, the Dooley columns function much as television's *The Colbert Report* did from 2005 to 2014, in which Stephen Colbert took on an exaggerated persona to mock the daily news for a popular audience. The periodical form organizes each installment, allowing the title character to respond nimbly to current events. The Mr. Dooley columns and *The Colbert Report* are also driven by their responses to media—how news events and politics are represented in journalism. In the same way that Colbert mimics Fox News, playing the role of a conservative news anchor, Mr. Dooley ostensibly advocates for Anglo dominance and imperialism. He takes on the style of "new" or "yellow" journalism.

Yellow journalism promoted U.S. imperial efforts abroad and a belligerent form of nationalism. This is most commonly exemplified by an apocryphal exchange between William Randolph Hearst, owner of the *New York Journal*, and artist Frederic Remington at the outset of the Spanish-American War. Supposedly, when Remington was sent to Cuba on assignment in 1897, he found no military conflict and cabled Hearst to say there was no war. Hearst infamously responded, "You furnish the pictures, and I will furnish the war." While this story is more myth than history, it nevertheless has become emblematic of the power of yellow journalism at the turn of the century, a topic that has since been explored by a number of scholars.[81] Charles Henry Brown's 1967 *The Correspondents' War*, for instance, analyzes the emergence of modern journalism in relation to the Spanish-American War.

At the same time, however, yellow journalism can also be defined through other innovations, such as its use of bold layouts and sensational writing styles. In his own study of yellow journalism, W. Joseph Campbell defines the genre through a variety of formal elements: use of multicolumn headlines and experimental layouts, the variety of topics reported on the front page, the frequent use of illustration, and a penchant for self-promotion.[82] As one example of these features, Joseph Pulitzer's *New York World* was stylized with "a colloquial tone, and a pioneering use of illustration, color ink, advertising, and entertaining weekend supplements."[83] Yellow journalism also included a great deal of sensationalistic reporting that focused on crime stories, gossip, scandals, sports, and bizarre pseudoscience. While sensationalism and yellow journalism are not entirely synonymous, newspapers such as Pulitzer's *New York World* and Hearst's *New York Journal* often focused on dramatic narratives that involved sports, crime, and celebrity personalities. Yellow journalism thus incorporated and reinvigorated sensational writing within the realm of U.S. newspapers, publishing exaggerated reports with bold typographies and layouts.

A specific example may help to illustrate how these features converge in yellow journalism and in the Mr. Dooley columns, and here I will return to Admiral Dewey and the Battle of Manila Bay. On Dewey's victory, the evening edition of Hearst's *New York Journal* took a sensational approach. Its front page for May 2, 1898, exclaims, "Have the Dons Had Enough! Powers Ready to Intervene" (figure 8). The headline itself is printed in bold font, in three different sizes of capitalization, spaced somewhat unevenly across the page. In fact, the headline is formatted to allow room for the box scores of the New York–Baltimore baseball game, so that the spectacle of war and the spectacle of domestic sports go hand in hand. The headline also takes a colloquial approach to this news, referring to the Spanish government as "the Dons." It mocks the Spanish defeat and defines the American forces as powerful, organized, and merely intervening on behalf of the Philippines. Notably, the front page also lists the newspaper's circulation at the top center: 1,408,200 copies.

Pages two and three of this issue of the *New York Evening Journal* continue coverage of Manila Bay with a headline running across the full width of the newspaper: "Spain Admits Complete Defeat!" A large illustration on page three shows an American ship with its flag raised

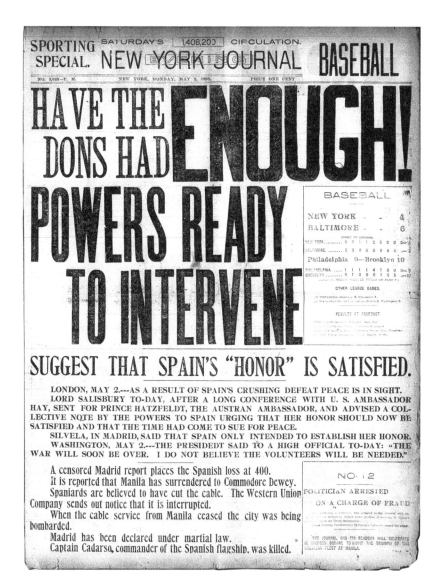

FIGURE 8. An example of yellow journalism published by William Randolph Hearst during the Spanish-American War. "Have the Dons Had Enough!," *New York Evening Journal,* May 2, 1898. Image courtesy of the Library of Congress.

high, centered amid explosions and collapsing vessels. The image is captioned, "The Big Naval Battle at Manila a Glorious Victory for Our War Ships." Columns on the page describe how "Dewey made a clean job of it," and is now "the subject of admiring comments from all Englishmen to-day." In all of this reporting, Hearst's *Journal* emphasizes U.S. militaristic power and victory. The destruction of the Spanish fleet and of Manila is described as a clean job, worthy of Anglo admiration. The *Journal* combines illustrations, large fonts, and sensational writing in praise of the U.S. war effort.

Dunne's column on Admiral Dewey in the Philippines, as I have shown, offers a critical response to American expansion and imperialism. It describes the destruction of Manila and how Dewey has "ilicted himself king iv the' F'lipine Islands."[84] The battle thus represents an illicit seizure of a foreign nation, tainting U.S. democracy with monarchical rule. At the conclusion of the piece, Mr. Dooley tells Hennessy that the government "will organize th' F'lipine Islands Jute an' Cider Comp'ny, an' th' rivolutchinists'll wish they hadn't." In other words, Dunne recognizes American expansion into the Philippines as an expansion of industrial interests into new markets for labor, raw goods, and trade. The U.S. government will exploit control of the Philippines, and the native population will be denied its own revolution against Spain.

It is also important, however, to consider how the column might actually reinforce imperialist attitudes for readers less attuned to these subversive elements. Taken as literal, rather than sarcastic hyperbole, Mr. Dooley's comments can be read as belligerent advocacy for American imperial expansion. Indeed, the quotations cited above can be read in the same style as those from the *New York Journal,* extolling Admiral Dewey's kinglike dominance over Spain and the Philippines. Elsewhere in the column, Admiral Dewey is praised for turning the harbor into a "Spanish stew" and for setting the town of Manila on fire.[85] When read alongside examples of yellow journalism, the description of Dewey as king of the islands is particularly troubling: "He'll be settin' up there undher a pa'm-three with naygurs fannin' him an' a drhop iv licker in th' hollow iv his arm, an' hootchy-kootchy girls dancin' befure him, an' ivry tin or twinty miyits some wan bringin' a prisoner in." How would a mass audience have read this description? Would the average reader have understood this as a subversive critique of U.S. imperialism and martial law? Some readers may have caught on, yes. But it is likely that many readers interpreted the column in agreement with the tenets of yellow journalism and Hearst's *New York Journal*. They would have been happy to picture the scene Dooley describes, complete with racial, sexual, and military violence. Indeed, the piece offers up the quintessential fantasy of Anglo supremacy: Admiral Dewey rules over prisoners in an exotic location, getting drunk, while girls dance for him and black servants keep him comfortable. Moreover, this very column established Mr. Dooley as a national sensation, serving as a spring-board for his mass popularity.

It is difficult to evaluate the nationwide reception of Mr. Dooley's work. In contrast to Chesnutt's career, the response does not delineate a linear trajectory over time. Instead, Mr. Dooley was understood in competing ways simultaneously. At times and among select readers, Mr. Dooley would have been read as radical satire, deconstructing ideas of race and nation. For others, he could be read as a voice of pro-gressivism, opposing corrupt politics and corporate greed.[86] For yet other readers, however, Mr. Dooley would have been read as neither progressive nor radical but as an active proponent of American impe-rialism. From this perspective, the Irish bartender was Americanized *through* his advocacy of war, participating in a culture of aggressive national expansion. Because Dunne, as an author, neither voiced his political criticisms explicitly nor "outed" himself as an ethnic author who opposed Anglo imperialism, these viewpoints coexisted and sus-tained his mass popularity. Such conflicting interpretations persisted for more than twenty years, as Dunne maintained the Dooley persona.

The most common reviews of Mr. Dooley are not critical but instead quote heavily from the columns themselves in order to repeat their ambiguity. These reviews praise Mr. Dooley as a humorist and phi-losopher, but do not analyze that humor or philosophy. Like Dunne's own writing, they avoid explications that might polarize or divide the audience, serving almost as advertisements for the series. For example, one response in the March 1899 edition of *Munsey's Magazine* claims that the columns are "so full of nuggets of wisdom and bits of the universal philosophy of life as to prove that Mr. Dunne has struck a vein of true humor."[87] Thus while the columns are described as universally wise and humorous, the reasons for making this claim are not provided. *Munsey's Magazine,* like Dunne, did not wish to alienate any subset of its reader-ship. Likewise, an article in the *Baltimore Sun* sidestepped any judgment of Mr. Dooley by reprinting the column instead of reviewing it: "Humor cannot be described—it must speak for itself."[88] In general, reviews often functioned in this way. They would briefly introduce Dunne and Mr. Dooley, and might describe the topic at hand, before quoting a substantial portion of a column. Without analysis, it is difficult to know how the reviewer is interpreting the humor. Indeed, such reviews merely repeat Dunne's own ambiguous tactics of representation.

Other reviews come closer to grasping Mr. Dooley's critique of the war and U.S. imperialism. One review published in the *Charlotte Daily Observer* serves as a good example. It describes Mr. Dooley's uncertainty regarding newly invaded U.S. territories, noting that he "does not seem to think well of expansion."[89] The use of the word "seem" is notable, as it refers to the ambiguity of the columns. The reviewer is relatively confident that Mr. Dooley opposes expansion into Cuba and the Philippines, but is not entirely certain. The review goes on to discuss Dooley's criticism of military leadership: "For General Miles and the strategy board Mr. Dooley . . . had only words of ridicule." Here, the reviewer clearly follows Dooley's "ridicule" of American strategy for the Spanish-American war. Mr. Dooley had mocked general Nelson A. Miles, who had led the invasion of Puerto Rico. (Nelson had also commanded the response to the Pullman Strike and overseen numerous battles against American Indians in the Great Plains.) For the *Charlotte Daily Observer*, Dunne's criticism of General Miles was at least clear.

However, there is good evidence that the columns were interpreted as advocating Anglo-American imperialism. For example, the *Munsey's* review that mentions Dooley's "universal philosophy" seems to take seriously Mr. Dooley's discussion of war. As they describe it, "All through the strenuous period of hostilities [Mr. Dooley] discoursed to his friends . . . of how it ought to be prosecuted, when it should begin and when stop, and what should be done with the spoils."[90] Again, *Munsey's* takes an objective and nonpartisan approach. It does not describe Mr. Dooley's response to the war as satiric hyperbole. A review in the *Literary Digest* likewise struggles to discern the meaning of Mr. Dooley's saloon conversations, especially with regard to imperial expansion. As this reviewer notes, "Peter Dunne's philosophical saloon-keeper whose observations on current topics continue to amuse, not to say instruct, the reading public, is still perplexed but hopeful concerning 'expansion.'"[91] Here, the *Literary Digest* very nearly recognizes the ambiguities of the columns, insofar as Mr. Dooley "continues to amuse" his readers without instructing them. Nevertheless, the review goes on to say that Mr. Dooley is "hopeful" for American expansion. If this reviewer recognized Mr. Dooley's sarcasm as political satire, they are unwilling to mention it.

Such were the hazards and benefits of writing in Irish dialect at the turn of the century. Mr. Dooley's vernacular allowed him to be read by different readers as white, as American, and as ethnic caricature—and to do so without explicitly crossing any boundaries. Thus, when reviews mention Dooley's Irish background, they describe his ethnicity as different but still essentially white. A review in the *Bookman* describes the saloonkeeper in this way: "Mr. Dooley is a type. He has all an Irishman's shrewdness, an Irishman's combativeness, an Irishman's independence, an Irishman's underlying appreciation of courage and loyalty, and also an Irishman's keen wit and picturesque phraseology, with that inevitable genius for blundering that is also Irish."[92] The Dooley caricature was attractive and nonthreatening to a popular audience. He was fascinating in his difference and yet inventive and humorous.

Much later in Dunne's career, in 1919, the *Outlook* would similarly reflect on Mr. Dooley's Irish American background, reclaiming him for the U.S. nation at large: "He is an American for all his brogue, for his humor is of the kind that Americans have delighted to honor these many generations. Salted with philosophy and satire, Gargantuan in mirth . . . the wit of this great protagonist of a once honored and prosperous profession is as racily American as that of any native son of New England."[93] Here, Mr. Dooley's dialect is absorbed as a fulfillment of the American dream. He becomes part of what John Higham has described as the "Crusade for Americanization" in the early twentieth century, when the term "American" was reencoded as white, Christian, and English-speaking.[94] The passage makes this explicit, so that Dooley is "as racily American" as "any native son of New England." In a painful irony of interpretation, Dooley's anti-imperial satire becomes the fulfillment of Anglo hegemony. Like Chesnutt's *Procrustes,* the subversive critique is understood as an exemplification of the white supremacist attitudes that are being criticized.

PLAYING WITH WHITENESS

In 1922, former editor of *Life* magazine, Thomas L. Masson, considered the legacy of the Mr. Dooley columns. In a provocative statement, Masson imagined that all documentary evidence from the first decade of the twentieth century could be replaced with Finley Peter Dunne's writing. As he put it, "If all the newspaper files and histories were destroyed between the years 1898 and 1910 and nothing remained but Mr. Dooley's observations, it would be enough."[95] The statement is clearly hyperbolic. Yet my argument takes Masson seriously, tracing the various ways Mr. Dooley became representative of U.S. national culture at this time. These columns could be read as local color, ethnic realism, and dialect fiction. They could enact modernist wordplay, clever puns that originated in the space between what Mr. Dooley said and how that speech was written on the page. They could serve as a sharp critique of Anglo-American racial imperialism. And yet, for an audience who did not read closely, the pieces could engage fantasies of global Anglo-American domination. These conflicting interpretations were not only common but were the basis for Mr. Dooley's mass popularity. Dunne's writing thus walked the line between journalism and literature, between news and a response to the news. As syndicated columns, they would have been reprinted alongside sensational yellow journalism and alongside the leading authorial figures of the era. As books, they sold hundreds of thousands of copies.

As an author figure, Dunne's Irish American background allowed such a variety of interpretations to coexist. Whereas the revelation of Charles W. Chesnutt's African American identity had foreclosed certain possibilities of interpretation—so that Chesnutt went from passing as white to being viewed as the champion of the black race—the revelation of Dunne's identity as Irish American did not necessarily "out" his critique of U.S. imperialism. The belligerent nationalist attitudes expressed satirically by Mr. Dooley were taken at face value by many Americans, almost by default. The example of Dunne thus elucidates the role of authorial whiteness in producing objects of U.S. popular culture. It was through his Irish American identity—through both his whiteness and his ethnicity—that Mr. Dooley stood for such a broad cross-section of American culture. While Dunne might have tested his audience by speaking more explicitly about his own political views, he was instead willing to maintain an ambiguous satire of whiteness in order to reach as many readers as possible.

CHAPTER 4

AGAINST BENEVOLENT READERS

The Souls of Black Folk, Mrs. Spring Fragrance,
and A. C. McClurg

In his collection of autobiographical essays *Dusk of Dawn*, W. E. B. Du Bois reflects on the initial 1903 publication of *The Souls of Black Folk.* In a matter-of-fact description, Du Bois reveals a striking feature about the origins of his best-known work. Namely, it was not his idea to gather several popular essays as a book. Instead the collection had been imagined and solicited by his publisher. As Du Bois describes,

> I had been asked sometime before by A. C. McClurg and Company of Chicago if I did not have some material for a book; I planned a social study which should be perhaps a summing up of the work of the Atlanta Conferences, or at any rate, a scientific investigation. They asked, however, if I did not have some essays that they might put together and issue immediately, mentioning my articles in the *Atlantic Monthly* and other places. I demurred because books of essays almost always fall so flat. Nevertheless, I got together a number of my fugitive pieces. . . . The "Souls of Black Folk" was published in 1903 and is still selling today.[1]

Here, Du Bois understates the amount of work and revision that went into *Souls.* He did not simply gather "fugitive pieces" but carefully edited and revised the collection, adding five previously unpublished chapters.[2] At the same time, the description emphasizes that the book and its essayistic form were actively solicited by A. C. McClurg and

Company. It was a project at which Du Bois initially "demurred," hoping instead to publish scholarship or a summary of the Atlanta Conferences. Ultimately, however, Du Bois was willing to collaborate with the publisher to provide material better suited to the popular market. The passage also indicates McClurg's efforts to compete against well-known publishers such as Houghton Mifflin, asking Du Bois specifically about essays he had written for the *Atlantic Monthly.* The company hoped to collect and publish Du Bois's essays "immediately," capitalizing on his potential as an emergent black intellectual.

In 1912, McClurg would publish another landmark book in American literature, Sui Sin Far's *Mrs. Spring Fragrance.*[3] This short story collection is one of the first books of Chinese American fiction, and it has garnered increasing scholarly attention in recent decades. The book itself was produced in a highly orientalized decorative edition. Its red cover was stamped with gilt lettering and images of water lilies and dragonflies. Sui Sin Far, like Du Bois, would also try to publish a book in which McClurg showed less interest. She had written and submitted a novel to the company at this same time. In March 1912, just as *Mrs. Spring Fragrance* was being printed, Sui Sin Far references this novel in a letter to friend and editor of the *Land of Sunshine,* Charles Lummis, "The other book, which I submitted to McClurg's, was not rejected by them absolutely. They want it, I think; but they have asked me to cut it down."[4] While McClurg did publish Sui Sin Far's collection of stories, it would not in the end publish her novel. Sui Sin Far died just two years after *Mrs. Spring Fragrance* was produced, and the manuscript for the novel has never been found.

This chapter examines the history by which McClurg published these two landmark texts of American literature—*The Souls of Black Folk* (1903) and *Mrs. Spring Fragrance* (1912). Under what business conditions and through what editorial arbitrations could a literary critique of racist attitudes be published for a popular white audience in the early twentieth century? How might authors of color anticipate and challenge this audience's attitudes about race? The histories of these two books, as they survived and influenced readers, seem to have very little in common. *The Souls of Black Folk* is a canonical work of American literature, one of the most influential African American texts of all time. *Mrs. Spring Fragrance* was published in a single small edition that had relatively little impact until its scholarly recovery in the 1980s.

To my knowledge, the two books have not been considered in direct comparison. And yet, as I will show, their histories are closely related, parallel tracks in early twentieth-century U.S. ethnic literature. Both authors collected their work from periodical publications. Both books use similar tactics to anticipate and respond to a predominantly white audience. And both were accepted for publication by the same editor, Francis G. Browne.

Because of McClurg's unusual business model—the company earned the vast majority of its revenue not as a publisher but as a wholesale distributor of retail goods to the expanding market of the western United States—Francis G. Browne had significant editorial freedom when he selected books for publication. Browne exercised his editorial freedom in a style of cross-racial exoticism. He published a variety of books that convey a sense of white sympathy and sentiment yet nevertheless reinscribe racial hierarchies, a genre that Yu-Fang Cho has described as "benevolent ethnography."[5] *The Souls of Black Folk* and *Mrs. Spring Fragrance* thus came into being at the margins of a massive distribution company, and both books played a similar role in the McClurg catalog, attracting the ethnographic curiosities of a national audience. It is no coincidence that *The Souls of Black Folk* begins with a plea for the reader's patience and forgiveness, or that Sui Sin Far's books was manufactured as a delicate collection of orientalized stories. Both books were produced to target white readers.

Comparing the work of Du Bois and Sui Sin Far, I show how both authors, in different ways, respond to this context of racial benevolence. Du Bois directs readers deeper and deeper into *The Souls of Black Folk*. Sui Sin Far shifts rapidly between Chinese and American subjects, in an effort to reorient her white audience. Both authors, in other words, trade on their white reader's cross-racial fascinations. Yet despite these efforts, *The Souls of Black Folk* and *Mrs. Spring Fragrance* were subject to harsh criticism and neglect. Indeed, because Du Bois and Sui Sin Far sought to challenge even their *sympathetic* white readers, they encountered especially virulent forms of rejection.

PART ONE: THE EARLY CIRCULATION OF
THE SOULS OF BLACK FOLK

On April 7, 1903, just as *The Souls of Black Folk* went to press, W. E. B. Du Bois wrote to the publishing manager at A. C. McClurg and Company, Francis G. Browne, asking to review the book's "forethought," which he had not received in proof copies. Browne responded apologetically, saying that the first edition of *The Souls of Black Folk* had already been printed (figure 9). He sent Du Bois an advance copy of the first edition, asking the author to mark changes on it so that McClurg might "have it corrected on the second edition."[6] Reviewing this copy, Du Bois edited the opening sentence of the forethought so that the book would show "the strange meaning of being black here at the dawning of the Twentieth Century" rather than "in the dawning of the twentieth century." Likewise, Du Bois revised the fourth paragraph of the forethought. To the sentence "All this I have ended with a tale twice told but seldom written" he appended the phrase "and a chapter of song." Du Bois also adjusted the title of this final chapter, which had been a late addition to the book. While it was called "The Sorrow Songs" in the first edition, it became "Of the Sorrow Songs" in subsequent printings, to align with the book's other chapter titles.[7] After the initial printing of 1,214 copies,[8] these revisions persisted from May 1903 through the 1953 Blue Heron Press edition (alongside revisions made at that time), and through the 1973 Kraus-Thomson edition. And yet these changes are noticeably absent in the current W. W. Norton and Oxford University Press editions of *The Souls of Black Folk*, which use the first edition as copy-text.[9]

On the most basic level, these changes affect the meaning of the collection. The book's revised opening sentence positions Du Bois and his interpretation of blackness not *within* "the dawning of the twentieth century" but *at* a dawning that is only beginning. It resituates the meaning of blackness during the turn-of-the-century era. The revised title "Of the Sorrow Songs" shows that the final chapter was meant to stand not apart from but alongside the other chapters. By reprinting the first state without commenting on these changes, the current Norton and Oxford editions restore a version of the book that did not circulate widely and that Du Bois had quickly corrected.

Beyond its effect on linguistic meaning, however, the reprinting of the first edition also indicates the extent to which *The Souls of Black Folk*

PUBLISHING DEPARTMENT
A.C.M^cCLURG & CO.
215-221 WABASH AVENUE,
CHICAGO.

April 10, 1903

Prof. W.E.B. Du Bois,
        Atlanta University,
                Atlanta, Georgia.

My dear Prof. Du Bois:

                I have your letter of the 7th, and am
surprised to learn that you did not see the proof of the "Forethought." The printed sheets of the book were off the press on
the 1st, and the bound books will be in our hands early next week,
and I am sorry that, through some oversight, the book went to press
without your seeing this matter. I am sending you a set of advance
sheets under separate cover, and I hope you will find the Preface
all right, but if there is anything wrong, please mark it, so that
we may have it corrected on the second edition. Through a mis-
calculation the first edition of the book was not as large as I had
planned, and I think we shall have to put a second edition to press
very shortly, and with that in view, I would like to have you go
through the sheets and mark anything that may have passed us in the
proofs. Please use the set I have sent you, as it has some marks
of my own. We have sent out a number of copies of the book in sheets
to editors, and I hope in a few days to begin to see notices in the
press. I am sure the book is one that will arouse a good deal of
interest.

        With my best regards, I am,

Dict. F.G.B.   Yours very truly,

FIGURE 9. Letter from A. C. McClurg and Company to W. E. B. Du Bois, April 10, 1903. Series 1A, W. E. B. Du Bois Papers, MS 312, Department of Special Collections and University Archives, University of Massachusetts Amherst.

is often viewed, retroactively, as an instant literary classic. Indeed, in his introduction to the Oxford University Press W. E. B. Du Bois series, Henry Louis Gates, Jr., describes how *The Souls of Black Folk* was "hailed as a classic even by his contemporaries."[10] David Levering Lewis offers a similar appraisal in his biography of Du Bois, claiming that, "for a controversial work," *The Souls of Black Folk* "enjoyed an impressive run" with exceptional sales.[11] To a certain extent, such an argument holds true. Among African American readers and in the longer history of the twentieth century, the book's importance can hardly be overstated, and Lewis emphasizes this reception. However, critical scholarship on the book's initial publication and circulation has been limited, and such a positive reception cannot be ascribed to the book's audience at the turn of the century. Indeed, claims regarding the book's favorable reception have a tendency to undercut both Du Bois's complex rhetorical strategies as an author and the hostile reviews and responses that the book withstood.

This is not to say that the book's publication history has gone unremarked. The initial publication of the book has been discussed in biographies written by Manning Marable and David Levering Lewis.[12] Changes to the 1953 jubilee edition of *Souls*—in which Du Bois revised several potentially antisemitic portions of the text—have been examined in detail. George Bornstein focused his attention on these 1953 revisions in a 2006 article for *Textual Cultures*,[13] and Henry Louis Gates, Jr., revisits them in the Norton Critical Edition.[14] In terms of the book's early circulation, the most significant work of scholarship was performed by Du Bois's literary executor, Herbert Aptheker, in his introduction to the 1973 Kraus-Thomson edition.[15] Aptheker's introduction closely examines the publication and reception of *Souls*. Yet despite this attention, Du Bois's revisions to the second printing have gone unmentioned. As such examples indicate, there is much more to be said about the publication of this foundational work of African American literature.

In this part of the chapter, I consider *The Souls of Black Folk* in its first year of publication: the history by which McClurg developed an interest in Du Bois, the solicitation of *The Souls of Black Folk* by Francis G. Browne and McClurg, the production of the text as it was collected and revised from previously published essays, the marketing and promotion of the book, and the reception of *Souls* among a contemporary audience. I look closely at the initial circulation of the text, historicizing the book's significance within the turn-of-the-century literary marketplace. In particular, I consider the fraught relationship between Du Bois, his Chicago publisher, and his predominantly white audience. Here, I am exploring the book's "early" circulation, both in terms of its initial publication at the dawning of the twentieth century and in terms of its prophetic vision, untimely for so many readers.

Such a dynamic, between African American authors and commercial literary publishers, has been explored most notably in John K. Young's *Black Writers, White Publishers.* As Young describes it, the relationship between black author and white publisher is distinctive because "the underlying social structure . . . transforms the usual unequal relationship [between author and publisher] into an extension of a much deeper cultural dynamic."[16] Young goes on to explore how white publishers in the United States are influenced by cultural forces to produce a one-dimensional and mythologized version of black experience. In a 2010 essay for *Book History,* Leon Jackson elaborates on this relationship. He argues that much of the scholarship on African American authors and white publishers falls into three categories: "publication-as-empowerment, publication-as-disempowerment, [and] publication-as-mediated-and-mediating process."[17] In the first two instances, scholars debate the extent of authorial empowerment and exploitation when black writers interact with predominantly white publishers. In the third instance, scholars take a factual approach that replaces intentionality with mediation. Even more recently, in her introduction to *Race, Ethnicity, and Publishing in America,* Cécile Cottenet has offered another possibility for exploring relationships between ethnic authors and mainstream publishers. Referring to both Young and Jackson, Cottenet argues that the goal of examining author-publisher relationships is not simply to disclose empowerment or disempowerment but to consider how authors "understood or did not understand" the book market, and how ethnic authors "work from *within,* although they continue to embody 'otherness.' "[18] This possibility, from Cottenet by way of Jackson and Young, strikes me as especially productive because it attends to authorial development *through* publication. As authors move through the communications circuit, from one project to the next, they develop new skills and strategies to understand the literary marketplace.

The publication of *The Souls of Black Folk* was an experiment in popular writing, as opposed to scholarly writing, which allowed Du Bois's authorial strategies to evolve in response to the commercial literary marketplace. Indeed, the book itself was imagined as a collection of popular essays, many of which had been previously published in magazines. In collecting and revising these essays in book form, Du Bois focused on the book's paratexts, especially its titles and epigraphs.[19] These materials, I argue, reappropriated benevolent fascinations with the racial other in an effort to lure the reader deeper within the veil of black experience. Put differently, Du Bois drew on his white reader's racist assumptions in an effort to share the history, literature, music, and spirituality of black culture. Du Bois and McClurg sought to target a national audience by simultaneously appealing to *and* subverting that audience's racial benevolence. Yet these efforts encountered dual forms of resistance among the vast majority of readers. On the one hand, Du Bois's argument for racial equality and social justice was explicitly rejected by white readers. On the other, the book was interpreted as confirming racial stereotypes and essential characteristics of the negro, and was even recommended for this feature. In his attempt to address a national, predominantly white audience, Du Bois came to better understand the extent of this audience's racist assumptions.

A. C. McClurg's Literary Interests

The history of A. C. McClurg and Company has rarely been discussed in critical scholarship yet provides important context for understanding *The Souls of Black Folk* and *Mrs. Spring Fragrance*.[20] McClurg had its origins in Chicago's oldest book and stationery store, W. W. Barlow and Company, which had been founded in 1844. In its early phases, the company changed hands several times: from W. W. Barlow to Samuel Chapman Griggs to Egbert L. Jansen and then Alexander Caldwell McClurg.[21] These changes in ownership frequently hinged on business losses, especially due to fire. Following the Chicago Fire of 1871, for example, S. C. Griggs sold his shares of the company to Egbert Jansen, Frederick B. Smith, and Alexander McClurg, so that the company became known as Jansen, McClurg, and Company. (It was not until 1886 that the firm would assume the name A. C. McClurg and Company.) Following another fire in 1899, McClurg considered dissolving the company but instead decided to maintain the business by incorporation and the sale of stock.[22] The company would survive as A. C.

McClurg and Company until 1962, so that its activities span nearly 120 years.

Alexander Caldwell McClurg himself was born in 1832 and grew up in Pittsburgh, Pennsylvania, before attending Miami University in Ohio. After graduating from Miami, McClurg returned to Pittsburgh to study law but soon decided his interests were better suited for publishing.[23] On March 4, 1859, McClurg wrote to S. C. Griggs's book business in Chicago, seeking employment as a family friend, and he joined the company soon afterward.[24] With the outbreak of the Civil War, however, McClurg left the business to enlist with the 88th Volunteer Illinois Infantry of the Union Army. During the war, McClurg fought in more than twenty-five battles and campaigns, including the Battle of Atlanta and Sherman's March to the Sea.[25] He was promoted to the brevet rank of colonel and then of brigadier general.[26] As the war concluded, McClurg was encouraged to remain in the service but chose to return to his business as a publisher. He was thus known to employees as "General McClurg," a title not only earned through military service but also indicative of the company's national ambitions. Working for McClurg was often imagined as a form of service to the nation. By 1893, General McClurg was president of Chicago's Commercial Club, vice president of the University Club and the Chicago Historical Society, trustee of the Newberry Library, and a former president of the Chicago Library Club.[27]

In his time as president of the company, until his death in 1901, General McClurg took special interest in the literary side of the business, rather than its work in wholesale distribution. In the mid-1870s, for example, working with George Millard, General McClurg organized the "English Book Department."[28] He and Millard made frequent trips to England and Europe to secure rare and fine books for the company and bookstore. This rare books section attracted a small group of writers and bibliophiles during the last decades of the nineteenth century. Indeed, throughout the 1890s, the A. C. McClurg and Company bookstore was a sort of literary landmark in Chicago, and George Millard's rare book section became known as the "Saints and Sinners Corner." It is described in a *New York Times* article, written shortly after the 1899 fire that destroyed the bookstore: "Clergymen, physicians, actors, newspapermen—men of all professions who loved books and the company of book lovers made that particular corner a kind of club for their leisure hours, and [Eugene] Field with characteristic wit, in a happy moment dubbed the coterie 'The Saints and Sinners.' "[29]

McClurg also established a house magazine, as a way to compete with the so-called quality publishers of New York and Boston. From 1880 to 1892, the company published the literary magazine the *Dial,* edited by Francis F. Browne. In its first issue, the magazine defined its own mission to serve as "an intelligent guide and agreeable companion to the book-lover and book-buyer."[30] Browne worked closely with General McClurg throughout the 1880s, serving not only as editor of the *Dial* but also as literary adviser for the company's publishing department.[31] In 1892, however, Browne purchased the *Dial* outright in order to manage it independently. The magazine would continue under Browne's guidance until 1913. As Frank Luther Mott describes, it would later become an important "literary, artistic, and critical organ of modernism," publishing work by T. S. Eliot, Ezra Pound, Gertrude Stein, and others.[32]

In his role as publisher, General McClurg expressed strong opinions about book publication. Although McClurg was not a prolific writer, he did publish a number of essays. He wrote more than ten articles for the *Dial* from 1880 to 1896, and published three essays with *Publishers Weekly.*[33] In May 1886, for instance, McClurg published an article with the *Dial* titled "Justice to Authors," advocating for international copyright law as it would be legislated in the Chace Act of 1891. In another article, "Of Making Many Books," McClurg criticized cheap bookmaking for its "stiff and common paper" as well as its "old and worn type."[34] He called, instead, for publishers "willing to pay for good, intelligent and workmanlike type-setting, and careful press-work." The article sets down standards for McClurg as quality bookmakers who pay careful attention to design and production.

General McClurg's essays with the *Dial* also include book reviews, which convey his values as a literary critic. In one, McClurg offers a strong recommendation for Joel Chandler Harris's *On the Plantation: A Story of a Georgia Boy's Adventures during the War.* McClurg says that it is "full of kindly and picturesque sketches . . . full of truth and nature but with no overstrained and degrading realism."[35] In another review, McClurg scathingly criticizes *The Red Badge of Courage* for its unbelievable depictions of Civil War battle scenes.[36] Between these two articles, it seems that General McClurg followed a common pattern of sectional reconciliation in the post-Reconstruction era, reimagining the war as a noble battle between white soldiers. As Jackson Lears describes this outlook, "Rather than a struggle to end slavery, the war became a testing ground for personal heroism . . . where white men, North and South, had repeatedly demonstrated their valor."[37] General McClurg's book reviews show that he is happy to reminisce about the "old time plantation" but is harshly critical of Crane's antiheroic war story.

Yet even as General McClurg himself was devoted to literary pursuits, his publishing company made the bulk of its money through the distribution and wholesale of books and other retail goods. Literary publication, in other words, functioned as just one aspect of a larger wholesale business, and was largely dependent on that business. According to one article in *Publishers Weekly*, for example, by 1899 the company "reached a total gross of $2,500,000 of which the publishing department accounted for $100,000."[38] Here, just four years prior to *The Souls of Black Folk*, at a time when the company was being incorporated, publishing represented only 4 percent of overall revenue. The larger side of the business, the retail department, had been managed by Frederick B. Smith since 1862.[39] Smith thus played a major role in the company. Just as McClurg had worked with George Millard to acquire rare and fine books internationally, Smith would travel to Europe looking for new retail goods to market in the western United States.[40] In fact, McClurg sold a wide variety of nonpaper retail goods, including pipes, glassware, pocket knives, prams, and lanterns.

In comparison to the bookstore's Saints and Sinners Corner, these retail and wholesale activities are less well known. As the head of the retail department, however, Smith did compile his own history of the company, *A Sketch of the Origin and History of the House of A. C. McClurg & Co.* The booklet details changes in company ownership and management from the mid-nineteenth century through the first years of the twentieth century, and is remarkable for its concise attention to place names, employee names, figures, and dates. For example, Smith describes how S. C. Griggs and Company ordered massive quantities of textbooks to be shipped westward prior to the Civil War: "Sanders's Spellers, 50,000; Sanders's Green Primer, 108,000; Sanders's Readers, 30,000 to 50,000."[41] By the time of the Civil War, the company became "easily the most important book concern west of New York." Whenever possible, Smith also provides the dimensions of the buildings occupied by the company. He describes the business as it moved to Booksellers Row in February 1869, where it occupied a 50-by-150-foot store at 117–119 State Street. In 1891, the company "purchased the entire stock of S. A. Maxwell & Co., their main Chicago Competitors."[42] In 1899, as the company was incorporated, it moved to 215–221 Wabash Avenue, occupying more than seven floors of an 80-by-160-foot building.

In the early twentieth century, the company continued to grow. As one report notes, "In 1907 the business had grown to such an extent that it was deemed best to conduct the retail and wholesale operations in separate buildings."[43] The company then moved to East Ohio Street, occupying buildings with 342,000 square feet of space and employing approximately seven hundred people. In place of McClurg's literary interests, Smith's history shows the progress of an industrial business, rapidly expanding through acquisitions, incorporation, and strategic use of its geographic location and infrastructure.

When it considers General McClurg's work for the publishing department, Smith's history describes the literary side of the business as a form of marketing. He points out, for instance, that General McClurg gave "special attention" to the publishing department, so that the *Dial* and the rare books section "attained during these years much importance."[44] Describing the Saints and Sinners Corner, Smith notes, "It became extensively known throughout the country through the prominence given by Eugene Field in a column of the Chicago 'Morning News.'"[45] Here, Smith recognizes the significance of the company's literary outlets for marketing purposes. The rare books section is not only a pet project subsidized by mass distribution, it is an "extensively known" representative of the company as a whole. The Saints and Sinners Corner thus functioned alongside the company's mass distribution to bolster McClurg's reputation. Overall, the company was set up—both physically, in its storefront location, and as a business—to promote the literary status of Chicago while earning revenue as a wholesale distributor.

From the early to mid-twentieth century, following the death of General McClurg in 1901, the company deemphasized its interest in fine books. In one meeting on January 11, 1910, the board of directors authorized a significant reduction in pay for George Millard and the rare books department, even as it increased the pay of numerous salesmen.[46] In early 1912, at the same time that *Mrs. Spring Fragrance* was being published, the company would form a committee to examine Millard's productivity, and would ultimately force his resignation.[47] In the second decade of the twentieth century, McClurg moved still further away from any interest in "high" literature, publishing popular genre fiction from authors such as Zane Grey, Clarence Mulford, and Edgar Rice Burroughs. From 1909 to 1922, the company published eleven books in Mulford's Hopalong Cassidy series, popular cowboy stories that sold more than 800,000 copies total and inspired numerous film adaptations.[48] Soon, Edgar Rice Burroughs became the company's touchstone author. From 1914 to 1929, Burroughs published twenty-nine books with McClurg, eleven in the Tarzan series. His 1914 *Tarzan of the Apes* was the company's most popular book of all time, selling 641,000 copies. Several of the Tarzan sequels sold nearly as well, and Burroughs's overall book sales for McClurg total more than 5,600,000 copies.[49]

Thus while McClurg had a modest history of publishing and promoting writers such as Du Bois and Sui Sin Far, this was only a small part of the business during a specific era. By the mid-1940s, McClurg would cease publishing books altogether, but would remain in business as a retail distributor. In this way, the company's revenue was always driven by its mass distribution of books and retail goods, capitalizing on Chicago's strategic location for the expanding United States. It was primarily from the late 1880s through the early 1900s, under the leadership of General McClurg himself, that the company expanded its role as a literary publisher. This involved the creation of a rare books section under George Millard, the publication of the *Dial* under Francis F. Browne, and (later on) the management of the publication department by Browne's son, Francis G. Browne. It was within this business structure, toward the Saints and Sinners Corner, that Du Bois and Sui Sin Far were published.

Solicitation of *The Souls of Black Folk*

It is not surprising that McClurg solicited *The Souls of Black Folk*. By the turn of the century, as Herbert Aptheker describes, Du Bois had already attracted national attention.[50] He had spoken at the Harvard graduation ceremonies in 1890, earned his doctorate at the university five years later, published his dissertation as a book, and conducted the first of the Atlanta Conferences. Indeed, Du Bois had already published essays with the *Atlantic Monthly,* the *Southern Workman,* the *Independent,* the *Nation, Harper's Weekly, World's Work,* and with Browne's the *Dial.* It seems natural, then, that Du Bois would transition from the *Dial* to publish with its parent company, A. C. McClurg and Company.

Yet the company's history, as outlined above, shows that the *Dial* was no longer directly affiliated with McClurg when *The Souls of Black Folk* was published. Rather, Browne had bought out stock for the magazine in 1892, separating himself from McClurg to publish the *Dial* independently. Indeed, McClurg took up a column in the July 1892 issue of the *Dial* to announce the magazine's independence.[51] By the time Du Bois published his book with McClurg, it had been dissociated from the magazine for nearly a decade.

This separation of the *Dial* from McClurg has alerted me to an error in scholarship regarding the publication of *The Souls of Black Folk.* Namely, the editor of *Souls* has been misidentified as Francis Fisher Browne, in place of Browne's son, Francis Granger Browne. Aptheker's introduction to the book makes this mistake in 1973, saying, "*The Dial* was owned by A. C. McClurg & Co. and its editors, the Brownes—W. R. and, especially important, Francis Fisher—were also the editors of the McClurg books, with the last named the editor of *Souls.*"[52] By the time *The Souls of Black Folk* was published in 1903, however, Francis F. Browne had moved on from his official affiliation with McClurg. Rather, Browne's son, Francis G. Browne, became manager of the company's publishing department from 1901 to 1912. Thus while the names, and even signatures, of father and son can be difficult to distinguish, it was the *younger* Francis Browne who served as editor for *Souls* and managed correspondence with Du Bois. Although archivists have been attuned to this distinction—special collections at the University of Massachusetts Amherst correctly attributes figure 9 to Francis G. Browne—a number of scholars working on the publication history of *Souls* have repeated Aptheker's error.[53] When Du Bois describes McClurg's solicitation of *The Souls of Black Folk,* he was therefore referring to Francis Granger Browne.

Biographical information on Francis G. Browne is scarce, especially in comparison to his father. But he was clearly invested in publishing multiethnic literature. Indeed, McClurg, as a publisher, is notable in this regard. In 1892, the company published Emma Wolf's *Other Things Being Equal,* arguably the first Jewish American novel from a mainstream press.[54] The company would publish two additional novels by Wolf within a decade, and Emma Wolf's novels are now being reprinted with extensive scholarly introductions by Barbara Cantalupo and Lori Harrison-Kahan.[55] As I will show, Browne was also responsible for publishing one of the earliest books of fiction by a Chinese North American author, *Mrs. Spring Fragrance.* These texts, much like *The Souls of Black Folk,* mediate between an ethnic author and a mainstream, predominantly white audience. Based on the titles published by McClurg under his leadership, Francis G. Browne had a serious interest in publishing the work of ethnic authors. At the same time, however, Browne's interests in ethnic literature were limited and often a product of racial exoticism. He published novels by Robert Ames Bennet, such as *For the White Christ* (1905) and *Into the Primitive* (1908). The first book is a historical romance set in the days of Charlemagne and Anglo-Saxon kings, when "the name of Muhammad [was] but little known."[56] The second is a modern adventure story set in Africa, taking its title from the first chapter of Jack London's *The Call of the Wild.* Both novels offered stereotyped depictions of nonwhite characters, and they prefigure McClurg's publication of the Tarzan series, romances that played on a white audience's fascinations with a heathen other.

As odd as it may seem to the twenty-first-century reader, *The Souls of Black Folk* should be read within this broader history whereby Francis G. Browne and McClurg directed ethnic literature toward a national, predominantly white audience. As Du Bois recognized when he initially demurred from writing a book for a popular audience, this cross-racial mediation was beset with potential and peril. Du Bois had planned to continue his scholarly work, yet agreed to collect his shorter essays in book form, for a more general audience. How could Du Bois adapt his writing for the commercial literary marketplace? What would white readers take from his ethnography of blackness?

Revisions and Additions

Assembling *The Souls of Black Folk,* Du Bois conducted varying levels of revision. Whereas some of the chapters were written exclusively for the book, several were republished almost directly from magazine essays. The first chapter, for example, had been originally published in the August 1897 *Atlantic Monthly* and is virtually unchanged. The opening paragraph, asking, "How does it feel to be a problem?," had been included in full in the *Atlantic* several years prior to the book's publication.[57] The second chapter on Reconstruction and the Freedman's Bureau, which had been published in the March 1901 *Atlantic,* underwent very slight revisions, most commonly adjusting the breaks between paragraphs.[58] As in *The Souls of Black Folk,* the original magazine article concluded with its central argument: "The problem of the Twentieth Century is the problem of the color line." Chapters 4 and 6 were also republished from the *Atlantic* with almost no revision.[59] In these instances, Du Bois was satisfied with his writing, and McClurg was happy to position itself alongside the *Atlantic* through republication.

The most significant, and uniform, revision to these chapters would be the framing materials that surrounded the text itself: the new titles, epigraphs, and musical notation given to each.[60] The opening chapter, for example, had been titled "Strivings of the Negro People" in its initial version, but was retitled "Of Our Spiritual Strivings" for the book. The chapter was thus given a "spiritual" emphasis that had not been included in the initial magazine essay title, reiterated by its musical notation. The revised title also identifies Du Bois as African American ("*Our* Spiritual Strivings"), speaking for collective action. It positions Du Bois himself as a spokesperson for African Americans, offering a spiritual perspective in contrast to Booker T. Washington's industrial education. Similarly, the title for the second chapter was changed from "The Freedman's Bureau" to "Of the Dawn of Freedom." As with many of the titles, the revision adds a mythic element to the essay's more descriptive title in the *Atlantic*; it uses the history of the Freedman's Bureau to address the emergence of African American freedom itself. This "Dawn of Freedom" is then reiterated in the forethought, where the book imagines itself "at the dawning" of the twentieth century.

Chapters taken from sources other than the *Atlantic Monthly* underwent more significant revision. While Du Bois had previously responded to Booker T. Washington in an article for the *Dial,* his chapter in *Souls* is significantly reorganized and expanded.[61] The chapter's sharper criticism of Washington foreclosed any possibility that Du Bois might work at the Tuskegee Institute. Chapters 7 and 8 were drawn from one essay in *World's Work,* and the shift in tone from essay to book publication is particularly evident in these examples. The initial piece had been titled "The Negro As He Really Is" with the subtitle "A Definite Study of One Locality in Georgia Showing the Exact Conditions of Every Negro Family—Their Economic Status—Their Ownership of Land—Their Morals—Their Family Life—The Houses They Live in and The Results of the Mortgage System."[62] The essay itself was published with numerous photographs of dwelling places, stores, women at work, and children in schools. Adapted for book publication, the content itself is similar. However, the chapter titles—"Of the Black Belt" and "Of the Quest for the Golden Fleece"—are repackaged in terms of color, metaphor, and myth. In such instances, Du Bois takes a more poetic approach, softening his academic terminology for a general audience. Repeated references to black and gold lend the book a sense of coherence and would be reinforced in the design of the book itself.

Composing new material for the book, Du Bois added chapter 5 ("Of the Wings of Atalanta") as well as chapters 11 through 14, the last four chapters of the book. These concluding chapters are especially important because they progress deeper into black experience. Indeed, Du Bois describes chapters 10 through 14 as follows: "Leaving, then, the white world, I have stepped within the Veil, raising it that you may view faintly its deeper recesses—the meaning of its religion, the passion of its human sorrow, and the struggle of its greater souls."[63] Du Bois thus structured *The Souls of Black Folk* so that it would move its readers from issues of history and education toward African American religion, family life, political activism, tragedy, and music. As these chapters move "within the veil," Du Bois again describes them in terms of "religion," "passion," and the "soul," drawing together the spiritual theme of the collection.

Of course, many critics have examined Du Bois's use of religious language and his personal religious beliefs.[64] My own point is that, by looking at the publication history of *Souls*, one can trace how Du Bois produced many of the text's religious elements *for* publication, as a way to unify the book and appeal to a national, predominantly white audience. He chose to privilege the idea of the "veil" in his opening chapter (a reference to the tabernacle's Holy of Holies),[65] to reframe black striving as "spiritual striving," to title his book itself *The Souls of Black Folk*. He chose to progress structurally toward "The Faith of the Fathers," and composed additional chapters titled "The Passing of the First Born," "The Coming of John," and "The Sorrow Songs." The process by which he collected, edited, and composed *The Souls of Black Folk* shows that, as it was being prepared for a general audience, Du Bois increasingly called on Christian sympathy.

This approach is especially evident in the parallelism of the forethought and the afterthought. In the opening, Du Bois uses direct address to target his predominantly white audience, offering the book respectfully to this "Gentle Reader," and explaining why it is "of interest" to them. Du Bois asks his white audience to "read with patience" and to forgive "mistake and foible for sake of the faith and passion that is in me."[66] Du Bois thus appeals to the reader in terms of his religious "faith and passion." He approaches his reader almost apologetically, asking forgiveness. By the book's conclusion, however, Du Bois shifts his attention from this "Gentle Reader" to the audience of "God the Reader." In doing so, Du Bois asserts his own sense of righteousness and providential justice. He replaces the judgment of a popular audience with a higher judgment, asking not for forgiveness but that "the ears of a guilty people tingle with truth."[67] Du Bois thus plays to his audience's benevolent sympathies in order to offer a critique of Jim Crow violence in the United States. In the afterthought, Du Bois boldly challenges this reader, praying that the long-term survival of his book foster social justice. Moreover, the strong parallelism between the forethought and afterthought shows how deliberately Du Bois had edited and revised the book so that it would call on its "Gentle Reader" in this way.

Editorial Correspondence, Publication, and Marketing

Publication with McClurg thus influenced Du Bois's writing style, as he sought to target a general audience. Yet at the same time, the company allowed Du Bois a great deal of authorial control. From the time the book entered production in January 1903 through the end of the year, Francis G. Browne wrote more than thirty letters to Du Bois, discussing contracts, revisions, book design, and advertisements. On January 21, for example, Browne wrote to Du Bois saying that he had read a revised manuscript of *Souls*, which they expected to publish in April.[68] The next week, Browne updated Du Bois on the printing and asked for approval of advertising material: "I enclose herein the first announcement we have made of the book. Please tell me frankly if these notes please you. I want the announcements to be satisfactory to you in every respect, but of course the work will require rather different handling from the ordinary book."[69] Here, Browne caters to Du Bois's preferences, asking for the author's honest opinion regarding marketing materials. Browne also recognizes the complex racial dynamics of the book's publication, which will require "rather different handling from the ordinary book." The tone of the passage assumes a shared understanding of this dynamic with Du Bois, as the publisher and author bring the book to a predominantly white audience. Indeed, this was an experimental project for both the author *and* publisher as they sought strategies to popularize Du Bois's sociological essays.

The advertisements approved in this correspondence emphasize both the book's push for equal rights and its passionate, poetic approach. One such ad, placed in the *New York Times,* promoted the book before its release, noting that it would be "Ready in April."[70] It describes *The Souls of Black Folk* in a short paragraph: "The new champion of the rights of the colored race is without doubt the most eloquent advocate that has yet come forward. It is expected that this remarkable collection of essays, which are quite unlike anything that has appeared for years, will have a perceptible effect on public opinion regarding the Negro question. Certainly it will be difficult for prejudice to contend against the impassioned plea that Professor Du Bois offers for the spiritual rights of his people." Like the book, the advertisement draws on religious language, describing Du Bois's "impassioned plea" and his advocacy "for the spiritual rights of his people." This last term, "spiritual rights," serves a variety of purposes in its imprecision. On the one hand, the phrase sets *The Souls of Black Folk* apart from the industrial education of Booker T. Washington. It positions Du Bois opposite Washington as a "new champion" for African Americans, more eloquent and poetic in his writing. On the other hand, "spiritual rights" also repeats the book's religious appeals without explicitly calling for social justice or legal rights. The book is original and provocative, but the exact effect it would have on public opinion was yet to be decided.

Subsequent advertisements would increasingly emphasize the book's call to social justice. A July announcement placed in the *Literary Digest* is more direct than the *New York Times'* advertisement for "spiritual rights," saying that the "author pleads for right and justice to his people."[71] The advertisement goes on to say, "Aside from its remarkable presentation of facts [*The Souls of Black Folk*] holds the reader—prejudiced or not—by its fascination of style and overpowering pathos." As in the previous advertisement, Du Bois's poetic style and "pathos" are emphasized. Readers will be drawn to the book and fascinated by Du Bois's expression of black feeling. At the same time, the book is described as true to "facts." It is not only original and provocative but true.

Correspondence with Francis G. Browne also indicates the timeline by which the book went to press. In a letter from March 5, 1903, Browne acknowledged Du Bois's preferences regarding the book's design.[72] It would be manufactured in a black cover, embossed with a rectangular pattern, with top edge gilt and gilt lettering on the cover and spine (figure 10). The book's golden soul would shimmer from inside its black cover. Du Bois approved this design. Similarly, correspondence with Browne reveals that the final chapter, "Of the Sorrow Songs," was a late addition to the book. Du Bois had wanted to conclude with the sorrow songs and was in the process of composing the chapter until just before the book was printed. In their letters, Browne and Du Bois discussed the timetable for submitting this piece, as well as its estimated page count. When Browne received "The Sorrow Songs," he wrote, "I have read the chapter through and like it very much, and it is now in the printer's hands. It seems to me it closes the book most appropriately, and I am very glad we carried out your original idea to have it in the volume."[73]

In general, Du Bois was given nearly full authority over the text itself. In one letter, Browne tells Du Bois he is "toning down a too strong word or phrase which . . . might unduly prejudice those we want to read, and learn from, your book."[74] He continues, "For instance, I took out your reference to Hawaii, Cuba, and the Philippines, with which I personally thoroughly agree, but which I know would arouse needless antagonism." Here, in an effort to appeal to a mainstream audience, Browne attempted to excise a discussion of U.S. imperialism. Yet it seems Du Bois contested the change, and won the argument. The line itself remains in chapter 3, criticizing the United States for its actions toward "the darker peoples in the West Indies, Hawaii, and the Philippines."[75] Given that many of the book's chapters were reprinted from previous publications without revision, and that Browne accepted "The Sorrow Songs" without criticism, it seems that Du Bois was allowed to compose and edit the book as he saw fit.

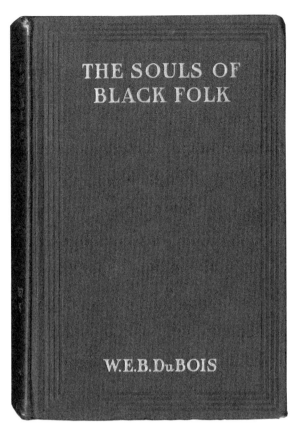

FIGURE 10. Cover of *The Souls of Black Folk,* 2nd ed. (Chicago: A. C. McClurg & Co., 1903). Image courtesy of the Newberry Library, Chicago.

Reception

On publication, *The Souls of Black Folk* garnered widespread review and discussion. Herbert Aptheker's introduction to the 1973 edition of the book discusses this reception extensively.[76] He categorizes the reviews according to various groups, and moves through these categories in order. According to Aptheker, publishers within the Tuskegee machine generally ignored the book, while other organs of the black press—especially Wendell Phillips Dabney in the *Ohio Enterprise* and William Monroe Trotter in the *Boston Guardian*—reviewed it enthusiastically. The Southern white press either ignored the book or reacted to it with hostile and explicit racism. Aptheker also describes the book's favorable reception among other writers such as Charles W. Chesnutt, Jessie Fauset, James Weldon Johnson, William James, and Langston Hughes.

Mainstream reviews from Northern publications are more complex, however. As Aptheker describes it, the *New York Times,* the *Chicago Tribune* and the *New York World* were all very harsh on Du Bois. The *Outlook* took sides with Booker T. Washington, whose work it frequently published. In contrast, the *Independent* and the *Nation* were sympathetic to Du Bois. Not surprisingly, the *Dial* reviewed *Souls* favorably, offering mild criticism of Booker T. Washington (and sharp disapproval of Thomas Dixon, who had begun his Ku Klux Klan trilogy in 1902). Indeed, Francis F. Browne's magazine gave one of the most enthusiastic reviews from the mainstream press.

While Aptheker describes this reception in detail, his summary often functions on a binary axis of positive and negative reception, considering how a review either favors or criticizes the book. Examining the reviews more closely, however, it becomes clear that Du Bois's revisions—toward mythic elements and religious passion—were influential for the reviews of Northern readers, which I would more often describe as mixed in their assessments. These tactics did not protect Du Bois from harsh criticism, but they allowed the book to be read in ways that would spark debate and promote sales.

Among the more positive reviews, Du Bois's emotional appeal was often seen as a central feature of the text. The *Nation,* for instance, describes how the book might surprise readers familiar with Du Bois's "coldly intellectual" style.[77] Such readers will not be prepared "for the emotion and the passion throbbing here in every chapter, almost every page." The review thus marks Du Bois's emotional appeal as a striking feature of the text, and an improvement on his scholarly work. Similarly, the *Los Angeles Times* declared *Souls* one of the best books of the year, calling it "the cry of a race struggling against fearful odds."[78] Beyond its positive evaluation, it is Du Bois's "cry" that registers with the reader, as an outburst of passion.

It is thus important to consider the type of reading that allowed Northern reviewers to praise the book. The review in the *Nation* that commends Du Bois's "passion," for instance, goes on to argue, "The features of Mr. Du Bois's mind are negro features." In other words, despite its generally positive assessment of the book, the review turns to scientific racism when describing Du Bois's ideas and perspective. It considers the book as a sort of curious expression of the negro mind.

(The review also forgets that Mr. Du Bois is a doctor and a professor.) Likewise, the review in the *Los Angeles Times*—which had called *Souls* one of the best books of the year—offers a peculiar comparison of Du Bois and Booker T. Washington, claiming that the negro race "need not fear for itself" under such leadership. Here, the review not only fails to recognize differences between Du Bois and Washington but relies on the mere existence of these leaders to assuage anxieties over racial inequality. In an era of legalized segregation and widespread lynching, the review argues that African Americans have nothing to fear. In this way, many of the seemingly positive reviews both criticize and misunderstand Du Bois's politics.

The more negative responses to Du Bois function almost in reverse. They criticize Du Bois's politics while admiring his passion and spirit. A review from Elia W. Peattie in the *Chicago Tribune,* for example, shifts between extreme bias and a recommendation of the book. At one point, Peattie argues that it is "the white man" in Du Bois that produces such writing; "the white man" has transcribed the unwritten sorrow songs and "caught their minor and melancholy cadences in the written note."[79] In this review, credit for Du Bois's literary achievement is transferred from the black folk to the white man; it is only "the white man" within Du Bois who can transcribe the notes of the sorrow songs. The review thus aligns whiteness with the written word and blackness with musicality, refusing to acknowledge African American literary success. Yet the review continues, "This passionate book, incomplete and sometimes self-conscious though it is, cannot but compel profound respect." In other words, despite her criticisms, Peattie recommends *The Souls of Black Folk* as passionate and compelling. Much as the forethought had asked, Peattie forgives "mistake and foible for sake of the faith and passion" in Du Bois.[80] The review shifts rapidly between unfair racist criticism and white benevolence and sympathy.

One more example, from the *New York Times,*[81] will exemplify my argument regarding the book's reception. The review is deeply prejudiced against Du Bois, emphasizing that he cannot understand the attitudes and customs of the South and is not qualified to criticize Booker T. Washington's policies. The article mocks Du Bois's advocacy for the "abolition of the social color-line." Nor is the reviewer impressed with Du Bois's writing style, claiming that his "attempt to be critically fair-minded is strangely tangled" with the "sentimental, poetical, picturesque" characteristics of the negro. Here, the writing is interpreted according to racial stereotype, as both picturesque and imitative of whiteness, or "fair-minded" thinking. Du Bois's hybrid voice does not produce anything of value but is "strangely tangled" between reason and poetry. Yet after all of these criticisms (and others), the *New York Times* goes on to recommend the book, calling it "interesting to the student of the negro character who regards the race ethnologically and not politically." Despite disagreeing with the book's argument and criticizing its poetic style, the reviewer nevertheless recommends *The Souls of Black Folk* for its insight on "negro character." According to this reviewer, Du Bois's politics can be disregarded and the book remains interesting as a study of the essential characteristics of the negro race.

Pointing to such a reading of *Souls*, I do not mean that the text itself presents black experience in terms of scientific racism. Rather, I am arguing that Du Bois's efforts to appeal to a benevolent audience *through* ethnographic writing and religious sympathy were interpreted according to racist assumptions and stereotypes. Assembling the book and composing new material for it, Du Bois constructed the text as a journey into the black soul. He appealed to his audience's curiosities regarding the "strange meaning of being black," and asked them to read with patience and charity. In doing so, Du Bois attempted to subvert his audience's racist assumptions in favor of a more complex ethnography, one that would pluralize the souls of black folk and express black consciousness as a gift of second sight. On the contrary, however, a white audience doubly rejected this message. Readers both North and South criticized the book's argument, misinterpreting the text to further reinforce racial stereotypes of imitation and pathos.

In a peculiar irony, however, such misreadings supported moderate sales for *The Souls of Black Folk*. These interpretations were expressed in mixed reviews, criticizing Du Bois's politics while nevertheless recommending the book for its representation of the seemingly essential characteristics of African Americans. Comparatively speaking, this is why Charles W. Chesnutt's *The Marrow of Tradition* was much more harshly reviewed than *The Souls of Black Folk*. As its title indicates, *The Marrow of Tradition* sought to confront the history of white supremacism. It directly addresses Jim Crow violence, exposing white power as a form of theft and disinheritance. *The Souls of Black Folk,* by contrast, was reviewed as a sort of tour of blackness.

The Souls of Black Folk sold steadily. In 1903, the book went through three editions totaling 4,764 copies. Four more editions were produced by the end of 1905, selling an additional 4,000 copies.[82] This was not a best seller, by any means; Booker T. Washington's *Up From Slavery* (1901) reportedly sold 30,000 copies in its first two years.[83] Yet *The Souls of Black Folk* did sell, and the number of small reprintings indicates that it sold better than anticipated by McClurg. In fact, it was reprinted twenty-four times by McClurg from 1903 to 1940, selling nearly 20,000 copies.[84] Throughout these years, Du Bois received numerous requests to quote from the book, which he readily granted. Du Bois also wrote to McClurg in later decades about purchasing the rights for the book, so that he might produce a less expensive edition.[85] McClurg responded frankly, telling Du Bois it preferred not to sell the rights because *Souls* was "what we call a good list book."[86] The company was happy to have

FIGURE 11. Original electrotype plates and cases for *The Souls of Black Folk.* Fisk University, John Hope and Aurelia E. Franklin Library, Special Collections, W. E. B. Du Bois Collection.

the book in its catalog, and would not release the copyright. It was not until 1946, after McClurg had closed its publishing department, that it would offer Du Bois the plates and rights of the book for $100.00.[87] After some delay, Du Bois bought the plates in January 1949, and prepared the jubilee edition in 1953 (figure 11). The original plates have survived and are now held in special collections at Fisk University.

Afterlife

Although Du Bois wrote three different autobiographical books and numerous autobiographical essays, he rarely discussed the publication of *The Souls of Black Folk*. His 1920 *Darkwater* revises the title of the book, in a chapter titled "The Souls of White Folk."[88] His *Autobiography* does not discuss *Souls* but focuses rather on his work as a professor in Atlanta.[89] The few passages in which Du Bois does mention *The Souls of Black Folk* indicate that he was satisfied with the book, yet wanted to push beyond its message. In the jubilee edition, Du Bois would publish a preface titled "Fifty Years After." Drawing on the passage cited in my introduction, Du Bois describes the publication of the book with reference to McClurg: "Late in the Nineteenth Century, there developed in Chicago a movement to build a literary and publishing center in the Mid-West."[90] He credits "the Brownes, father and son," for supporting this movement, and reiterates that *The Souls of Black Folk* was "aimed at a popular audience." Du Bois's own descriptions of the book thus emphasize its relationship to McClurg, to the Brownes, and to a popular audience.

"Fifty Years After" goes on to consider the writing itself, mentioning two issues that, at the time of composition, Du Bois had not fully realized in his own intellectual development. The first "realization," as Du Bois describes it, draws on Freud: "*The Souls of Black Folk* does not adequately allow for unconscious thought and the cake of custom in the growth and influence of race prejudice."[91] Here, Du Bois admits that he had underestimated the tenacity of his audience's racism. The book did not fully recognized its white audience's resistance to criticism, and encountered a psychological denial for which the author was unprepared. Du Bois's second "realization" refers to Marx, noting that racial injustice is underwritten by so-called civilized life and a willingness to live in comfort at the expense of "poverty, ignorance, and disease" for others.[92] In both of these areas, Du Bois claims, *The Souls of Black Folk* could have better foreseen the context within which it was published. While the book had aimed to depict black humanity for a benevolent audience, it had not fully anticipated the psychology of racism nor the economic and institutional structures founded on racial inequality.

These "realizations" might, in turn, be applied to the dual misreadings of the text among its popular white audience. On the one hand, the vast majority of readers viewed Du Bois through the lens of white supremacism, interpreting *The Souls of Black Folk* as confirming stereotypes of black musicality, spirituality, and emotion. On the other hand, white readers openly refused to accept the book's critique of racial capitalism, rejecting the text in a hostile backlash of reentrenched racist attitudes. They harshly criticized the book's message while nevertheless recommending, and reimagining, *Souls* as a study that confirmed racial stereotypes. Indeed, many reviewers interpreted the book positively *in terms* of scientific racism, as a description of the essential characteristics of the negro race. In its early years, the potential for such a misreading helped the book to be widely read, reviewed, and reprinted within a predominantly white publishing industry. It was only among black readers and reviewers that the book was recognized as an instant classic. In the wake of this reception, Du Bois would adjust his authorial strategies. Instead of describing black culture for white readers to study, he would interrogate "The Souls of White Folk." Despite Du Bois's efforts to approach a benevolent audience, the publication of *The Souls of Black Folk* revealed the extent to which white supremacist misreadings dominated the turn-of-the-century literary marketplace, both North and South.

PART TWO: *MRS. SPRING FRAGRANCE,* IMMORTAL BOOK

Less well known than Du Bois, Edith Maude Eaton (who would write under the pen name Sui Sin Far) has received increasing scholarly attention since her work was recovered in the 1980s. Born in England in 1865, she was the child of Edward Eaton, an artist and clerk who was estranged from his British merchant family, and of Achuen "Grace" Amoy, an enslaved member of an acrobatic troupe rescued by a group of London missionaries.[93] Edith Eaton's parents met in Shanghai during one of her father's business trips and were married there before returning to England.[94] Edith was the second child and the eldest daughter in a family of fourteen siblings. In the early 1870s, after preliminary trips across the Atlantic, the family settled in Montreal, where Edith Eaton coined her pen name, a Chinese term for "water lily."[95] Throughout her life Eaton would return to Montreal to visit her family, and she died in the city in 1914. In her years as a writer, however, she moved between cities in Canada, the United States, and Jamaica.

Like many women writers at the turn of the century, Eaton made a living through a variety of journalistic activities: publishing freelance stories and reports, typing correspondence, and working as a stenographer.[96] As described in Annette White-Parks's biography, Eaton moved rapidly between various jobs and locations. At the age of eighteen she began work at the *Montreal Star*, "picking and setting type" in the composing room.[97] There, she taught herself typewriting and stenography, a trade that most of her sisters would practice until their marriages.[98] In the mid-1880s, Eaton placed articles in U.S. newspapers and soon published short stories in the *Dominion Illustrated*, a Canadian periodical. By the time she was in her thirties, Eaton was able to separate herself from serving as caretaker for her siblings and family. She took up work for *Gall's Daily Newsletter* in Jamaica.[99] She traveled to San Francisco, typing correspondence for the *Canadian Pacific*, and continued work for that newspaper in San Diego and Los Angeles, where she met *Land of Sunshine* editor Charles Lummis.[100] In the fall of 1900 she moved to Seattle, where she would live, at various addresses, for the first decade of the twentieth century, before moving to Boston in 1910. Throughout her adult life, Sui Sin Far's migrations were frequent and cosmopolitan, transitioning from one job and one city to the next.

At the same time, Sui Sin Far fostered long-standing ambitions to publish a book. In a brief biographical piece, written late in her career for the *Boston Globe*, Far says that she "must have been about 8 years old" when she "conceived the ambition to write a book about the half Chinese."[101] Far goes on to describe how, when caring for her younger siblings, she sought contentment by imagining herself in a more comfortable future, as an author. She concludes the essay by looking forward to the publication of *Mrs. Spring Fragrance*: "I am myself quite excited over the prospect. Would not any one be who had worked as hard as I have—and waited as long as I have—for a book!" The biographical article thus promotes the forthcoming short story collection, describing *Mrs. Spring Fragrance* as the work of a lifetime. Far also seems aware of the ways that book publication, as opposed to articles placed in a variety of periodicals, would collect her work more permanently and bolster her status as an author.

Much like Du Bois, Sui Sin Far used her writing to subvert and challenge the assumptions of her white readers. Both writers draw on their white audience's benevolence and cross-racial fascinations to lure the reader further into the text. Yet for Sui Sin Far, a Chinese North American woman, these cross-racial fascinations were quite different than for Du Bois, an African American man. In her case, reader interest hinged on racist conceptions of yellow peril, the heathen Chinese, and the inscrutable oriental. This last category, inscrutability, is particularly relevant for Edith Eaton/Sui Sin Far, who manipulated her public persona in ways that challenge any simple understanding of her identity. Indeed, critics to this day debate whether she should be referred to as Edith Eaton or Sui Sin Far.

Yet if Sui Sin Far's background was generally unknown to her readers, the author had a much better idea of the audience she targeted. Indeed, Sui Sin Far was deliberate in submitting her work to McClurg, aware of the company's complex relationship to orientalist literature. In what follows, I show that Francis G. Browne played an important role in the book's publication, both comparable to and quite different from his influence on *The Souls of Black Folk.* I conclude by examining the ways publication is represented within the collection itself, looking especially at a story called "The Inferior Woman," in which the character of Mrs. Spring Fragrance plans to write an "immortal book" about Americans.[102] As a Chinese immigrant writer, Mrs. Spring Fragrance thus reverses the ethnographic gaze by studying white Americans. She shows that race is a relative phenomenon and ethnographic writing depends on the perspective of the author and their subject. This book, in turn, is directed at a benevolent white neighbor, who is the antagonist of "The Inferior Woman." In the story's idealized happy ending, this benevolent audience listens to the immortal book of Mrs. Spring Fragrance and is reoriented by its Chinese American perspective.

Who Was Sui Sin Far?

Edith Eaton's decision to write as a Chinese "Eurasian" challenged prevailing sinophobia in her era. Whereas her sister, Winnifred Eaton, wrote popular novels under the Japanese pen name Onoto Watanna, Edith Eaton (writing as Sui Sin Far) chose to identify with the more socially outcast Chinese.[103] In one passage from her autobiographical essay "Leaves from the Mental Portfolio of an Eurasian," Far describes this identification explicitly. In the scene, she sits down to dinner with her employer and co-workers, who do not realize that she is Chinese. As the subject of conversation turns to the "Chinamen" who work on the transcontinental railroad, the party offers a slew of racial stereotypes. The Chinese give one young girl "such a creepy feeling." Sui Sin Far's employer can barely believe "that the Chinese are humans like ourselves." For the town clerk, they are "more repulsive" than African Americans.[104] The scene thus depicts a range of anti-Chinese attitudes and stereotypes in the form of condensed dialogue. Some Americans express contempt for Chinese labor; others consider the Chinese inhuman, inscrutable, and emotionless; still others express physical revulsion against the Chinese body. This malicious racism does not, however, extend to the Japanese. Rather, one man at the party describes how "there is something bright and likeable about [Japanese] men." Far listens to the discussion silently at first, but soon stands up against this racism, telling her boss, "I am a Chinese."[105] The anecdote exemplifies the strength of conviction that has drawn critics to Eaton's work. Though she would have been able to pass as white or as Japanese, Edith Eaton actively adopted her Chinese heritage as Sui Sin Far.

During Sui Sin Far's lifetime, such stereotypes were widespread. As Ronald Takaki notes, in the late nineteenth century, "racial qualities previously assigned to blacks quickly became 'Chinese' characteristics," so that the Chinese "were described as heathen, morally inferior, savage, childlike, and lustful."[106] Chinese women were seen as depraved, and Chinese men as sensuously interested in white women.[107] Chinese Americans were also depicted as exotic and mysterious, in the style that Edward Said has called "orientalism."[108] These stereotypes were depicted prominently in political cartoons, and in writing such as Bret Harte's "Plain Language from Truthful James," a poem that was intended as satire but became popular for its repeated descriptions of "the heathen Chinee." Because Chinese immigrants constituted only 0.002 percent of the U.S. population in 1880, Takaki argues that such widespread caricatures, disproportionate to the Chinese American population, were "symptomatic of a larger conflict between white labor and white capital."[109] In other words, anti-Chinese racism became an outlet for the expression of white working-class anxieties. As one result of this dynamic, the Chinese Exclusion Act of 1882 prevented Chinese laborers and women from immigration into the United States, allowing entry only to merchants and able-bodied professionals. The act also denied citizenship to Chinese American immigrants, codifying their second-class status in American culture. The Exclusion Act was then expanded and renewed in the Geary Act of 1892 and was further reinforced with the Immigration Act of 1924. Indeed, Chinese Exclusion set the precedent for U.S. immigration restriction. It was not until 1944, in response to China's role in World War II, that the Exclusion Act would be repealed.

Recovery of Sui Sin Far has often focused on her subversive response to this culture. Several early academic critics praised Sui Sin Far for taking up her Chinese identity and advocating for an oppressed and excluded minority. In 1990, Amy Ling joined S. E. Solberg in this appraisal, claiming, "The personal story of what life was like for the Chinese and Eurasians in America at the turn of the century is Sui Sin Far's special contribution to American letters."[110] Annette White-Parks's biography tracks Eaton's "rising voice as a defender of Chinese immigrants" as well as "the development of her identity as a writer of Chinese heritage."[111] Lori Jirousek has written about the ways Eaton combats a culture of "spectacle ethnography" that examined the Chinese body as a foreign object.[112] Dominika Ferens has similarly written a comparative analysis describing the ways Edith and Winnifred Eaton responded to ethnographies of orientalism at the turn of the century.[113]

Yet the story in which Sui Sin Far announces her Chinese background to her co-workers also reveals that she had been willing, at times, to pass as white. The depiction of Sui Sin Far as "defender of Chinese immigrants" has thus been challenged by several scholars, skeptical of her ability to represent the Chinese American experience. The editors of *Aiiieeeee!*, a 1974 anthology of Asian American literature that had initially recovered Sui Sin Far's writing, argued that her depictions of Chinese Americans worked "within the terms of the stereotype as laundryman, prostitute, smuggler, [and] coolie."[114] Sean McCann has even argued that Sui Sin Far's writing is not so much an influence on mid-century Asian American writers—who would not have known her work—as a predecessor for the values of neoliberal capitalism, using its characters to advocate for free market exchange.[115]

More recent scholarship has settled somewhere between such extremes, recognizing Sui Sin Far's hybrid position. Mary Chapman's edited collection *Becoming Sui Sin Far* has greatly expanded the author's legacy, recovering more than seventy previously unknown journalistic reports and short stories. As Chapman points out, many of these works do not fit easily into Sui Sin Far's established canon of Chinatown fiction. Chapman thus sees it fitting to identify Edith Eaton with her birth name, emphasizing the performative aspects of the name Sui Sin Far—as well as other pen names the author used, such as Fire Fly, Sui Seen Far, and Wing Sing. Chapman describes Edith Eaton as "an important transnational, or even post-national, author who questioned the coherence of ideas about ethnic and national identity."[116]

In many ways, the difficulty of determining the real name of Edith Eaton/Sui Sin Far is, itself, the point. The author cultivated this hybrid identity, describing herself as a "connecting link" between the Orient and the Occident.[117] The most significant aspect of her name is not Eaton or Far but the separatrix between them, which defies boundaries. (Coincidentally, this idea of the separatrix has been crucial to the philosophy of deconstruction.) Indeed, within the text of *Mrs. Spring Fragrance,* there is a proliferation of names that play on the interpretive possibilities of Eurasian identity. The book's title is derived from the main character of the first two stories in the collection, whose name is a transliteration from Chinese. This name, Mrs. Spring Fragrance, echoes the consonant and vowel sounds of the author's pen name, Sui Sin Far, and becomes not only a protagonist in the stories but also the book itself.

To further complicate the issue, the title page of *Mrs. Spring Fragrance* includes the name Edith Eaton enclosed parenthetically under the byline of Sui Sin Far. In other words, the title page includes both Sui Sin Far's birth name and her assumed authorial persona. Hsuan Hsu's Broadview edition of *Mrs. Spring Fragrance* argues that the inclusion of both names "reveals the artifice behind the author's Chinese pen name."[118] Hsu's interpretation points out that readers may have interpreted the book as a white-authored text, written by Edith Eaton under the pen name Sui Sin Far. In this interpretation, the book serves as a relatively standard ethnography—an exploration of Chinese American culture from a sympathetic white author. Yet the inclusion of both names cannot be interpreted so easily. As Martha Cutter has noted, Sui Sin Far was not simply a "pen name" for Edith Eaton but was an "assumed name" with which Eaton would increasingly identify in personal correspondence.[119] The pen name was not merely artificial. Moreover, it is equally possible that a general audience would have read the parenthetical byline Edith Eaton as the American name of an assimilated Chinese American author, comparable to the book's title character. Indeed, when McClurg published Clara Kathleen Rogers's book *My Voice and I* in 1910, it placed the author's *pseudonym*, Clara Doria, in the same parenthetical position as Edith Eaton.[120]

Notably, the few reviews of the book—collected in Hsuan Hsu's Broadview edition—avoid explicit discussion of Sui Sin Far's race or ethnicity. Much as critics struggle with the name today, reviewers variously identified the author as Sui Sin Far, Miss Edith Eaton, Sui Sin Far (Edith Eaton), and "Sui Sin Far." This liminal authorial identity might thus be compared to Charles W. Chesnutt's in the middle stages of his career with Houghton Mifflin, relying on ambiguous descriptions in an effort to attract a wider audience. In the same way that Chesnutt was marketed at the time he published *The House Behind the Cedars*, Sui Sin Far was positioned on the color line and between worlds.

Of course, some readers would have known Sui Sin Far's background. Those who had come across her autobiographical essay in the *Boston Globe,* or those who had read "Leaves of the Mental Portfolio of a Eurasian" in the *Independent,* would have been aware of her Chinese American heritage. Discussing these essays, White-Parks argues that they present Sui Sin Far as both "exotic" and "safe," both half-Chinese and white.[121] White-Parks even suggests that this presentation of Sui Sin Far as a "safe ethnic" was part of a long-term marketing campaign to promote the author for a white audience. Yet because these autobiographical essays were printed years apart from each other—"Leaves" was published in 1909, and the *Boston Globe* essay in 1913—it is virtually impossible that any one publisher guided Sui Sin Far's autobiographical representations from one to the next. This is especially true because she worked for so many different periodicals, and did not have repeated contracts with a single publisher. As a result, it is likely that Sui Sin Far decided on her own self-presentation for how these essays would depict her "Eurasian" background. (In portraits included with these articles, it is noteworthy that Sui Sin Far wore lace, a material that she made and sold as a child, when she was called "the Little Chinese Lace Girl."[122]) Any censorship in these articles would have been self-imposed, and certainly did not prevent Sui Sin Far from criticizing prevailing sinophobia. "Leaves from the Mental Portfolio of a Eurasian" is quite explicit in expressing such criticism.

Many readers, however, would have approached *Mrs. Spring Fragrance* unaware of the author's background, and it is interesting to consider how such readers would understand the book's opening paragraph: "When Mrs. Spring Fragrance first arrived in Seattle, she was unacquainted with even one word of the American language. Five years later her husband, speaking of her, said, 'There are no more American words for her learning.' And everyone who knew Mrs. Spring Fragrance agreed with Mr. Spring Fragrance."[123] The book thus introduces its title character as a fully Americanized Chinese immigrant. She is intelligent and capable of assimilation, and importantly, she assimilates by learning to speak "the American language." At the same time, this opening allows for skepticism regarding this process of assimilation. The Spring Fragrances have a peculiar name, and Mrs. Spring Fragrance's husband has a peculiar speech pattern. He refers to English as "the American language," and formulates his wife's language acquisition in reverse order; she does not learn all of the words, but instead "there are no more words for her learning." Mr. Spring Fragrance's dialect, in the quotation, then carries over to the narrator, who begins a sentence with a conjunction and repeats the unusual name of the Spring Fragrance family three times.

Much like *The Souls of Black Folk,* the introductory paragraph of the book thus sets up the "problem" of the ethnic American, allowing Eaton to address readers who are both sympathetic and skeptical of Chinese assimilation. Yet whereas Du Bois identifies himself as African American and asks his readers to forgive his mistakes, Mrs. Spring Fragrance claims full control of the American language. In doing so, the opening implies that Chinese immigrants can learn "American," even if they cannot conform to Anglo definitions of American culture.

As twenty-first-century readers of the text, we approach Sui Sin Far's writing through biographical awareness. Her work is significant, in large part, because it is one of the earliest examples of Asian American literature. At the time of publication, however, Sui Sin Far used her own relative anonymity to open up possibilities regarding the book's authorship. This opening of possibilities regarding the author's background is especially significant because inscrutability was one of the most central stereotypes of the Chinese. Many of Sui Sin Far's readers would have assumed that Chinese people were mysterious, shifty, and unknowable. *Mrs. Spring Fragrance* both engages and subverts this stereotype. On the one hand, its author's identity is difficult to determine. On the other, this indeterminacy compels readers to consider issues of Chinese American hybridity and cross-racial mediation. Sui Sin Far thus deployed tactics of inscrutability and exoticism in order to lure a wider variety of readers. Whether a reader approached the text as written by a Chinese author, a Eurasian author, or a white author—the book itself would challenge anti-Chinese stereotypes.

Orientalist Designs

As a book, *Mrs. Spring Fragrance* took on a highly orientalized style. It was bound in red cloth with green and white imagery: a scene of

FIGURE 12. Cover of *Mrs. Spring Fragrance* (Chicago: A. C. McClurg & Co., 1912). Image courtesy of the Library of Congress.

dragonflies hovering past water lilies in front of a rising sun (figure 12). As Annette White-Parks points out, the imagery reiterates the author's pen name, which translates as "water lily."[124] The spine of the book repeats this design, with an image of a water lily in white, and the name of the book, author, and publisher in gold. The title of the book is written in gilt lettering above this image. Along the lower right side of the cover, Chinese characters approximate the phrase "Signed by Sui Sin Far."[125] The book's colors, fonts, and title all reiterate its status as an exotic, oriental text. Set within this stylized cover, the pages themselves are also decorated. As Hsuan Hsu describes it, "Every recto page is imprinted with images of flowers, birds, and the characters 'Fu Lu Shou' (Good Fortune, Prosperity, Longevity)."[126] This imagery is continued onto the verso pages as well, minus the Chinese characters, so that the flowers and branches create a landscape image that spans the pages. The book was thus marked with Chinese writing and imagery at every turn, literally shifting the background on which it was read.

Discussions of the book have at times responded to this materiality. In one early consideration, Elizabeth Ammons contemplates whether or not Sui Sin Far would have approved the cover, saying, "It is not at all clear whether the most obvious and inescapable formal choice of the book—its insistently 'Orientalized,' hyper-feminized pages—came from the author or the publisher."[127] Annette White-Parks's biography also goes into some detail regarding the production of the book. As she notes, *Mrs. Spring Fragrance* was manufactured by Plimpton Press, a Massachusetts-based company whose motto was "perfect book-making in its entirety."[128] White-Parks also notes, correctly, that the book's first and only print run was 2,500 copies.[129]

McClurg company business records help to reveal some of the forces that influenced the form *Mrs. Spring Fragrance* would take. At a very basic level, for instance, company records detail Sui Sin Far's earnings. A "Statement of Royalties" shows that Edith Eaton was advanced $100 on August 16, 1912, a few months after the book was published.[130] By January 1913, however, the book had sold copies that amounted to $89.46 worth of royalties. This amount is recorded underneath the $100 payment, to show that the Eaton's royalty had already been covered. The "Statement of Royalties" continues for several years, and includes even small payments to other authors under contract with McClurg. Yet Eaton's name disappears from the records, indicating that she was never paid any money beyond the initial $100 advance. If we assume that Eaton was paid the standard royalty of 10 percent—which McClurg paid to almost all of its authors—on a book priced at $1.40, the January 1913 royalty statement indicates that *Mrs. Spring Fragrance* sold only 639 copies in total. In its first year, then, the book significantly underperformed expectations, selling only 25 percent of its print run.

The $100 advance also points to Sui Sin Far's vulnerable financial status. In her article for the *Boston Globe,* Sui Sin Far mentions that she had relied on patrons to fund her writing, and that she hoped "soon to be in a position to repay them."[131] In another letter to Charles Lummis, Eaton mentions that she had expected to have money from McClurg almost immediately on the book's publication.[132] Beyond her own dream to publish a book, then, Eaton sought publication for monetary compensation as well. Eaton's letters indicate that she had written the book in hopes of commercial success.

Beyond this information, however, the McClurg company archives rarely provide concrete answers regarding the company's relationship to Eaton. My own research found only three instances in which the McClurg records mention Eaton directly: twice in the royalty statements, and once in a list of publications, confirming that the company printed 2,500 copies of *Mrs. Spring Fragrance.*[133] This is partly because McClurg records are not comprehensive, and partly because Sui Sin Far was seen as a minor author for the company. Extant records reflect the challenges she faced as a woman of color. To the best of my knowledge, any correspondence between Sui Sin Far and McClurg has not been retained in the company archives. Whether Sui Sin Far made an effort to preserve her own papers and manuscripts is also unclear. In another letter to Lummis, Sui Sin Far indicates that many of her papers were destroyed in a railway fire.[134] Because of this absence of primary materials, a broader knowledge of McClurg company practices becomes especially useful for reconstructing the publication history of *Mrs. Spring Fragrance.*

With regard to the cover, for instance, it is very likely Eaton would have been informed of the book's design, without having significant input or oversight. This contrasts sharply with the case of W. E. B. Du Bois, who was mailed potential designs from which to choose. But again, McClurg was actively soliciting Du Bois's work as a well-known author with extraordinary potential. The typical McClurg contract did not grant authors any rights or influence over cover design. In one example, for a 1911 book called *The Scout of Pea Ridge* by Byron Dunn, the contract states, "The said Publisher agrees upon its part to print and publish said manuscript <u>in illustrated form</u> at its own expense in such style and manner and in such quantity as it deems most expedient."[135] Here, the language of the contract is boilerplate, but the underlined portions allow for the particular book to be described more specifically. The contract for *Mrs. Spring Fragrance* might have specified that the book would be published "<u>in regular book form.</u>" The boilerplate contract also indicates that the book will be produced "in such a style and manner" as decided by McClurg. As a courtesy, the company would often correspond with its authors to describe the "style" a book would take.[136] Such letters would not ask for feedback or commentary, but would generally assume cooperation from the author. McClurg would thus keep its authors apprised of publication details, without allowing significant input.

Because *Mrs. Spring Fragrance* and many other McClurg books were produced by Plimpton Press, the company could remotely manage its book manufacturing decisions. The *Plimpton Press Year Book,* mentioned by White-Parks, is actually a sort of sales catalog, allowing publishers to make design choices à la carte. The catalog not only describes Plimpton's commitment to the "book beautiful" but also provides samples of typography, paper, layout, and bindings.[137] The catalog emphasizes the ability of Plimpton Press to manage all of these aspects in a process of "complete manufacture."[138] This idea of "complete manufacture" is then repeated throughout the *Year Book,* so that Plimpton Press advertises both its quality and convenience. In other words, publishers such as McClurg could easily interact with Plimpton by proxy, to have a book designed and manufactured in its entirety. In a March 23, 1912, letter to Charles Lummis, Eaton mentions her awareness of the book's production, but she stops short of commenting on its design: "My book is being printed at Norwood, Mass. It will have a red cover and will be entitled 'Mrs. Spring Fragrance.'"[139]

Yet if Sui Sin Far would not have had significant influence on the design of the book, she would have been aware of McClurg's catalog, which included a number of books engaged in orientalism and primitivism. Before accepting *Mrs. Spring Fragrance,* for instance, McClurg had already published exotic novels by Robert Ames Bennet such as

For the White Christ (1905) and *Into the Primitive* (1908). In 1910, McClurg also published a Japanese romance novel by Bennet titled *The Shogun's Daughter*. Like *Mrs. Spring Fragrance,* this book was manufactured by Plimpton Press in an orientalized style; it was given a purple cloth cover with images of gold samurai swords on the front and spine.

Sui Sin Far was likely aware of these and other orientalist titles in the McClurg catalog. In addition to Bennet's romance novels, the McClurg catalog included nonfiction ethnography such as Sarah Pike Conger's 1909 *Letters from China.* Conger was the wife of Edwin H. Conger, a political diplomat to China during the time of the Boxer Rebellion, and her *Letters* offer a benevolent depiction of Chinese culture. At the con- clusion of the book, for example, in contrast to prevailing stereotypes of the mysterious and unfeeling Chinese, Conger notes, "I find that the Chinese have deep feelings, and they express them."[140] She goes on to exclaim, "May the Oriental 'dawn' and the Occidental 'twilight' be effaced by the constant sunshine of one eternal day, alike for all."[141] Conger's *Letters from China* included eighty half-tone photographic images and was produced as a special edition with a red and gold cover, comparable to *Mrs. Spring Fragrance.* Approaching McClurg with her manuscript, Sui Sin Far addressed a company with established inter- ests in a range of orientalized texts. Indeed, it is almost certain that she submitted her book manuscript to McClurg *because* of the company's investment in orientalism.

Targeting White Readers

Not surprisingly, then, *Mrs. Spring Fragrance* can be read as address- ing a predominantly white audience. In several stories, Sui Sin Far even includes the figure of the white reader as a major character within the text. For example, the second story in the collection, "The Inferior Woman," focuses on Mrs. Spring Fragrance's ability to communicate with and persuade a white audience. In the story, Mrs. Spring Fragrance's neighbor Will Carman is in love with "the inferior woman" Alice Winthrop. The two are kept apart, however, because Will's mother insists that he marry "the superior woman," Ethel Evebrook. Ethel is a well-educated and moneyed suffragette, whereas Alice has earned her own living since the age of fourteen, working in law offices and secretary positions alongside numerous businessmen. Alice is not ashamed of this background but is proud of her accomplishments, and she will not accept Will Carman's proposal until his mother openly agrees to their marriage. The story thus centers on a romantic relationship across lines of class, with Mrs. Spring Fragrance supporting "the inferior woman." Throughout the story, Mrs. Spring Fragrance functions as a matchmaker, working to connect Will Carman with the young woman he loves.

Mrs. Spring Fragrance sets out to match Will and Alice by writing a book about Americans, a study of American culture written from the Chinese perspective. The story opens with Mrs. Spring Fragrance considering this immortal book. She thinks to herself, "Many American women wrote books. Why should not a Chinese? She would write a book about Americans for her Chinese woman friends. The American people were so interesting and mysterious."[142] The passage thus expands on Mrs. Spring Fragrance's literacy so that she is not only speaking the American language but also has ambitions to write a book. It also reverses the white ethnographic gaze so that a Chinese protagonist will write a book about American people. In doing so, the passage also reverses stereotypes of the "interesting and mysterious" Chinese, applying these ideas to Americans. In a gesture of cultural relativism, mystery and interest are not inherent to the Chinese subject but are defined by the position of the ethnographic observer.

Mrs. Spring Fragrance returns to this idea when she learns of the trouble between Will Carman and Alice Winthrop. She exclaims to her husband, "Ah, these Americans! These mysterious, inscrutable, incomprehensible Americans!"[143] Here, even more explicitly, the story reverses the stereotype of the "inscrutable" oriental and applies it to Americans. Importantly, however, this outburst also indicates real difficulties that can arise in cross-cultural interactions. Mrs. Spring Fragrance is actually struggling to understand the obstacles that separate Will Carman and Alice Winthrop, and finds Mrs. Carman's class bias mysterious.

In order to explore this mystery, Mrs. Spring Fragrance decides to focus her book on the topic of "the inferior woman." At her husband's suggestion, she plans to research the topic by first meeting with Ethel Evebrook, using research for the book as a pretext to interact with "the superior woman." When she arrives at the Evebrook house, before entering, Mrs. Spring Fragrance overhears Ethel and her mother discussing Alice Winthrop. She waits outside, eavesdropping, and the reader listens to the conversation from the same perspective. As the mother and daughter talk, Mrs. Spring Fragrance learns that Ethel Evebrook admires Alice Winthrop a great deal. Indeed, Ethel defends Alice as hardworking and respectable, and recognizes her own privileged status, since she has never had to work for a living.[144]

At this point, the Evebrooks notice Mrs. Spring Fragrance outside of the house and invite her in. She explains that she is working on a "book about the Americans" and wants to include their conversation in her writing.[145] In fact, she has transcribed the conversation in Chinese, and asks to read it back to the Evebrooks: "With your kind permission, I will translate for correction."[146] In this passage, Mrs. Spring Fragrance takes on Sui Sin Far's own abilities as a stenographer.[147] She records the Evebrooks' conversation, translating it into Chinese, and then reads it back to them in English, asking for corrections. In doing so, Mrs. Spring Fragrance models an alternative version of ethnography, based not on racist assumptions but on direct observation and the consent of those observed. She reflects U.S. culture back to the Americans, and asks for approval in what she has composed. Moreover, because these transcriptions are written for a book, they provide a metatextual reference to *Mrs. Spring Fragrance* itself. The story shows how reading can help its audience see U.S. culture from the Chinese American perspective.

In the next scene, Mrs. Spring Fragrance meets with Will Carman's mother to report on her book project regarding "the inferior woman." Mrs. Carman is not happy with the topic but is fascinated by the overall project and eager to know what the Evebrooks have said. As Mrs. Spring Fragrance reads her transcription, the story reaches its climax and its resolution: Mrs. Carman decides that she does "admire" Alice Winthrop, after all, and decides to meet with Alice directly and welcome her into the family.[148] Mrs. Spring Fragrance thus succeeds in her project as matchmaker. She establishes her own authority as ethnographer by choosing her interviews strategically and accurately transcribing them. Moreover, Mrs. Spring Fragrance progresses beyond her frustrations with "inscrutable Americans" to demonstrate an excellent sense of American culture, its class biases, and how they might be addressed. The Americans, it turns out, are not entirely mysterious. Knowing them simply requires some attention and interpretive skill.

In contrast to Mrs. Spring Fragrance as heroine-matchmaker, Mrs. Carman is clearly the story's antagonist. It is Mrs. Carman who drives the story's conflict by standing for hereditary wealth against "the inferior woman." In a provocative maneuver, this upper-middle-class white woman becomes the central point of tension in the story. Along these lines, Sui Sin Far offers a careful description of Mrs. Carman's background and attitudes: "Having lived in China while her late husband was in the customs service there, Mrs. Carman's prejudices did not extend to the Chinese, and ever since the Spring Fragrances had become the occupants of the villa beside the Carmans, there had been social good feeling between the American and Chinese families. Indeed, Mrs. Carman was wont to declare that amongst all her acquaintances there was not one more congenial and interesting than little Mrs. Spring Fragrance."[149] Here, Sui Sin Far offers subtle criticism of condescending attitudes toward the Chinese. Mrs. Carman is not aggressively prejudiced against Mrs. Spring Fragrance but is overly benevolent. Her perspective is marked by exaggerated fascination toward her Chinese neighbor, who is seen as "interesting" and "little." Indeed, Mrs. Carman dominates the conversation with Mrs. Spring Fragrance for more than a half hour before noticing that her guest is "uninterested and unresponsive."[150]

This description of Mrs. Carman's experience with the customs service in China is especially significant because it alludes to fellow McClurg author Sarah Pike Conger, who had been the wife of a U.S. diplomat in China. In other words, Sui Sin Far brings the McClurg catalog—the books alongside which *Mrs. Spring Fragrance* would have been sold—into the story and positions these texts as antagonistic to the goals of Mrs. Spring Fragrance. The story conflates Mrs. Carman and Mrs. Sarah Pike Conger, representing them as a single character whose friendship with the Chinese is also a source of conflict. It responds to books such as *Letters from China* by allowing the Chinese immigrant to speak back to American culture, taking on the position of the ethnographer. This perspective is unfamiliar to Mrs. Carman, who responds to Mrs. Spring Fragrance's book idea with amazement: "What an original idea!"[151] Despite her deep sympathies and her history of international travel, this woman has never considered the possibility that a Chinese American might study American culture.

Mrs. Spring Fragrance is patient and polite in responding to Mrs. Carman's orientalism, working carefully to advocate for the inferior woman. As the story reaches its conclusion, it imagines that this subtle rebuke can influence a benevolent white audience. Indeed, the stories in *Mrs. Spring Fragrance* often turn toward pure tragedy or comedy, resulting in death or marriage, respectively. The ease with which Mrs. Spring Fragrance influences Mrs. Carman, and the happy ending of the story, mark "The Inferior Woman" as an idealized model for social interaction across lines of race and class.

When the story ends, Mrs. Spring Fragrance's book is left unfinished. The project has evolved through several phases. At the outset of the story, Mrs. Spring Fragrance aims to write a book about Americans for the Chinese, and imagines reading the book with Chinese American neighbors. As she begins to write her book, however, Mrs. Spring Fragrance finds it will be more helpful to present American culture not to the Chinese but to Americans. She translates conversations into Chinese and back into English, asking her neighbors to reflect on their own ideas and culture. In this way, "The Inferior Woman" highlights the goals of reading and writing *Mrs. Spring Fragrance* itself. The story presents the book as one that could be written for a Chinese audience or an American audience, and even translated from the Chinese. Yet among these possibilities, the book is written especially for benevolent readers such as Mrs. Carman. It hopes to introduce this audience to the relative virtues of "the inferior." When Mrs. Spring Fragrance's book achieves this goal and disappears from view, *Mrs. Spring Fragrance* remains in the hands of its reader.

Francis G. Browne's Ethnic Literary Interests

As with *The Souls of Black Folk,* Francis G. Browne was centrally responsible for the publication of *Mrs. Spring Fragrance* as well as the orientalist texts alongside which it was sold. Browne managed the McClurg publishing department through 1911, when the company would have reviewed and accepted Sui Sin Far's manuscript. Although there is no record of their correspondence in the McClurg archives, Browne managed correspondence with almost all of the company's authors at the time, and he most likely worked with Sui Sin Far as the book was submitted. Browne resigned from the company in December 1911, however, just months before *Mrs. Spring Fragrance* was printed.[152] Based on this timeline, Browne would have accepted *Mrs. Spring Fragrance* for publication but would not have supervised its printing and production.

This coincidence, by which Francis G. Browne accepted *Mrs. Spring*

Fragrance and then resigned before it was printed, may have influenced the appearance of the book. (Few of the books published under Browne reach this level of stylized orientalism.) Browne's resignation from McClurg may also have played a role in Sui Sin Far's novel remaining unpublished, since Browne would not have been in an editorial position to accept the book. Indeed, just as Browne left McClurg, the company was making a major shift toward more popular fiction. It was during the very same month *Mrs. Spring Fragrance* was published that the long-time manager of the rare books department, George Millard, was forced to resign from the company.[153] From 1909 onward, the Hopalong Cassidy series was being published, and *Tarzan of the Apes* would debut in 1914.

Browne left McClurg to form his own publishing business that would demonstrate continued interest in orientalism. The company itself was short-lived. It was established as F. G. Browne and Company in early 1913, changed its name to Browne and Howell Company in the same year,[154] and went bankrupt in January 1915.[155] During its brief term as a publisher, the company collaborated with the Plimpton Press on almost all of the books it produced. Moreover, out of the company's short list of titles, several deal with orientalist subjects. In 1913, F. G. Browne and Company published Byron E. Veatch's *The Two Samurai* as well as another book from Sarah Pike Conger titled *Old China and Young America*. Under the name Browne and Howell, the company published another romance novel from Robert Ames Bennet titled *The Quarterbreed*. It also published a series of illustrated books that included *Our Neighbors: The Japanese; Our Neighbors: The Fillipinos;* and *Our Neighbors: The Chinese.* This last book opens with a discussion of the "yellow race," speculating on its origins among the "several types of mankind."[156] In the absence of direct correspondence between McClurg and Sui Sin Far, Browne's work as an independent publisher provides further evidence that he would have been responsible for accepting *Mrs. Spring Fragrance.*

It is difficult to judge Francis G. Browne's objectives when publishing the range of orientalist texts that he selected: ethnographic nonfiction and exotic romance novels alongside *Mrs. Spring Fragrance.* In comparison to his father, Francis F. Browne, there is very little biographical information available about him. However, in the March 30, 1913, *Chicago Tribune,* Browne did write a brief article on his work as a publisher, "A Big Job to Put a Novel on the Market." In distinct sections, the article moves through the phases of publication. He discusses book sales and distribution, merchandising, review copies for editors, and expenses. Browne describes how he personally reads all of the books that are published under his management. In one passage, Browne describes his selection process as an editor, and he does so in terms of business rather than literature: "From a mass of a hundred manuscripts [the editor] selects perhaps one that he believes has 'the punch' and may become a good 'seller.' For the publication of fiction no longer is considered from the literary standpoint: it is published from the viewpoint of dollars and cents, what it will make for the author and what it will net the publisher. It has developed into a commercial proposition pure and simple—the merchandising of literature."[157] Here, Browne gives us the logic behind his editorial selections, driven by sales, dollars, net profits, and merchandising. At the same time, Browne recognizes the risk of selecting which books "may" become good sellers. Browne concludes the article by describing the publishing trade as "a gamble." As the title of the article indicates, this is especially true in the case of novels, because each book must be marketed and sold on its own terms. Selling books is a commercial endeavor, but it also involves prediction and judgment.

As Browne left McClurg to establish his own publishing company, he gambled heavily on the success of well-manufactured orientalist books. Such books offered varying degrees of exoticism, ethnography, and benevolent sympathy. Sarah Pike Conger's work, while sympathetic to Chinese culture, nevertheless advocates for imperialist trade policies with China. Other books, such as those written by Robert Ames Bennet, trafficked more explicitly in oriental exoticism and romance. The Our Neighbors series is steeped in late nineteenth-century scientific racism. Overall, the catalog assembled by Francis G. Browne's company reflects an upper-middle-class concern for relationships between the United States and Asia.

The results of this venture, however, show that Browne was actually a poor judge of the commercial literary marketplace. Despite having $60,000 in capital at the company's founding,[158] Browne and Howell went bankrupt in just two years. Browne's "gamble" to publish beautiful books focused on Asian American culture had failed. In contrast, his success with these types of books at McClurg had been enabled by the company's unusual business model, earning the vast majority of its revenue from wholesale distribution. In a complicated corporate relationship, the legacy of General McClurg had allowed Browne to operate on principals that would bankrupt him as an independent publisher. Browne's sensibilities as an editor were fraught with racial exoticism, but he was also proactive in recruiting ethnic authors, and both aspects of his career should be recognized. *The Souls of Black Folk* and *Mrs. Spring Fragrance* were thus shaped by the efforts of an ethnographically inclined publishing manager whose position was subsidized by corporate funding derived from wholesale distribution revenue.

FOR DIFFERENT READERS

Publishing with McClurg, Du Bois and Sui Sin Far both recognized the potential and peril of addressing a white audience. In collaboration with Francis G. Browne, both authors collected and edited previously published writing into the form of a complete book. Because he was responsible for publishing both books, Browne is a particularly important figure for understanding them. He was in the position of what we might today call a white ally—supporting authors of color and publishing foundational works of U.S. ethnic literature, yet doing so imperfectly, with his own sensibilities of racial exoticism. In many ways, Browne embodied the benevolent white reader targeted by these books. This editorial apparatus was, in turn, supported by McClurg's Chicago location in an era when the U.S. nation expanded into the American West. Du Bois and Sui Sin Far entered into this complicated dynamic as a way to reach a wider national audience.

Reading these books in light of their historical and social production can also change their meaning as literature. With *The Souls of Black Folk,* Du Bois made a conscious decision to offer his readers an ethnographic view of African American culture, as a way to challenge racist stereotypes and assumptions. The book's framing devices, written specifically for the collection, were meant to accomplish this goal. They simultaneously rely on and challenge his white audience's fascination with blackness. These efforts allowed Du Bois to achieve moderate sales among a white audience, but not for the reasons he had hoped. Rather, the book's ethnographic approach was interpreted as evidence for an essentially imitative, albeit poetic, black race. Ironically, this interpretation of *The Souls of Black Folk*—as confirming African American stereotypes—became crucial for promoting further reviews, sales, and distribution of the book during its first years of publication. It was not the success Du Bois anticipated, but it allowed him to reach a national audience and to adjust his own authorial strategies in subsequent work. Indeed, it is remarkable that the book we know as *The Souls of Black Folk* passed through such a crucible.

Examining *Mrs. Spring Fragrance* with a mind for its audience at the time of publication, one finds the text increasingly disorienting. Is it written by an Americanized Chinese immigrant such as Mrs. Spring Fragrance? By Sui Sin Far? By Miss Edith Eaton? The book attempted to use these various possibilities to attract a wider audience. Like Du Bois, Sui Sin Far traded on cross-racial fascination as a means of subversion. Unlike *The Souls of Black Folk*, however, *Mrs. Spring Fragrance* resists explaining the dynamic between ethnic author, ethnic content, and white reader. The book allows a variety of cross-racial relationships to coexist and multiply. As I have shown, this strategy was not commercially successful. The book significantly underperformed McClurg's expectations and was generally neglected by contemporary readers. To their credit, however, both Du Bois and Sui Sin Far recognized that the published book would take on a life of its own.

THE FUTURE AMERICAN

This book has argued that, at the time of initial publication and reception, the subversive potential of the ethnic trickster was denied by a predominantly white audience. The book further proposes that this rejection, within the literary marketplace, was characteristic of race relations in this era. Whereas select publishers did invest in authors of color, hoping that their work might attract a national audience, this antiracist literature was nevertheless rejected within commercial literary culture. In terms of reception, my project has articulated a pattern of defensive misreading in response to emergent multiethnic literature. On the one hand, what authors of color intended as hyperbolic racial caricature was often interpreted as literary realism, fulfilling and confirming white fantasies of racial domination. On the other hand, texts understood as explicitly critical of white supremacism were rejected openly, in a hostile backlash of reentrenched racist attitudes. The response to *The Souls of Black Folk* is most notable in this regard. Reacting against W. E. B. Du Bois's explication of race relations, a white audience harshly criticized its central message while nevertheless recommending the book as a study that confirmed racial stereotypes.

Such interpretations also hinge on depictions of the author, since knowledge of a writer's background would influence how their work was perceived. For example, from the outset of his career, Du Bois was advertised as a champion of the negro race. In *The Souls of Black Folk,* he would use the forethought to identify himself as "bone of the bone and flesh of the flesh" of the African American community.[1] This identification attracted readers, but it also guided their interpretations toward familiar patterns. A contemporary white audience did not read the book "with patience," as Du Bois hoped, but interpreted it as confirming the essential characteristics of the negro. Charles W. Chesnutt's African American heritage, in contrast, was revealed gradually, in alignment with his literary output. He began his career as an author who could pass for white but was soon advertised, like Du Bois, as a champion of the colored race. In time, Chesnutt's writing progressed toward a more explicit critique of whiteness—*The Marrow of Tradition*—that doomed his career within the contemporary literary establishment.

Because this book examines how ethnic literature circulated within the predominantly white publishing trade at a time of intense racism, I have often returned to issues of miscommunication and misreading. While I have occasionally considered more favorable receptions in posterity and among readerships of color, the project's rhythm is one of repeated frustration. It cycles through new case studies with comparable results and rejections of the ethnic trickster. This repeated frustration is important for understanding a literary culture that did not view multiethnic texts as we view them today. It allows us to consider the turn-of-the-century literary marketplace for its biases and hostilities—casting appropriate suspicion on the industry of literary culture. Having offered this view of turn-of-the-century reading formations, however, I want to return now to this literature's potential for subversion and disruption. What of artistic ingenuity? What of cross-racial entanglement? What of change over a longer duration of time?

The artistic achievement of these authors, I would argue, is made *more* impressive when we consider their position within such a hostile culture. Indeed, in response to this culture, their manipulations of language and authorial identity are wonderfully inventive. I think of María Amparo Ruiz de Burton, for example, planning for her book to be camouflaged within J. B. Lippincott's catalog of sensational novels, revealing its Mexican American perspective covertly. I think of Chesnutt's portrait in those Houghton Mifflin fliers, with its Mona Lisa smile. His own body and image challenged the notion of the color line, and this same photograph would invoke different meanings in advertisements for *The Conjure Woman* and *The Wife of His Youth*. Or I think of Mr. Dooley speaking as Admiral Dewey, hoping that U.S.

citizens are "injyin" the peace that comes when a nation's enemies are shattered to pieces. It is an extraordinary critique of U.S. empire—from the genocide of indigenous people to the Spanish-American War—accomplished through a dialect that blurs the boundaries of the written and spoken word. Regarding *The Souls of Black Folk,* my focus on publication indicates the extent to which it was tailored to a predominantly white audience. These efforts made *Souls* especially appealing, even as it remained openly resistant. Du Bois, more than any of the authors I examine, achieved a popular resistance in his writing. Similarly, *Mrs. Spring Fragrance* seems to respond to the circumstances of its own publication. It comments on the role of the Chinese American author, particularly when this author addresses benevolent white readers. Taken together, these examples point not only toward historical modes of reading but also toward the ways a literary text might circumvent such readings. While my project has often focused on the commercial literary marketplace, it is my hope that this interest can enliven the text itself. Indeed, these social histories take part in the meaning making of literature.

Another point that bears emphasis is the emergent nature of this writing at the turn of the century. Needless to say, these were not the first authors of color to publish literature in the United States. They were, however, the first to have access to commercial literary publication as a means to address a national audience. As such, they created a form of antiracist literature that was directed at white readers, challenging this audience to reimagine its own racial identity. For Ruiz de Burton, white womanhood and domestic sentiment were defined by a faith in manifest destiny; for Chesnutt, whiteness was the blank book of *Procrustes,* valuable but empty; for Finley Peter Dunne, the Anglo-Saxon was a child that had forgotten its parents; for Du Bois, the ears of a guilty audience should tingle with truth; for Sui Sin Far, a sympathetic white woman could very well be a story's antagonist. Based on these challenges to the white reader, I have come to see these authors as constituting a sort of multiethnic avant-garde. The writers I examine developed metatextual strategies to reflect on the production of racial discourse itself. They sought literary techniques that would not only attract a white audience but would also pressure this audience to question its own beliefs. They confronted white readers in an effort to shift the onus of racial inequality back across the color line.

Chesnutt describes this dynamic explicitly in "The Future American," a series of three essays published in the *Boston Evening Transcript* in the summer of 1900. As indicated by its title, the series makes predictions regarding U.S. race relations in the twentieth century. It predicts gradual ethnic admixture, describing "a future ethnic type" that shall inhabit the "northern hemisphere of the western continent."[2] Throughout the series, Chesnutt's writing moves between speculative predictions, anthropological science, census data, legal cases, and anecdotes of ethnic hybridity. As with so much of his work, Chesnutt confronts fears of miscegenation, criticizing an Anglo-European definition of American identity. At one point, in the third article of the series, Chesnutt discusses how racial progress is already underway: "The outbreaks of race prejudice in recent years are the surest evidence of the Negro's progress. No effort is required to keep down a race which manifests no desire nor ability to rise; but with each new forward movement of the colored race it is brought into conflict with the whites at some fresh point, which evokes a new manifestation of prejudice until custom has adjusted things to the new condition."[3] This passage, it seems to me, predicts the more confrontational approach Chesnutt would take in *The Marrow of Tradition.* He would press on the "forward movement of the colored race" in order to bring it into conflict with whites. While this work might encounter a prejudiced response, it would also create a "fresh point" of pressure. Although Chesnutt's writing should not be reduced to political propaganda, it was part of this antiracist movement. Indeed, turn-of-the-century authors of color sought to create a form of writing that was at once literary, antiracist, and meant for an expansive national audience. If the quality of this literature was not fully recognized by contemporary readers, perhaps it could create new forms of conflict and have a more lasting influence on future Americans.

Sui Sin Far took solace in such a conception of historical time and futurity. She hoped her work would have an effect in the long term and articulated this sense of posterity. In an essay for the *Boston Globe,* for example, Far describes how she was taught at a young age that "the true fathers and mothers of the world were those who battled through great trials and hardships to leave to future generations noble and inspiring truths."[4] Here, Sui Sin Far replaces a notion of sexually reproductive futurity with a sense of *textually* reproductive futurity. Without marrying or having children, she might still become a true mother of the world and a witness to future generations.[5] Sui Sin Far expressed similar ideas about futurity in her biographical essay "Leaves from the Mental Portfolio of an Eurasian." In a passage that bears striking similarities to Chesnutt's "The Future American," she notes, "I believe some day a great part of the world will be Eurasian. I cheer myself with the thought that I am but a pioneer. A pioneer should glory in suffering."[6] Here, Sui Sin Far predicts a globalized interracial future. She views the racist challenges in her own personal life as an aspect of trail blazing.

In her 2006 book *Through Other Continents,* Wai Chee Dimock offers a similar view of American literature across "deep time." Dimock reconceptualizes the American literary canon by tracing references and allusions around the globe and across the history of world literature. As Dimock puts it, "Literature is the home of nonstandard space and time."[7] The writers I examine, like many writers, thought of their work in this way; they hoped to survive the culture industries as literature. Du Bois told his readers, "I sit with Shakespeare and he winces not."[8] Alienated from full citizenship in the United States, he is nevertheless at home alongside the world's greatest authors. Indeed, as I have tried to show, *The Souls of Black Folk* is profoundly invested in this dual sense of literary time. From the outset, it calls on a contemporary "Gentle Reader," asking to be "read with patience." Du Bois recognized this reader as a gatekeeper to literary status, and so he proceeds with caution. By the conclusion, however, Du Bois more explicitly describes his ambitions in what Dimock would call deep time. He directs the afterthought at "God the Reader," in hopes that "these crooked marks on a fragile leaf be not indeed The End." *The Souls of Black Folk* thus progresses from the contemporary literary marketplace toward righteous judgment and unknown futurity.

My own project has explored how U.S. writers of color sought to achieve such recognition through a predominantly white publishing industry. Even as they sought status among canonical works of literature, these authors interacted with industrial print manufacturers and were deeply engaged with contemporary racial ideologies and with popular culture. I have returned to this era of initial publication to consider how the literary text was historically produced, distributed, and received. In doing so, I have considered how racist attitudes—that dominated the literary marketplace—repeatedly denied the subversive meanings of these texts. At the same time, however, the project also elaborates on an emergent literary critique of white supremacism. It restores the work accomplished by these texts *in being rejected* within the realm of commercial literary culture. In this way, I hope my book historicizes not only the patterns of white supremacism within the literary marketplace at the turn of the century but also one process by which a dominant culture might be changed.

NOTES

INTRODUCTION

1. Zitkala-Ša, "Impressions of an Indian Childhood," *Atlantic Monthly* (January 1900): 37–47; "The School Days of an Indian Girl," *Atlantic Monthly* (February 1900): 185–94; "An Indian Teacher among Indians," *Atlantic Monthly* (March 1900): 381–87.
2. Dexter Fisher, foreword to *American Indian Stories* (Lincoln: University of Nebraska Press, 1985), vi.
3. William B. Parker to Zitkala-Ša, September 20, 1899, Houghton Mifflin Company, MS Am 2030 (207), Houghton Library, Harvard University (hereafter Houghton Mifflin Records).
4. Ruth Spack, "Dis/engagement: Zitkala-Ša's Letters to Carlos Montezuma, 1901–1902," *MELUS* 26, no. 1 (2001): 172–204, quote on 187.
5. Bliss Perry to Zitkala-Ša, October 4, 1899, Houghton Mifflin Records.
6. Barbara Chiarello has discussed how these essays contrast with stereotypical depictions of Native Americans in Mary Johnston's *To Have and To Hold*, a hugely popular romance novel that was serialized in the *Atlantic Monthly* alongside Zitkala-Ša. Barbara Chiarello, "Deflective Missives: Zitkala-Ša's Resistance and its (Un)Containment," *Studies in American Indian Literatures* 17, no. 3 (2005): 1–26.
7. Richard H. Brodhead, *Cultures of Letters: Scenes of Reading and Writing in Nineteenth-Century America* (Chicago: University of Chicago Press, 1993), 121.
8. Gavin Jones, *Strange Talk: The Politics of Dialect Literature in Gilded Age America* (Berkeley: University of California Press, 1999), 8–12.
9. Elizabeth Ammons and Annette White-Parks, eds., *Tricksterism in Turn-of-the-Century American Literature* (Hanover, NH: University Press of New England, 1994); Henry B. Wonham, *Playing the Races: Ethnic Caricature and American Literary Realism* (New York: Oxford University Press, 2004).
10. Wonham, *Playing the Races*, 31.
11. Bret Harte, "Plain Language from Truthful James," *Overland Monthly* (September 1870): 287–88.
12. Hsuan L. Hsu, ed., *Mrs. Spring Fragrance* (Ontario: Broadview, 2011), 239.
13. As its name suggests, Amy Kaplan's *The Anarchy of Empire in the Making of U.S.*

Culture describes an ambiguous and "unstable paradox at the heart of U.S. imperial culture" (Cambridge: Harvard University Press, 2002), 3. Borrowing a phrase from Teddy Roosevelt for his title, Matthew Frye Jacobson makes a comparable argument regarding the ambiguities of empire: *Barbarian Virtues: The United States Encounters Foreign People at Home and Abroad, 1876–1917* (New York: Hill and Wang, 2001), 4–5.

14. Robert Darnton, "What Is the History of Books?" *Daedalus* 111, no. 3 (1982): 65–83.

15. Here I am drawing on the language of Michael Warner's *Publics and Counterpublics* (New York: Zone Books, 2002).

16. George Hutchinson and John K. Young, eds., *Publishing Blackness: Textual Constructions of Race Since 1850* (Ann Arbor: University of Michigan Press, 2013), 2.

17. On text technologies, see N. Katherine Hayles and Jessica Pressman, eds., *Comparative Textual Media: Transforming the Humanities in the Post-Print Era* (Minneapolis: University of Minnesota Press, 2013); Lisa Gitelman and Geoffrey B. Pingree, eds., *New Media, 1740–1915* (Cambridge, MA: MIT Press, 2003); Matthew G. Kirschenbaum, *Track Changes: A Literary History of Word Processing* (Cambridge, MA: Belknap Press of Harvard University Press, 2016).

18. The foundational bibliographical writing of both Fredson Bowers and W. W. Greg emphasized the role of authorial intentions in editorial decision making.

19. See Jerome McGann, *A Critique of Modern Textual Criticism* (Charlottesville: University of Virginia Press, 1983); Peter L. Shillingsburg, *Resisting Texts: Authority and Submission in Constructions of Meaning* (Ann Arbor: University of Michigan Press, 1998); Paul Bryant, *The Fluid Text: A Theory of Revision and Editing for Book and Screen* (Ann Arbor: University of Michigan Press, 2002).

20. John Sekora, "Black Message/White Envelope: Genre, Authenticity, and Authority in the Antebellum Slave Narrative," *Callaloo* 10, no. 3 (1987): 482–515.

21. With the term "threshold," I am drawing on Gérard Genette, *Paratexts: Thresholds of Interpretation,* trans. Jane E. Lewin (Cambridge: Cambridge University Press, 1997).

22. On American ethnic print cultures, see Lara Langer Cohen and Jordan Alexander Stein, eds., introduction to *Early African American Print Culture* (Philadelphia: University of Pennsylvania Press, 2012), 1–16; Raúl Coronado, *A World Not to Come: A History of Latino Writing and Print Culture* (Cambridge, MA: Harvard University Press, 2013); Cécile Cottenet, ed., *Race, Ethnicity, and Publishing in America* (New York: Palgrave Macmillan, 2014); Frances Smith Foster, "A Narrative of the Interesting Origins and (Somewhat) Surprising Developments of African-American Print Culture," *American Literary History* 17, no. 4 (2005): 714–40; Elizabeth McHenry, *Forgotten Readers: Recovering the Lost History of African American Literary Societies* (Durham: Duke University Press, 2002); Joycelyn Moody and Howard Rambsy II, "Guest Editors' Introduction: African American Print Cultures," *MELUS* 40, no. 3 (Fall 2015): 1–11; Philip H. Round, *Removable Type: Histories of the Book in Indian Country, 1663–1880* (Chapel Hill: University of North Carolina Press, 2010).

23. Johanna Drucker, "Distributed and Conditional Documents: Conceptualizing

Bibliographical Alterities," *MATLIT: Materialities of Literature* 2, no. 1 (2014): 11–29.

24. This is sometimes described as the "sociology of texts." D. F. McKenzie, *Bibliography and the Sociology of Texts* (Cambridge: Cambridge University Press, 1999), 12–16.
25. María Amparo Ruiz de Burton, *Who Would Have Thought It?* (Philadelphia: J. B. Lippincott, 1872).
26. Charles W. Chesnutt, *The Conjure Woman,* large-paper ed. (Boston: Houghton Mifflin, 1899), 84HM-38, Houghton Library, Harvard University.
27. Charles W. Chesnutt, "Baxter's Procrustes," *Atlantic Monthly* (June 1904): 823–29.
28. As described in chapter 4, the editor of *The Souls of Black Folk,* Francis G. Browne, has repeatedly been mistaken for his father, Francis F. Browne, editor of *The Dial.*
29. These early books of Jewish American and Asian American fiction include Emma Wolf, *Other Things Being Equal* (Chicago: A. C. McClurg & Co., 1892), and Sui Sin Far, *Mrs. Spring Fragrance* (Chicago: A. C. McClurg & Co., 1913).
30. Rosaura Sánchez and Beatrice Pita, "María Amparo Ruiz de Burton and the Power of Her Pen," in *Latina Legacies: Identity, Biography, and Community*, ed. Vicki L. Ruiz and Virginia Sánchez Korrol (New York: Oxford University Press, 2005), 72–83.
31. Charles W. Chesnutt, "Remarks of Charles Waddell Chesnutt, of Cleveland, in Accepting the Spingarn Medal at Los Angeles," in *Essays and Speeches*, ed. Joseph R. McElrath, Jr., Robert C. Leitz III, and Jesse S. Crisler (Stanford: Stanford University Press, 1999), 510–15, quote on 514.
32. For more on how nineteenth-century Irish Americans were labeled as "colored" and yet also granted rights that were denied to African Americans, see Noel Ignatiev, *How the Irish Became White* (New York: Routledge, 1995).
33. Annette White-Parks, *Sui Sin Far/Edith Maude Eaton: A Literary Biography* (Urbana: University of Illinois Press, 1995).
34. Susan Rose Dominguez, "Zitkala-Ša: The Representative Indian," in *American Indian Stories* (Lincoln: University of Nebraska Press, 2003), v–xxv.
35. Sandra Gunning, *Race, Rape, and Lynching: The Red Record of American Literature, 1890–1912* (Cambridge: Oxford University Press, 1996), 4–8; Jackson Lears, *Rebirth of a Nation: The Making of Modern America, 1877–1920* (New York: Harper Perennial, 2009), 92–110.
36. Joy Porter, "Historical and Cultural Contexts to Native American Literature," in *The Cambridge Companion to Native American Literature*, ed. Joy Porter and Kenneth M. Roemer (Cambridge: Cambridge University Press, 2005).
37. Erika Lee, *At America's Gates: Chinese Immigration during the Exclusion Era, 1882–1943* (Chapel Hill: University of North Carolina Press, 2003), 9–11.
38. "General & Publication Ledger No. 5, Special No. 1," vol. 71, J. B. Lippincott Company Archives, pp. 466, Collection 3104, Historical Society of Pennsylvania.
39. Charles Fanning, *Finley Peter Dunne and Mr. Dooley: The Chicago Years* (Lexington: University of Kentucky Press, 1978), 4–5; Emery Ellis, *Mr. Dooley's America: A Life of Finley Peter Dunne* (New York: Knopf, 1941), 9–12.

40. White-Parks, *Sui Sin Far*, xvi.
41. William L. Andrews, *The Literary Career of Charles W. Chesnutt* (Baton Rouge: Louisiana State University Press, 1980), 3.
42. "Who Would Have Thought It?: A Native Californian Authoress—A Literary Incognito Lost in an Interview—A New Sensation for the Public," *Daily Alta California* (San Francisco), September 15, 1872.
43. *Holiday Bulletin 1899* (Boston: Houghton Mifflin, 1899), 18, call no. 2003–197, box 7, Houghton Library, Harvard University.
44. Elizabeth Hutchinson, *The Indian Craze: Primitivism, Modernism, and Transculturation in American Art, 1890–1915* (Durham: Duke University Press, 2009).
45. W. E. B. Du Bois, *The Souls of Black Folk* (Millwood, NY: Kraus-Thomson, 1973), 13.
46. Charles W. Chesnutt, *The Journals of Charles W. Chesnutt*, ed. Richard H. Brodhead (Durham: Duke University Press, 1993), 139–40.
47. James P. Danky, "Reading, Writing, and Resisting: African American Print Culture," in *A History of the Book in America*, vol. 4, *Print in Motion: The Expansion of Publishing and Reading in the United States, 1880–1940*, ed. Carl F. Kaestle and Janice A. Radway (Chapel Hill: University of North Carolina Press, 2009), 339–58.
48. Ibid., 344.
49. Sally M. Miller, "Distinctive Media: The European Ethnic Press in the United States," in Kaestle and Radway, *History of the Book in America*, 4:299–311.
50. Ibid., 4:301.
51. Ruth Spack, "Zitkala-Ša, The Song of Hiawatha, and the Carlisle Indian School: A Captivity Tale," *Legacy* 25, no. 2 (2008): 211–24, quote on 214.
52. Parker to Zitkala-Ša, *Houghton Mifflin Records*.
53. Ellery Sedgwick, *A History of the "Atlantic Monthly," 1857–1909: Yankee Humanism at High Tide and Ebb* (Amherst: University of Massachusetts Press, 2009), 310.
54. Ibid.
55. Perry to Zitkala-Ša, *Houghton Mifflin Records*.
56. Darnton, "History of Books," 74.
57. Thomas R. Adams and Nicolas Barker, "A New Model for the Study of the Book," in *A Potencie of Life: Books in Society*, ed. Nicolas Barker (London: British Library, 1993), 5–43, relevant portion on 27–30.
58. Nina Baym, *Novels, Readers, and Reviewers: Responses to Fiction in Antebellum America* (Ithaca: Cornell University Press, 1984).
59. Leah Price, "Reading: The State of the Discipline," *Book History* 7 (2004): 303–20.
60. Carlo Ginzburg, *The Cheese and the Worms: The Cosmos of a Sixteenth-Century Miller* (Baltimore: John Hopkins University Press, 1980); Jonathan Rose, *The Intellectual Life of the British Working Class* (New Haven: Yale University Press, 2010).
61. Janice Radway, *Reading the Romance: Women, Patriarchy, and Popular Culture* (Chapel Hill: University of North Carolina Press, 1984).
62. McHenry, *Forgotten Readers*.
63. On whiteness studies, see Ian Haney-Lopez, *White by Law: The Legal Construction of Race* (New York: New York University Press, 2006); Cheryl L. Harris,

"Whiteness as Property, *Harvard Law Review* 106, no. 8 (June 1993): 1707–91; Matthew Frye Jacobson, *Whiteness of a Different Color: European Immigrants and the Alchemy of Race* (Cambridge, MA: Harvard University Press, 1998); Toni Morrison, *Playing in the Dark: Whiteness and the Literary Imagination* (Cambridge, MA: Harvard University Press, 1992); David R. Roediger, *The Wages of Whiteness: Race and the Making of the American Working Class* (New York: Verso, 1991).

64. Ralph Ellison, *Invisible Man* (New York: Vintage, 1995), 3–5.

65. Warner, *Publics and Counterpublics*, 63.

66. William L. Andrews, foreword to *The House Behind the Cedars* (Athens: University of Georgia Press, 1988), xxi.

67. John Lowe, "Newsprint Masks: The Comic Columns of Finley Peter Dunne, Alexander Posey, and Langston Hughes," in *Beyond the Binary: Reconstructing Cultural Identity in a Multicultural Context,* ed. Timothy B. Powell (New Brunswick: Rutgers University Press, 1999), 205–35.

68. John Daniels, review of *The Souls of Black Folk,* by W. E. B. Du Bois, *Alexander's Magazine* (September 15, 1905): 10–11.

69. Edith Maude Eaton, *Becoming Sui Sin Far: Early Fiction, Journalism, and Travel Writing,* ed. Mary Chapman (McGill-Queen's University Press, 2016).

CHAPTER 1: SENSATIONAL JOB

1. *Who Would Have Thought It?* (Philadelphia: J. B. Lippincott & Co., 1872).

2. Klara Bauer, *Must It Be?* (Philadelphia: J. B. Lippincott & Co., 1873); J. C. Heywood, *How Will It End?: A Romance* (Philadelphia: J. B. Lippincott & Co., 1872).

3. The terminology of book "jobbing" was used broadly in the nineteenth century. "Job printing" often described when publishers produced business cards, fliers, and letterhead. Meanwhile book "jobbers" were companies that helped to distribute books printed elsewhere or by other presses. As I describe, Lippincott published full books and novels for a commission, and its records list these publications under the "Job Printing Department."

4. Rosaura Sánchez and Beatrice Pita, "María Amparo Ruiz de Burton and the Power of Her Pen," in *Latina Legacies: Identity, Biography, and Community,* ed. Vicki L. Ruiz and Virginia Sánchez Korrol (New York: Oxford University Press, 2005), 72–83, quote on 73.

5. José F Aranda, Jr., *When We Arrive: A New Literary History of Mexican America* (Tucson: University of Arizona Press, 2003), 93.

6. Sánchez and Pita, "María Amparo Ruiz de Burton," 75.

7. "Recovery Program: Recovering the U.S. Hispanic Literary Heritage," Arte Público Press, 2019, last accessed March 12, 2020, https://artepublicopress.com/recovery-program/.

8. Jesse Alemán, "Citizenship Rights and Colonial Whites: The Cultural Work of María Amparo Ruiz de Burton's Novels," in *Complicating Constructions: Race, Ethnicity, and Hybridity in American Texts,* ed. David S. Goldstein and Audrey B. Thacker (Seattle: University of Washington Press, 2007), 3–30; John Morán González, *The Troubled Union: Expansionist Imperatives in Post-Reconstruction*

American Novels (Columbus: Ohio State University Press, 2010); Amelia María de la Luz Montes and Anne Elizabeth Goldman, eds., *María Amparo Ruiz de Burton: Critical and Pedagogical Perspectives* (Lincoln: University of Nebraska Press, 2004).

9. María Amparo Ruiz de Burton, *Who Would Have Thought It?* (Houston: Arte Público Press, 1995), 19–26.

10. Rosaura Sánchez and Beatrice Pita, introduction to *Who Would Have Thought It?* (Houston: Arte Público Press, 1995), xvi.

11. Ruiz de Burton, *Who Would Have Thought It?*, 78, 269.

12. Ibid., 100.

13. Raúl Coronado, *A World Not to Come: A History of Latino Writing and Print Culture* (Cambridge: Harvard University Press, 2013).

14. Rodrigo Lazo, "Confederates in the Hispanic Attic: The Archive against Itself," *Unsettled States: Nineteenth-Century American Literary Studies*, ed. Dana Luciano and Ivy G. Wilson (New York: New York University Press, 2014), 31–54, quote on 47.

15. José F. Aranda, Jr., "Contradictory Impulses: María Amparo Ruiz de Burton, Resitance Theory, and the Politics of Chicano/a Studies," *American Literature* 70, no. 3 (September 1998): 551–79, quote on 563.

16. The J. B. Lippincott Company Records refer to her as "Mrs. María A. Burton," excluding the Spanish preposition altogether. This may have been a decision made by the company and not Ruiz de Burton. I also recognize that Ruiz de Burton would have chosen to deemphasize her Spanish heritage due to social pressures. Nevertheless, as with all of the authors I consider, I am interested in the ways she strategically adapted her name and authorial persona.

17. Here, I am drawing on the language of the essay collection edited by Rodrigo Lazo and Jesse Alemán, *The Latino Nineteenth Century* (New York: New York University Press, 2016).

18. C. T. Hinckley "A Visit to the Book Bindery of Lippincott, Grambo, and Company," *Godey's Lady's Book* (November 1852): 403–12.

19. Hinckley, "Visit to the Book Bindery," 412.

20. Michael Winship and Matthew Lyons, finding aid for J. B. Lippincott Company Records, Collection 3104, Historical Society of Pennsylvania (hereafter Lippincott Records).

21. *The Publishers' Trade List Annual* (New York: Office of the Publishers Weekly, 1874), ix–xii.

22. J. Stuart Freeman, *Toward a Third Century of Excellence* (Philadelphia: J. B. Lippincott & Co., 1992), 24.

23. Rosaura Sánchez and Beatrice Pita, introduction to *The Squatter and the Don* (Houston: Arte Público Press, 1992), 13.

24. Aranda Jr., *When We Arrive*, 95–97.

25. Allison E. Fagan, *From the Edge: Chicana/o Border Literature and the Politics of Print* (New Brunswick: Rutgers University Press, 2016), 101–12.

26. *The Author and His Audience, with a Chronology of Major Events in the Publishing History of J. B. Lippincott Company* (Philadelphia: Lippincott, 1967).

27. Winship and Lyons, finding aid, Lippincott Records.

28. Oscar Wilde, *The Picture of Dorian Gray: An Annotated, Uncensored Edition*, ed. Nicholas Frankel (Cambridge, MA: Belknap Press, 2011).

29. J. B. Lippincott & Co. to Mrs. M. A. Burton, May 20, 1872, box 1.3, p. 248, Lippincott Records.

30. J. B. Lippincott & Co. to Mrs. M. A. Burton, January 29, 1873, box 1.6, p. 267, Lippincott Records.

31. J. B. Lippincott & Co. to Mrs. M. A. Burton, November 19, 1872, box 1.6, p. 33, Lippincott Records.

32. "Obituary: Samuel L. M. Barlow," *New York Times,* July 11, 1899.

33. María Amparo Ruiz de Burton to S. L. M. Barlow, September 9, 1872, in *Conflicts of Interest: The Letters of María Amparo Ruiz de Burton* (Houston: Arte Público Press, 2001), 433–34.

34. In 1883, Ruiz de Burton's ledger account was transferred to "Publication Dept. Special Ledger [No. 2]," vol. 82, pp. 798–99, Lippincott Records. Information on Ruiz de Burton was also listed in the "Inventory Book" under the date January 31, 1888.

35. One such advertisement for *Who Would Have Thought It?* appears in the back pages of the Lippincott translation of Eugenie Marlitt, *The Second Wife* (Philadelphia: Lippincott, 1874). Similarly, the 1874 *Publishers' Trade List Annual* includes a J. B. Lippincott & Company catalog from September 1874 that advertises Ruiz de Burton's novel on page 35.

36. J. B. Lippincott & Co. to Mrs. María R. Burton, February 24, 1894, box 10.5, p. 171, Lippincott Records.

37. "Publication Dept. Special Ledger [No. 2]," vol. 82, pp. 799, Lippincott Records.

38. J. B. Lippincott & Co. to Mrs. M. A. Burton, November 19, 1872, Box 1.6, p. 33, Lippincott Records.

39. Ibid.

40. Ruiz de Burton, *Who Would Have Thought It?* (1872).

41. *The Uniform Trade List Annual* (New York: Office of the Publishers Weekly, 1873).

42. "Publication Dept. Special Ledger [No. 2]," vol. 82, pp. 234–35, 238–39, 990–91, 996–97, Lippincott Records.

43. Ruiz de Burton, *Who Would Have Thought It?*, 138.

44. Ibid., 92.

45. Ibid., 159.

46. Emily Steinlight, "Why Novels Are Redundant: Sensation Fiction and the Overpopulation of Literature," *ELH* 79, no. 2 (2012): 501–35, quote on 502.

47. Andrew Radford, *Victorian Sensation Fiction* (New York: Palgrave MacMillan, 2009), 3.

48. Michael Denning, *Mechanic Accents: Dime Novels and Working-Class Culture in America* (London: Verso, 1987), 46.

49. Jesse Alemán and Shelley Streeby, introduction to *Empire and the Literature of Sensation: An Anthology of Nineteenth-Century Popular Fiction* (New Brunswick:

Rutgers University Press, 2007), xviii. Also see Shelley Streeby, *American Sensations: Class, Empire, and the Production of Popular Culture* (Berkeley: University of California Press, 2002).

50. Ruiz de Burton, *Who Would Have Thought It?*, 38.

51. Reviews of the novel include "Who Would Have Thought It?" *Lippincott's Magazine* (November 1872): 607; "Literary Notices," *Godey's Lady's Book* (September 1872): 273; "Current Literature," *Literary World* (August 1872): 33–34. Reviews in both *Lippincott's Magazine* and *Godey's* refer to the author as a man.

52. "Who Would Have Thought It?: A Native Californian Authoress—A Literary Incognito Lost in an Interview—A New Sensation for the Public," *Daily Alta California* (San Francisco), September 15, 1872.

53. Eric Gardner, "'The Attempt of Their Sister': Harriet Wilson's *Our Nig* from printers to Readers," *New England Quarterly* 66, no. 2 (June 1993): 226–46.

CHAPTER 2: ACROSS THE COLOR LINE

1. Gérard Genette, *Paratexts: Thresholds of Interpretation* (Cambridge: Cambridge University Press, 1997), 12.

2. Beth A. McCoy, "Race and the (Para)Textual Condition," *PMLA* 121, no. 1 (January 2006): 156–69 quote on 156.

3. John Sekora, "Black Message/White Envelope: Genre, Authenticity, and Authority in the Antebellum Slave Narrative," *Callaloo* 10, no. 3 (1987): 482–515. On author portraiture and the slave narrative, see Lynn A. Casmier-Paz, "Slave Narratives and the Rhetoric of Author Portraiture," *New Literary History* 34, no. 1 (Winter 2003): 91–116; and Augusta Rohrbach, *Truth Stranger Than Fiction: Race, Realism, and the U.S. Literary Marketplace* (New York: Palgrave, 2002), 29–50.

4. In contrast to the example of the slave narrative, Genette writes, "I know of only one case . . . in which the author feels the need to assert in the preface that he is the author of the text, but this case is obviously playful." Genette, *Paratexts*, 184.

5. Leon Jackson, "The Talking Book and the Talking Book Historian: African American Cultures of Print," *Book History* 13 (2010): 251–308, quote on 252.

6. Robert Darnton, "What Is the History of Books?" *Daedalus* 111, no. 3 (1982): 65–83, quote on 68.

7. Jerome J. McGann, *The Textual Condition* (Princeton: Princeton University Press, 1991), 13.

8. William L. Andrews, *The Literary Career of Charles W. Chesnutt* (Baton Rouge, Louisiana State University Press, 1980), 274.

9. Richard H. Brodhead, ed., *The Journals of Charles W. Chesnutt* (Durham: Duke University Press, 1993); Richard H. Brodhead, introduction to *The Conjure Woman and Other Conjure Tales* (Durham: Duke University Press, 1993); Richard H. Brodhead, *Cultures of Letters: Scenes of Reading and Writing in Nineteenth-Century America* (Chicago: University of Chicago Press, 1993), 177–210.

10. In addition to Andrews and Brodhead, see Helen M. Chesnutt, *Charles Waddell Chesnutt: Pioneer of the Color Line* (Chapel Hill: University of North Carolina Press, 1952); Joseph R. McElrath, Jr., "Collaborative Authorship: The Charles W.

Chesnutt-Walter Hines Page Relationship," in *The Professions of Authorship: Essays in Honor of Matthew J. Bruccoli,* ed. Richard Layman and Joel Myerson (Columbia: University of South Carolina Press, 1996), 150–68.

11. Hannah Crafts's *The Bondwoman's Narrative* was not originally printed but rather survived as a manuscript until its recovery and publication in 2002. Harriet Wilson's *Our Nig* was published by Rand, Avery, and Company in 1859. However, the book was neither marketed nor distributed but was only printed for Wilson herself to sell; Eric Gardner, "'The Attempt of Their Sister': Harriet Wilson's *Our Nig* from Printers to Readers," *New England Quarterly* 66, no. 2 (June 1993): 226–46. William Wells Brown's *Clotel* appears to be the first African American novel that was both formally published and distributed. It was produced by a London company in 1853 before being published three times in the United States. The closest comparable texts to Chesnutt's *The House Behind the Cedars* include Frances Harper's *Iola Leroy* (1892), Paul Lawrence Dunbar's *The Uncalled* (1899), Sutton E. Griggs's *Imperium in Imperio* (1899), and Pauline E. Hopkins's *Contending Forces* (1900). As the introduction to the Schomburg edition of *Iola Leroy* notes, the book underwent five printings in its first year and was quite popular; Frances Smith Foster, introduction to *Iola Leroy, or Shadows Uplifted* (New York: Oxford University Press, 1988), xxvii.

12. Charles W. Chesnutt, *"To Be an Author": Letters of Charles W. Chesnutt, 1899–1905,* ed. Joseph R. McElrath, Jr., and Robert C. Leitz III (Princeton: Princeton University Press, 1997), 139–40.

13. Chesnutt, *To Be an Author,* 133, 137.

14. Cécile Cottenet, ed., *Race, Ethnicity, and Publishing in America* (New York: Palgrave Macmillan, 2014), 9.

15. Here, I am drawing on Kenneth Warren's claims regarding the periodization of African American literature in *What Was African American Literature?* (Cambridge: Harvard University Press, 2011), 1–6. Warren argues that African American literature, understood as a coherent body of imaginative writing, did not emerge until the late nineteenth century. This question of periodization is further explored in Lara Langer Cohen and Jordan Stein's introduction to *Early African American Print Culture* (Philadelphia: University of Pennsylvania Press, 2014), 4–6. Cohen and Stein similarly argue that African American writing from the late nineteenth century may still be considered "early."

16. Among other correspondence, Langston Hughes sent Helen a signed print of *The Negro Speaks of Rivers* in 1941 and a handmade Christmas card in 1942. Charles W. Chesnutt Collection, box 15, folder 5, Special Collections, John Hope and Aurelia E. Franklin Library, Fisk University.

17. Dean McWilliams, introduction to *The Quarry* by Charles Chesnutt (Princeton: Princeton University Press, 1999), xii–xvii.

18. Chesnutt, *Journals,* 154. The passage's exclamation "To be an Author!" now serves as the title for the edited collection of Chesnutt's early letters.

19. Chesnutt, *Journals,* 139.

20. Andrews, *Charles W. Chesnutt,* 13.

21. Sylvia Lyons Render tracks this development in her edition of *The Short Fiction of Charles W. Chesnutt* (Washington, D.C.: Howard University Press, 1981);

Henry B. Wonham also focuses on Chesnutt's early career in *Playing the Races: Ethnic Caricature and American Literary Realism* (New York: Oxford University Press, 2004), 152–72.

22. Frank Luther Mott, *A History of American Magazines*, vol. 3, *1865–1885* (Cambridge, MA: Harvard University Press, 1938), 494.

23. Chesnutt, *To Be an Author*, 75.

24. Ibid., 75.

25. Ibid., 44.

26. Brodhead, "Introduction," 16.

27. Heather Tirado Gilligan, "Reading, Race, and Charles Chesnutt's 'Uncle Julius' Tales," *ELH* 74, no. 1 (2007): 195–215, quote on 203.

28. In his letters, Chesnutt insisted that he was compelled to write his conjure tales in opposition to the plantation tradition of Harris and Page; Chesnutt, *To Be An Author*, 167–68. Likewise, in his essay "Post-Bellum — Pre-Harlem," Chesnutt wrote, "The name of the storyteller, 'Uncle' Julius, and the locale of the stories, as well as the cover design were suggestive of Mr. Harris's Uncle Remus, but the tales were entirely different." *Essays and Speeches*, ed. Joseph R. McElrath, Jr., Robert C. Leitz III, and Jesse S. Crisler (Stanford: Stanford University Press, 1999), 544.

29. Brodhead, "Introduction," 5.

30. Bill Hardwig, "Who Owns the Whip?: Chesnutt, Tourgée, and Reconstruction Justice," *African American Review* 36, no. 1 (2002): 5–20; Paul Outka, *Race and Nature from Transcendentalism to the Harlem Renaissance* (New York: Palgrave MacMillan, 2008), 103–26; John Levi Barnard, "Ancient History, American Time: Chesnutt's Outsider Classicism and the Present Past," *PMLA* 129, no. 1 (January 2014): 71–86.

31. Eric J. Sundquist, *To Wake the Nations: Race in the Making of American Literature* (Cambridge, MA: Harvard University Press, 1993), 264.

32. Kenneth M. Price, "Charles Chesnutt, the *Atlantic Monthly*, and the Intersection of African-American and Elite Culture," in *Periodical Literature in Nineteenth-Century America* (Charlottesville: University of Virginia Press, 1995).

33. David D. Britt, "Chesnutt's Conjure Tales: What You See Is What You Get," *CLA Journal* 15, no. 3 (March 1972): 269–83, quote on 271. For another interpretation of Chesnutt and the plantation tradition, see Tynes Cowan, "Charles Waddell Chesnutt and Joel Chandler Harris: An Anxiety of Influence," *Resources for American Literary Study* 25, no. 2 (1999): 232–53.

34. Chesnutt, *Journals*, 140.

35. Houston A. Baker, Jr., *Modernism and the Harlem Renaissance* (Chicago: University of Chicago Press, 1987), 41.

36. Jean Lee Cole, "Coloring Books: The Forms of Turn-of-the-Century American Literature," *Papers of the Bibliographical Society of America* 97, no. 4 (December 2003): 461–93, quote on 470.

37. *Uncle Remus* itself sold between 1,246 and 2,050 copies per year from 1898 to 1907. "Record of Book Sales, 1891–1907," Houghton Mifflin Company, MS Am 2030: I (32). Houghton Library, Harvard University (hereafter Houghton Mifflin Records).

38. "Book Showings, O-R," Houghton Mifflin Records, 55–58.

39. Charles B. Gullans and John J. Espey, *The Decorative Designers, 1895–1932: An Essay* (Los Angeles: University of California Library, 1970), 1.

40. Wonham, *Playing the Races,* 39.

41. Wolfgang Iser, *The Implied Reader: Patterns of Communication in Prose Fiction from Bunyan to Beckett* (Baltimore: Johns Hopkins University Press, 1974), xii.

42. Gullans and Espey, *Decorative Designers,* 4.

43. Chesnutt, *To Be an Author,* 75.

44. *A Catalog of Authors Whose Works Are Published by Houghton, Mifflin and Company* (Cambridge, MA: Houghton Mifflin, 1901), 2003–197, box 7, Houghton Library, Harvard University.

45. "History of Fayetteville State University," Charles W. Chesnutt Library Archives and Special Collections, Fayetteville State University, 2019, last accessed March 12, 2020, http://library.uncfsu.edu/archives/fsu-history.

46. The Charles Chesnutt Digital Archive, developed by Stephanie Browner and now edited in collaboration with Kenneth M. Price and Matt Cohen, has an excellent collection of reviews of Chesnutt's work. For portions of this essay focused on reception, I have used the digital archive as a reference. Whenever possible, I have verified the primary source and cited it directly. Reviews accessed only through the digital archive are noted.

47. "New Books," review of *The Conjure Woman, Philadelphia Times,* April 2, 1899, 24, Charles Chesnutt Digital Archive.

48. "More Fiction," *Nation* (June 1, 1899): 421.

49. "Recent Works of Fiction," *Springfield Sunday Republican,* April 30, 1899, 15.

50. "The Conjure Woman," *New York Times,* April 15, 1899, RBA246, New York Times Digital Archive.

51. Promotional flier, *The Conjure Woman,* Houghton Mifflin Records, 244.

52. Chesnutt, *To Be an Author,* 133.

53. "Chronicle and Comment," *Bookman* (August 1898): 449–68.

54. Chesnutt, *To Be an Author,* 109–10.

55. Frank Luther Mott, *A History of American Magazines,* vol. 4, *1885–1905* (Cambridge, MA: Harvard University Press, 1957), 436.

56. "Literary Items," *Boston Evening Transcript,* November 11, 1899, 20.

57. Charles W. Chesnutt, *The Wife of His Youth and Other Stories of the Color Line* (Ann Arbor: University of Michigan Press, 1968), 8.

58. Chesnutt, *The Wife of His Youth,* 10.

59. Chesnutt, *The Wife of His Youth,* 23.

60. Lorne Fienberg, "Charles W. Chesnutt's *The Wife of His Youth:* The Unveiling of the Black Storyteller," *American Transcendental Quarterly* 4, no. 3 (1990): 219–37, quote on 219.

61. Anne Fleischmann, "Neither Fish, Flesh, nor Fowl: Race and Region in the Writings of Charles W. Chesnutt," *African American Review* 34, no. 3 (2000): 461–73, quote on 463.

62. W. D. Howells, "Mr. Charles W. Chesnutt's Stories," *Atlantic Monthly* (May 1900): 699–701.

63. William Andrews, "William Dean Howells and Charles W. Chesnutt: Criticism

and Race Fiction in the Age of Booker T. Washington," *American Literature* 48, no. 3 (1976): 327–39; Joseph R. McElrath, Jr., "W. D. Howells and Race: Charles W. Chesnutt's Disappointment of the Dean," *Nineteenth-Century Literature* 51, no. 4 (1997): 474–99.

64. Howells, "Mr. Charles W. Chesnutt's Stories," 699, 701.

65. "A Year's Best Books," *New York Times Review of Books*, June 30, 1900, 442–43.

66. Howells, "Mr. Charles W. Chesnutt's Stories," 699.

67. Promotional leaflet, *The Wife of His Youth*, Houghton Mifflin Records, 244.

68. The cover design for *The Wife of His Youth* featured an abstract interwoven line, reiterating the book's "color line" theme; Cole, "Coloring Books," 484–85.

69. John K. Young, *Black Writers, White Publishers: Marketplace Politics in Twentieth-Century African American Literature* (Jackson: University Press of Mississippi, 2006), 4.

70. Rohrbach, *Truth Stranger Than Fiction*, 31.

71. Chesnutt, *To Be an Author*, 115.

72. Ibid.

73. Hamilton Wright Mabie, "Two Novelists," *Outlook* (February 24, 1900): 440–41.

74. Howells, "Mr. Charles W. Chesnutt's Stories," 701.

75. Chesnutt, *To Be an Author*, 152.

76. Ibid., 162.

77. On racial masquerade in *The Marrow of Tradition*, see Sundquist, *To Wake the Nations*, 271–454. On racial violence, Andrew Hebard, "Romance and Riot: Charles Chesnutt, the Romantic South, and the Conventions of Extralegal Violence," *African American Review* 44, no. 3 (2011): 471–87; Bryan Wagner, "Charles Chesnutt and the Epistemology of Racial Violence," *American Literature* 73, no. 2 (2001): 311–37. On the novel's discourse of whiteness, Stephen P. Knadler, "Untragic Mulatto: Charles Chesnutt and the Discourse of Whiteness," *American Literary History* 8, no. 3 (1996): 426–48.

78. Chesnutt, "Chesnutt's Own View of His New Story," 169.

79. Chesnutt, *To Be an Author*, 162.

80. Ibid., 165.

81. "Book Showings, O-R," Houghton Mifflin Records, 55–58.

82. Promotional leaflet, *The Marrow of Tradition*, Houghton Mifflin Records, 245, p. 72.

83. As Ellen Gruber Garvey points out, "Until the 1900s and later, class . . . magazines [such as the *Atlantic Monthly*] genteely segregated ads from what was known as reading matter, placing the ads in separate sections in the front and back of the magazines, thus making it easy to remove them." Ellen Gruber Garvey, "What Happened to the Ads in Turn-of-the-Century Bound Magazines, and Why," *Serials Librarian* 37, no. 1 (1999): 83–91. Partly because of this separation, advertisements from turn-of-the-century magazines are often missing from library collections. The *Atlantic Monthly Advertiser* discussed here is the copy scanned to Hathi Trust from the University of Michigan.

84. *The Marrow of Tradition*, advertisements, *Atlantic Monthly Advertiser* (December 1901): 56, 86.

85. George Hutchinson, "Representing African American Literature: Or, Tradition

against the Individual Talent," in *Publishing Blackness: Textual Constructions of Race Since 1850* (Ann Arbor: University of Michigan Press, 2013), 39–66, quote on 40.

86. *The Marrow of Tradition*, advertisement, *Atlantic Monthly Advertiser* (December 1901): 86.

87. "'The Marrow of Tradition': Race Problems in the South," *Argonaut,* May 5, 1902, 301, Charles Chesnutt Digital Archive.

88. "A Short Guide to New Books," *World's Work* (February 1902): 1786–90.

89. "Books & Writers," *Outlook* (November 16, 1901): 681–721.

90. Chesnutt, *To Be an Author,* 139.

91. "Literature," *Independent,* March 1902, 582.

92. Chesnutt, *To Be an Author,* 174.

93. W. D. Howells, "A Psychological Counter-Current in Recent Fiction," *North American Review* (December 1901): 872–88, quote on 882.

94. Promotional leaflet, *The House Behind the Cedars,* Houghton Mifflin Records, 244.

95. Chesnutt, *To Be an Author,* 171.

96. "Book Showings, O-R," Houghton Mifflin Records, 55–58.

97. "Record of Book Sales, 1891–1907," Houghton Mifflin Records.

98. "Book Showings, O-R," Houghton Mifflin Records.

99. William Andrews, introduction to *The House Behind the Cedars* (Athens: University of Georgia Press, 1988), xxi.

100. "Book Showings, O-R," Houghton Mifflin Records.

101. "Record of Book Sales, 1891–1907," Houghton Mifflin Records.

102. Sandra Gunning, *Race, Rape, and Lynching: The Red Record of American Literature, 1890–1912* (Oxford: Oxford University Press, 1996), 30.

103. Claire Parfait, *The Publishing History of Uncle Tom's Cabin, 1852–2002* (Abingdon, UK: Ashgate Publishing Group, 2008), 158.

104. Rayford Whittingham Logan, *The Negro in American Life and Thought: The Nadir, 1877–1901* (New York: Dial Press, 1954).

105. Charles W. Chesnutt, "Baxter's Procrustes," *The Short Fiction of Charles W. Chesnutt,* ed. Sylvia Lyons Render (Washington, D.C.: Howard University Press, 1981), 416.

106. Ibid., 422.

107. Ibid., 416.

108. McGann, *Textual Condition,* 13.

109. Chesnutt, "Baxter's Procrustes," 420.

110. William Andrews, "'Baxter's Procrustes': Some More Light on Biographical Connection," *Black American Literature Forum* 11, no. 3 (Autumn 1977): 75–78, quote on 76.

111. Chesnutt, "Baxter's Procrustes," 415.

112. Andrews, "Baxter's Procrustes," 76.

113. Robert Hemenway, "Baxter's Procrustes": Irony and Protest," *CLA Journal* 18, no. 2 (1974): 172–85, quote on 174.

114. Hemenway, "Baxter's Procrustes," 173.

115. Chesnutt, "Post-Bellum—Pre-Harlem," 544.

116.Chesnutt's story also borrows language from Houghton Mifflin's advertisements for these limited editions from the Riverside Press. In a 1901 *Holiday Bulletin*, for example, Houghton Mifflin advertises limited editions of "Dr. Brown's edition of the *Rubáiyát* and . . . Thoreau's *Essay of Friendship*." Houghton, Mifflin and Company, *Holiday Bulletin* (Cambridge, MA: Riverside Press, 1901), xli, 2003–197, box 7, Houghton Library, Harvard University. In Chesnutt's story, the Bodleian Club similarly publishes a translation of the *Rubáiyát* and an "essay . . . by Thoreau." Thus within the story itself, Chesnutt makes explicit connections between the Bodleian Club and Houghton's Riverside Press.

117.Houghton Mifflin Records, "Book Showings, O-R."

118.I have examined other copies of the book that have been opened, including one at the Library Company of Philadelphia. Nevertheless, it is clear that the opening was done by hand, and the book itself was produced and distributed with the pages unopened, as a sort of collector's edition for members of the Rowfant Club.

119.Chesnutt, "Baxter's Procrustes," 418.

120.Charles W. Chesnutt, *The House Behind the Cedars*, 161–63.

121.Charles W. Chesnutt, *The Quarry* (Princeton: Princeton University Press, 1999), 240–54.

122.Chesnutt, "Baxter's Procrustes," 416.

123.Charles W. Chesnutt, *The Marrow of Tradition* (New York: W. W. Norton, 2012), 40–41.

124.Cheryl L. Harris, "Whiteness as Property," *Harvard Law Review* 106, no. 8 (June 1993): 1707–91.

125.Chesnutt, "Baxter's Procrustes," 415.

126.Ibid., 417.

127.Ibid., 420.

128.Ibid., 422.

129.Ibid., 421–22.

CHAPTER 3: SATIRE OF WHITENESS

1. Matthew Frye Jacobson, *Whiteness of a Different Color: European Immigrants and the Alchemy of Race* (Cambridge, MA: Harvard University Press, 1998), 7–8.

2. Elmer Ellis, *Mr. Dooley's America: A Life of Finley Peter Dunne* (New York: Knopf, 1941), 120.

3. Ibid., 133.

4. This scene is described in Edith Wharton, *A Backward Glance* (New York: D. Appleton, 1934), 178.

5. For more on Dunne's comic influence, see John Lowe, "Newsprint Masks: The Comic Columns of Finley Peter Dunne, Alexander Posey, and Langston Hughes," in *Beyond the Binary: Reconstructing Cultural Identity in a Multicultural Context*, ed. Timothy B. Powell (New Brunswick: Rutgers University Press, 1999), 205–35.

6. Lawrence J. McCaffrey et al., eds., *The Irish in Chicago* (Urbana: University of Illinois Press, 1987), 1–3.

7. David Noel Doyle, "The Irish as Urban Pioneers in the United States, 1850–1870," *Journal of American Ethnic History* 10, no. 1–2 (1990): 36–59. James Barrett and David R. Roediger, "The Irish and the 'Americanization' of the 'New Immigrants' in the Streets and in the Churches of the Urban United States, 1900–1930," *Journal of American Ethnic History* 24, no. 4 (2005): 3–33.

8. Noel Ignatiev, *How the Irish Became White* (New York: Routledge, 1995), 34–59.

9. For the "Paddy" stereotype, see Dale T. Knobel, *Paddy and the Republic: Ethnicity and Nationality in Antebellum America* (Middletown: Wesleyan University Press, 1986). For a discussion of representations of the Irish in literature, see Jack Morgan and Luis Renza's introduction to *The Irish Stories of Sarah Orne Jewett* (Carbondale: Southern Illinois University Press, 1996). Notably, the stories by Jewett offer a more complex depiction of Irish American immigrants.

10. Henry Childs Merwin, "The Irish In American Life," *Atlantic Monthly* (March 1896): 289–301, quote on 289.

11. Jacobson, *Whiteness of a Different Color*, 8.

12. "Men New Prominent in the Passing Show," *Idaho Daily Statesman*, February 15, 1907.

13. Ellis, *Mr. Dooley's America*, 56.

14. Ibid., 3–15.

15. Shelley Fisher Fishkin, *Was Huck Black? Mark Twain and African American Voices* (New York: Oxford University Press, 1993).

16. Hugh J. Dawson, "The Ethnicity of Huck Finn—and the Difference It Makes," *American Literary Realism* 30, no. 2 (1998): 1–16, quote on 7.

17. Ignatiev, *Irish*, 3.

18. Thomas Giglielmo, *White on Arrival: Italians, Race, Color, and Power in Chicago, 1890–1945* (New York: Oxford University Press, 2003), 7.

19. Ian Haney-Lopez, *White by Law: The Legal Construction of Race* (New York: NYU Press, 1996).

20. William V. Shannon, *The American Irish* (New York: MacMillan, 1963).

21. Kerby A. Miller, "Urban Immigrants: The Irish in the Cities," *Urban History* 16, no. 4 (1990): 428–41, quote on 436.

22. Timothy Meagher, ed., *The Columbia Guide to Irish American History* (New York: Columbia University Press, 2005), 85.

23. Charles Fanning, *Finley Peter Dunne and Mr. Dooley: The Chicago Years* (Lexington: University of Kentucky Press, 1978), 4.

24. Doyle, "Irish as Urban Pioneers," 40.

25. Fanning, *Finley Peter Dunne*, 4.

26. Ellis, *Mr. Dooley's America*, 5.

27. Biographical information throughout this paragraph is taken from Ellis, *Mr. Dooley's America*, 16–25, 34, 54–65.

28. Fanning, *Finley Peter Dunne*, 29–30.

29. Finley Peter Dunne, *Mr. Dooley at His Best*, ed. Elmer Ellis (New York: C. Scribner's Sons, 1938), xxiii.

30. Reprinted in Ellis, *Mr. Dooley's America*, 85.

31. Kevin J. Hayes, "A Note on the Text," in *Maggie: A Girl of the Streets*, by Stephen Crane (Boston: Bedford/St. Martin, 1999), 34.

32. Reprinted in Ellis, *Mr. Dooley's America*, 86.

33. Fanning, *Finley Peter Dunne*, 176–77.

34. Ellis, *Mr. Dooley's America*, 113.

35. Ibid., 114–16.

36. Ibid., 120.

37. "The Best Selling Books," *Bookman* (December 1899): 408.

38. Prior to Charles Fanning's 1978 book, Dunne's writing received occasional attention. For popular articles, see Philip Dunne, "Mr. Dooley's Friends: Teddy Roosevelt and Mark Twain," *Atlantic Monthly* (September 1963): 77–99; and John V. Kelleher, "Mr. Dooley and the Same Old World," *Atlantic Monthly* (June 1946): 119–25. For scholarship, see Walter Blair, *Horse Sense in American Humor: From Benjamin Franklin to Ogden Nash* (Chicago: University of Chicago Press, 1942), 247–50; Barbara Schaaf, *Mr. Dooley's Chicago* (Garden City, NY: Anchor Press, 1977); Norris W. Yates, "Mr. Dooley of Archer Road," *The American Humorist: Conscience of the Twentieth Century* (Ames: Iowa State University Press, 1964), 85–87.

39. Charles Fanning, *The Exiles of Erin: Nineteenth-Century Irish American Fiction* (Chester Springs, PA: Dufour Editions, 1997), 265.

40. W. D. Howells, "Certain of the Chicago School of Fiction," *North American Review* (May 1903): 734–36.

41. Finley Peter Dunne, "From the Bleachers," *Metropolitan* (January 1912): 14–15.

42. Ibid., 15.

43. Quoted in Ellis, *Mr. Dooley's America*, 64.

44. Ibid., 39, 103.

45. Arthur Power Dudden, "The Record of Political Humor," *American Quarterly* 37, no. 1 (1985): 50–70, quote on 54.

46. John Rees, "An Anatomy of Mr. Dooley's Brogue," *Studies in American Humor* 5, no. 2–3 (1986): 145–57, quote on 149.

47. For another analysis of Dunne's literary dialect, see Clyde Thogmartin, "Mr Dooley's Brogue: The Literary Dialect of Finley Peter Dunne," *Visible Language* 16, no. 2 (1982): 184–98.

48. Quoted in Ellis, *Mr. Dooley's America*, 115.

49. Dunne often emphasized American imperialism in this way. His first book, *Mr. Dooley in Peace and in War*, was divided into sections titled "On War" and "On Peace." In the section "On Peace," Dunne inserts a column titled "On the Indian War," so that American peace encompasses violence against Native Americans.

50. Grace Eckley, *Finley Peter Dunne* (Boston: Twayne, 1981), 148–49.

51. James Joyce, *The Critical Writings of James Joyce*, ed. Ellsworth Mason and Richard Ellman (Ithaca: Cornell University Press, 1989), 246–48.

52. James Joyce, *The Critical Writings of James Joyce*, ed. Ellsworth Mason and Richard Ellmann (New York: Viking Press, 1959).

53. Terry Eagleton, Fredric Jameson, and Edward W. Said, *Nationalism, Colonialism, and Literature* (Minneapolis: University of Minnesota Press, 1990).

54. Michael North, *The Dialect of Modernism: Race, Language, and Twentieth-Century*

Literature (New York: Oxford University Press, 1998), v. For more on blackface minstrelsy, see Eric Lott, *Love and Theft: Blackface Minstrelsy and the American Working Class* (New York: Oxford University Press, 1993); and Michael Rogin, *Blackface, White Noise: Jewish Immigrants in the Hollywood Melting Pot* (Berkeley: University of California Press, 1996).

55. Gavin Jones, *Strange Talk: The Politics of Dialect Literature in Gilded Age America* (Berkeley: University of California Press, 1999), 179.

56. James P. Byrne, "The Genesis of Whiteface in Nineteenth-Century American Popular Culture," *MELUS* 29, no. 3/4 (2004): 133–49, quote on 138.

57. William R. Linneman, "Immigrant Stereotypes: 1800–1900," *Studies in American Humor* 1, no. 1 (1974): 28–39, quote on 29.

58. Byrne, "Genesis of Whiteface," 138.

59. Finley Peter Dunne, *Mr. Dooley in Peace and in War* (Boston: Small, Maynard & Co., 1898), 54.

60. Ibid., 55.

61. Ibid.

62. Homi K. Bhabha, *The Location of Culture* (New York: Routledge, 1994), 122.

63. Amy Kaplan, *The Anarchy of Empire in the Making of U.S. Culture* (Cambridge, MA: Harvard University Press, 2002), 1.

64. For more on the Spanish-American War and U.S. imperialism, see Philip Sheldon Foner, *The Spanish-Cuban-American War and the Birth of American Imperialism, 1895–1902* (New York: Monthly Review Press, 1972).

65. Kaplan, *Anarchy of Empire*, 124.

66. Ibid., 134. For more on black soldiers in Cuba, see Willard B. Gatewood, *"Smoked Yankees" and the Struggle for Empire: Letters from Negro Soldiers, 1898–1902* (Urbana: University of Illinois Press, 1971).

67. Kaplan, *Anarchy of Empire*, 127.

68. Finley Peter Dunne, *Mr. Dooley's Philosophy* (New York: R. H. Russell, 1900), 13.

69. Ibid., 16.

70. Richard Ohmann, *Selling Culture: Magazines, Markets, and Class at the Turn of the Century* (New York: Verso, 1996), 20–25.

71. Richard Ohmann, "Diverging Paths: Books and Magazines in the Transition to Corporate Capitalism," in *A History of the Book in America*, vol. 4, *Print in Motion*, ed. Carl F. Kaestle and Janice A. Radway (Chapel Hill: University of North Carolina Press, 2009), 102–15.

72. Ibid., 103.

73. On the magazine transition to mass culture, see also Ellen Gruber Garvey, *The Adman in the Parlor: Magazines and the Gendering of Consumer Culture, 1880s–1910s* (New York: Oxford University Press, 1996); Christopher P. Wilson, *The Labor of Words: Literary Professionalism in the Progressive Era* (Athens: University of Georgia Press, 1985).

74. Charles Johanningsmeier, *Fiction and the American Literary Marketplace: The Role of Newspaper Syndicates, 1860–1900* (New York: Cambridge University Press, 1997), 31.

75. Johanningsmeier, *Fiction*, 223.

76. Richard L. Kaplan, "From Partisanship to Professionalism: The Transformation of the Daily Press," in Kaestle and Radway, *History of the Book in America,* 4:123.

77. Johanningsmeier, *Fiction,* 107–25.

78. Ohmann, "Diverging Paths," 108.

79. Dunne, *Mr. Dooley in Peace and in War,* x.

80. In an excellent analysis of the columns, John Rees finds clues that Mr. Dooley is surprisingly well-read; John Rees, "A Reading of Mr. Dooley," *Studies in American Humor* 7 (1989): 5–31.

81. On yellow journalism and imperialism, see John Patrick Leary, "America's Other Half: Slum Journalism and the War of 1898," *Journal of Transnational American Studies* 1, no. 1 (2009), https://escholarship.org/uc/item/0v654 385; Michael Robertson, *Stephen Crane, Journalism, and the Making of American Literature* (New York: Columbia, University Press, 1997); John Seelye, *War Games: Richard Harding Davis and the New Imperialism* (Amherst: University of Massachusetts Press, 2003); Nirmal Trivedi, "Staging Unincorporated Power: Richard Harding Davis and the Critique of Imperial News," *Journal of Transnational American Studies* 3, no. 2 (2011), https://escholarship.org/uc/item/0o40jokc; Christopher P. Wilson, "Stephen Crane and the Police," *American Quarterly* 48, no. 2 (1996): 273–315.

82. Joseph W. Campbell, *Yellow Journalism: Puncturing the Myths, Defining the Legacies* (Westport, CT: Praeger, 2001), 8.

83. Leary, "America's Other Half," 2009.

84. Ellis, *Mr. Dooley's America,* 115–16.

85. Ibid., 115.

86. For Dunne's relationship to progressives and muckrakers, see *Mr. Dooley's America,* 201–58; and John M. Harrison, "Finley Peter Dunne and the Progressive Movement," *Journalism Quarterly* 44 (1967): 475–81.

87. "Literary Chat," *Munsey's Magazine* (March 1899): 974–78, quote on 976.

88. "New Publications," *Baltimore Sun,* November 3, 1899, 6.

89. "Books and Periodicals," review of *Mr. Dooley in the Hearts of His Countrymen, Charlotte Daily Observer,* April 22, 1899, 2.

90. "Literary Chat," *Munsey's Magazine,* 975.

91. "Mr. Dooley on Expansion Again," *Literary Digest,* February 11, 1899, 155.

92. H. T. P., "A New Humorist," review of *Mr. Dooley in Peace and in War, Bookman* (February 1899): 574–76.

93. "Mr Dooley Returns," review of *Mr. Dooley on Making a Will and Other Necessary Evils, Outlook,* September 17, 1919, 94–95.

94. John Higham, *Strangers in the Land: Patterns of American Nativism, 1860–1925* (New Brunswick: Rutgers University Press, 2008), 234–64.

95. Thomas L. Masson, *Our American Humorists* (New York: Moffat, Yard and Company, 1922), 119.

CHAPTER 4: AGAINST BENEVOLENT READERS

1. W. E. B. Du Bois, *Dusk of Dawn: An Essay Toward an Autobiography of a Race Concept,* 1940 (Millwood, NY: Kraus-Thomson, 1975), 80.

2. Herbert Aptheker, introduction to *The Souls of Black Folk* (Millwood, NY: Kraus-Thomson, 1973), 5–46, quote on 10.

3. Critics have debated whether it is best to use the name Edith Eaton or Sui Sin Far. Martha Cutter and Hsuan L. Hsu use Sui Sin Far. Mary Chapman has recently made a case for using Edith Eaton. As I discuss later in the chapter, I find it appropriate to alternate between the two names, though I more frequently rely on "Sui Sin Far."

4. Martha Cutter, "Sui Sin Far's Letters to Charles Lummis: Contextualizing Publication Practices for the Asian American Subject at the Turn of the Century," *American Literary Realism* 38, no. 3 (Spring 2006): 259–75, quote on 271.

5. Yu-Fang Cho, "Domesticating the Aliens Within: Sentimental Benevolence in Late Nineteenth-Century California Magazines," *American Quarterly* 61, no. 1 (March 2009): 113–36, quote on 118.

6. A. C. McClurg to W. E. B. Du Bois, April 10, 1903, W. E. B. Du Bois Papers (MS 312), Special Collections and University Archives, University of Massachusetts Amherst Libraries (hereafter Du Bois Papers). The collection has been digitized and is available online.

7. W. E. B. Du Bois, *The Souls of Black Folk,* 2nd ed. (Chicago: A. C. McClurg, 1903).

8. A. C. McClurg & Co., semiannual statement of sales, May 1, 1903, Du Bois Papers.

9. The Norton edition includes a "Note on the Text," indicating that it was reprinted from the first edition but does not mention changes to the second printing. W. E. B. Du Bois, *The Souls of Black Folk,* ed. Henry Louis Gates, Jr., and Terri Hume Oliver (New York: W. W. Norton, 1999), xl–xli. The Oxford edition reproduces the first printing without any bibliographical description or note on the text. W. E. B. Du Bois, *The Souls of Black Folk,* ed. Henry Louis Gates, Jr. (New York: Oxford University Press, 2007).

10. Henry Louis Gates, Jr., "The Black Letters on the Sign: W. E. B. Du Bois and the Canon," *The Souls of Black Folk* (New York, Oxford University Press, 2007), xiii.

11. David Levering Lewis, *W. E. B. Du Bois: Biography of a Race* (New York: Henry Holt, 1993), 291.

12. Manning Marable, *W. E. B. Du Bois: Black Radical Democrat* (Boston: Twayne Publishers, 1986), 47–49; Lewis, *W. E. B. Du Bois,* 265–96.

13. George Bornstein, "W. E. B. Du Bois and the Jews: Ethics, Editing, and *The Souls of Black Folk,*" *Textual Cultures* 1, no. 1 (2006): 64–74.

14. Henry Louis Gates, Jr., and Terri Hume Oliver, "Note on the Text," in *The Souls of Black Folk* (New York: W. W. Norton, 1999), xl–xli.

15. Herbert Aptheker, "Introduction," 38–43.

16. John K. Young, *Black Writers, White Publishers: Marketplace Politics in Twentieth Century African American Print Culture* (Jackson: University Press of Mississippi, 2006), 4.

17. Leon Jackson, "The Talking Book and the Talking Book Historian: African American Cultures of Print," *Book History* 13 (2010): 251–308, quote on 275.

18. Cécile Cottenet, introduction to *Race, Ethnicity, and Publishing in America* (New York: Palgrave Macmillan, 2014), 9.

19. Gérard Genette, *Paratexts: Thresholds of Interpretation*, trans. Jane E. Lewin (New York: Cambridge University Press, 1997).

20. A brief history of the publisher is available in the Newberry Library's online finding aid, A. C. McClurg & Co. Records, processed by Adrian Alexander and Roberta Kovitz, 2008, last accessed March 12, 2020, https://mms.newberry.org /xml/xml_files/McClurg.xml. For the publisher's early history, see Jack Cassius Morris, "The Publishing Activities of S. C. Griggs and Company, 1848–1896; Jansen, McClurg and Company, 1872–1886; and A. C. McClurg and Company, 1886–1900," master's thesis, University of Illinois, Urbana, 1939.

21. "A. C. McClurg," *Publishers Weekly* (February 18, 1893): 322–33.

22. Frederick B. Smith, *A Sketch of the Origin and History of the House of A. C. McClurg & Co.* (Chicago: A. C. McClurg, c.1902), 13.

23. "A. C. McClurg," *Publishers Weekly*, 322–33.

24. A. C. McClurg & Co. Records, The Newberry Library, Chicago (hereafter McClurg Records), folder 515.

25. "In Memorium," funeral Pamphlet for general Alexander C. McClurg, *Military Order of the Loyal Legion of the U.S.*, October 20, 1901, folder 519, McClurg Records.

26. "General Alexander Caldwell McClurg," *Publishers Weekly* (April 20, 1901): 1022–23.

27. "A. C. McClurg," *Publishers Weekly* (February 18, 1893): 322–33.

28. Smith, *History of the House*, 11–12.

29. J. Francis, "Saints and Sinners," *New York Times, Saturday Review of Books and Art*, December 29, 1900, BR7. In his book *Midwest Portraits*, Harry Hansen notes, "The proudest boast of McClurg's has been its 'amen corner' . . . many influential men of the middle west found its rare book section as important a place to visit on a trip to Chicago as the stockyards"; Harry Hansen, *Midwest Portraits* (New York: Harcourt Brace, 1923), 196.

30. "Our Intent," *Dial* (May 1880): 17–18.

31. Smith, *History of the House*, 12.

32. Frank Luther Mott, *A History of American Magazines*, vol. 3, *1865–1885* (Cambridge, MA: Harvard University Press, 1938), 543.

33. McClurg's essays with *Publishers Weekly* are printed in volumes 23, 28, and 29. McClurg also wrote one essay for the *Atlantic Monthly*, regarding his wartime experience with General Sherman, "The Last Chance of the Confederacy," *Atlantic Monthly* (September 1882): 389–400. For a full bibliography of A. C. McClurg's writings, see Morris, "Publishing Activities," 132–35.

34. Alexander C. McClurg, "Of Making Many Books" *Dial* (May 1885): 8–10.

35. Alexander C. McClurg, "Old Time Plantation Life," review of *On the Plantation* by Joel Chandler Harris, *Dial* (June 1892): 46–47.

36. Alexander C. McClurg, "The Red Badge of Hysteria," review of *The Red Badge of Courage* by Stephen Crane, *Dial* (April 16, 1896): 227–28.

37. Jackson Lears, *Rebirth of a Nation: The Making of Modern America, 1877–1920* (New York: Harper Perennial, 2009), 26.
38. "A Half Century of Chicago Publishing" *Publishers Weekly* (August 16, 1941): 456–59.
39. Smith, *History of the House,* 16.
40. John Drury, *A. C. McClurg & Co. Centennial, 1844–1944* (Chicago: A. C. McClurg & Co., 1944).
41. Smith, *History of the House,* 6.
42. Ibid., 11.
43. "A. C. McClurg & Co. Chicago's Largest Bookseller," *Publishers Weekly* (June 29, 1918): 1970.
44. Smith, *History of the House,* 11–12.
45. Ibid.
46. Record Book 1, McClurg Records.
47. Record Book 2 (March 5, 1912), McClurg Records.
48. Folder 516, McClurg Records.
49. Ibid.
50. Aptheker, "Introduction," 7–9.
51. A. C. McClurg & Co., "The Dial: Change of Ownership," *Dial* (July 1892): 85.
52. Aptheker, "Introduction," 8.
53. Francis F. Browne is described as the editor of *Souls* in Brent Hayes Edwards, introduction to *The Souls of Black Folk* (New York: Oxford University Press, 2007), xx; Shamoon Zamir, *The Cambridge Companion to W. E. B. Du Bois* (New York: Cambridge University Press, 2008), 10; and Henry Louis Gates, Jr., introduction to *The Souls of Black Folk* (New York: W. W. Norton, 1999), xviii. In another essay, Susan Belasco makes the reverse error, identifying Francis G. Browne as the founder of the *Dial*: "The Cultural Work of National Magazines," *A History of the Book in America*, vol. 3, *The Industrial Book, 1840–1880* (Chapel Hill: University of North Carolina Press, 2007), 259.
54. Barbara Cantalupo, introduction to *Other Things Being Equal* (Detroit: Wayne State University Press, 2002), 9–58.
55. Emma Wolf, *The Joy of Life* (Chicago: A. C. McClurg & Co., 1896); Emma Wolf, *Heirs of Yesterday* (Chicago: A. C. McClurg & Co., 1900). The latter novel includes Jewish content, but *Joy of Life* does not. Barbara Cantalupo and Lori Harrison-Kahan have a forthcoming edition of *Heirs of Yesterday*, with an introduction that discusses the novel's publication history. Harrison-Kahan is also working on a book, *West of the Ghetto*, that will examine Emma Wolf among a group of San Francisco-based Jewish writers.
56. Robert Ames Bennet, *For The White Christ* (Chicago: A. C. McClurg & Co., 1905), 11.
57. W. E. B. Du Bois, "Strivings of the Negro People," *Atlantic Monthly* (August 1897): 194–98.
58. W. E. B. Du Bois, "The Freedman's Bureau," *Atlantic Monthly* (March 1901): 354–65.

59. W. E. B. Du Bois, "A Negro Schoolmaster in the New South," *Atlantic Monthly* (January 1899): 99–104; W. E. B. Du Bois, "Of the Training of Black Men," *Atlantic Monthly* (September 1902): 287–97.

60. On Du Bois and music, see Jack Kerkering, "Of Me and Mine: The Music of Racial Identity in Whitman and Lanier, Dvorak and Du Bois," *American Literature* 71, no. 1 (2001): 147–84; Eric J. Sundquist, *To Wake the Nations: Race in the Making of American Literature* (Cambridge, MA: Harvard University Press, 1993), 271–454.

61. W. E. B. Du Bois, "The Evolution of Negro Leadership," *Dial* (July 16, 1901): 53–55.

62. W. E. B. Du Bois, "The Negro as He Really Is," *World's Work* (June 1901): 848–66.

63. W. E. B. Du Bois, *The Souls of Black Folk* (Millwood, NY: Kraus-Thomson, 1973), viii. Subsequent quotations of the text are from this Kraus-Thomson edition.

64. On Du Bois and religion, see Edward J. Blum, *W. E. B. Du Bois: American Prophet* (Philadelphia: University of Pennsylvania Press, 2007); Jonathon S. Kahn, *Divine Discontent: The Religious Imagination of W. E. B. Du Bois* (Oxford: Oxford University Press, 2009); Jerold J. Savory, "The Rending of the Veil in W. E. B. Du Bois's *The Souls of Black Folk*," *CLA Journal* 15 (1972): 334–37; Shamoon Zamir, *Dark Voices: W. E. B. Du Bois and American Thought, 1888–1903* (Chicago: University of Chicago Press, 1995).

65. Shamoon Zamir, "*The Souls of Black Folk:* Thought and Afterthought," in *The Cambridge Companion to W. E. B. Du Bois* (New York: Cambridge University Press, 2008), 7–36.

66. Du Bois, *Souls of Black Folk* (1973), vii.

67. Ibid., 265.

68. A. C. McClurg & Co. to Du Bois, January 21, 1903, Du Bois Papers.

69. A. C. McClurg & Co. to Du Bois, January 30, 1903, Du Bois Papers.

70. "The Souls of Black Folk," advertisement, *New York Times*, March 21, 1903, BR12.

71. "The Souls of Black Folk," advertisement, *Literary Digest* (July 11, 1904): 56.

72. A. C. McClurg & Co. to Du Bois, March 5, 1903, Du Bois Papers.

73. A. C. McClurg & Co. to Du Bois, March 16, 1903, Du Bois Papers.

74. A. C. McClurg & Co. to Du Bois, March 9, 1903, Du Bois Papers.

75. Du Bois, *Souls of Black Folk* (1973), 52. I am indebted to Christopher Dingwall for pointing out that this line remains in the text. His book in progress, *Selling Slavery: Race and the Industry of American Culture*, includes excellent research on the marketing of *Souls.*

76. Aptheker, "Introduction," 14–34.

77. Review of *The Souls of Black Folk, Nation,* June 11, 1903, 481–82.

78. Review of *The Souls of Black Folk, Los Angeles Times,* July 27, 1903, 8.

79. Elia W. Peattie, "Souls of Black Men," *Chicago Daily Tribune,* May 2, 1903, 17.

80. Du Bois, *Souls of Black Folk* (1973), vii.

81. "The Negro Question," *New York Times,* April 25, 1903, BR7.

82. Aptheker, "Introduction."

83. Louis R. Harlan, introduction to *The Booker T. Washington Papers,* vol. 1, *The Autobiographical Writings* (Urbana: University of Illinois Press, 1972), xxxiv.

84. Aptheker, "Introduction," 45.

85. Du Bois to A. C. McClurg & Co., March 4, 1926, Du Bois Papers.

86. Folder 112, McClurg Records.

87. Ibid.

88. W. E. B. Du Bois, *Darkwater: Voices from Within the Veil* (Millwood, NY: Kraus-Thomson, 1975), 29–52.

89. W. E. B. Du Bois, *The Autobiography of W. E. B. Du Bois* (New York: International Publishers, 1968), 205–35.

90. Du Bois, *Souls of Black Folk* (1973), ix.

91. Ibid., x–xi.

92. Ibid.

93. Mary Chapman, introduction to *Becoming Sui Sin Far: Early Fiction, Journalism, and Travel Writing* by Edith Maude Eaton (Toronto: McGill-Queen's University Press, 2016), xvi.

94. "Sui Sin Far, the Half Chinese Writer, Tells of Her Career," *Boston Globe*, May 5, 1912, SM6.

95. Annette White-Parks, *Sui Sin Far/Edith Maude Eaton: A Literary Biography* (Urbana: University of Illinois Press, 1995), 15–18.

96. For more on women writers and journalism at the turn of the century, see James P. Danky and Wayne Wiegand, eds., *Women in Print: Essays on the Print Culture of American Women from the Nineteenth and Twentieth Centuries* (Madison: University of Wisconsin Press, 2006); Sharon M. Harris, ed., *Blue Pencils and Hidden Hands: Women Editing Periodicals, 1830–1910* (Boston: Northeastern University Press, 2004); Jean Marie Lutes, "Beyond the Bounds of the Book: Periodical Studies and Women Writers of the Late Nineteenth and Early Twentieth Centuries," *Legacy: A Journal of American Women Writers* 27, no. 2 (2010): 336–56; Karen Roggenkamp, *Narrating the News: New Journalism and Literary Genre in Late Nineteenth-Century American Newspapers and Fiction* (Kent, OH: Kent State University Press, 2005).

97. "Sui Sin Far," *Boston Globe*, May 5, 1912.

98. White-Parks, *Sui Sin Far*, 26.

99. Mary Chapman, "Finding Edith Eaton," *Legacy: A Journal of Women Writers* 29, no. 2 (2012): 263–69, quote on 264.

100. White-Parks, *Sui Sin Far*, 36–42.

101. "Sui Sin Far," *Boston Globe*, May 5, 1912.

102. Sui Sin Far, *Mrs. Spring Fragrance*, ed. Hsuan L. Hsu (Ontario: Broadview Press, 2011), 53. All citations of the text of *Mrs. Spring Fragrance* refer to this 2011 Broadview edition.

103. Although Winnifred Eaton has sometimes been criticized for choosing to pass as Japanese, a number of critics have offered more sympathetic perspectives: Diana Birchall, *Onoto Watanna: The Story of Winnifred Eaton* (Urbana: University of Illinois Press, 2006); Huining Ouyang, "Ambivalent Passages: Racial and Cultural Crossings in Onoto Watanna's the Heart of Hyacinth," *MELUS* 34, no. 1 (2009): 211–29; Karen E. H. Skinazi, "'As to Her Race, Its Secret Is Loudly Revealed': Winnifred Eaton's Revision of North American Identity," *MELUS* 32, no. 2 (2007): 31–53.

104. Sui Sin Far, *Mrs. Spring Fragrance*, 227.

105. Ibid.

106.Ronald Takaki, *Strangers From a Different Shore: A History of Asian Americans* (Boston: Little Brown, 1989), 101.

107.For more on Chinese exclusion and anti-Chinese racism, see Erika Lee, *At America's Gates: Chinese Immigration During the Exclusion Era, 1882–1943* (Chapel Hill, University of North Carolina Press, 2003); Josephine Lee, Iomgene H. Lim, and Yuko Matsukawa, eds., *Re/Collecting Early Asian America: Essays in Cultural History* (Philadelphia: Temple University Press, 2002); Lisa Lowe, *Immigrant Acts: On Asian American Cultural Politics* (Durham: Duke University Press, 1996).

108.Edward Said, *Orientalism* (New York: Vintage, 1979), 38–41.

109.Takaki, *Strangers*, 110–11.

110.Amy Ling, "Pioneers and Paradigms: The Eaton Sisters," *Between Worlds: Women Writers of Chinese Ancestry* (New York: Pergamon Press, 1990), 21–55, quote on 21.

111.White-Parks, *Sui Sin Far*, 5.

112.Lori Jirousek, "Spectacle Ethnography and Immigrant Resistance: Sui Sin Far and Anzia Yezierska," *MELUS* 27, no. 1 (Spring 2002): 25–52.

113.Dominika Ferens, *Edith and Winnifred Eaton: Chinatown Missions and Japanese Romances* (Urbana: University of Illinois Press, 2002).

114.Frank Chin et al., eds., *Aiiieeeee! An Anthology of Asian-American Writers* (Garden City: Anchor-Doubleday, 1973), 4.

115.Sean McCann, "Connecting Links: The Anti-Progressivism Of Sui Sin Far," *Yale Journal of Criticism* 12, no. 1 (1999): 73–88, quote on 87.

116.Chapman, *Becoming Sui Sin Far*, xix.

117.Sui Sin Far, "Leaves of a Mental Portfolio of a Eurasian," in *Mrs. Spring Fragrance*, 233.

118.Hsuan L. Hsu, *Mrs. Spring Fragrance* (Ontario: Broadview Press, 2011), 233–34.

119.Cutter, "Sui Sin Far's Letters," 272.

120.Clara Kathleen Rogers, *My Voice and I* (Chicago: A. C. McClurg & Co., 1910).

121.White-Parks, *Sui Sin Far*, 199.

122.Sui Sin Far, "Leaves of a Mental Portfolio of a Eurasian," in *Mrs. Spring Fragrance*, 225.

123.Sui Sin Far, *Mrs. Spring Fragrance*, 35.

124.White-Parks, *Sui Sin Far*, 198.

125.Ibid.

126.Hsu, *Mrs. Spring Fragrance*, 233–34.

127.Elizabeth Ammons, *Conflicting Stories: American Women Writers at the Turn of the Twentieth Century* (New York: Oxford University Press, 1991), 119.

128.White-Parks, *Sui Sin Far*, 197.

129.Ibid., 202.

130.Folder 461, McClurg Records.

131."Sui Sin Far," *Boston Globe*, SM6.

132.White-Parks, *Sui Sin Far*, 202.

133.Folder 516, McClurg Records.

134.Cutter, "Sui Sin Far's Letters," 275.

135.Folder 115, McClurg Records.

136.In 1907, for example, McClurg arranged to collaborate with Small, Maynard &

Co. to reprint two of their titles by Ottilie Liljencrantz. Writing to Liljencrantz about the new editions, the company notes, "The form in which the books would be issued will be subject to our approval, so that there need be no fear of anything discreditable in their appearance. The main difference would be one picture instead of four, a slightly smaller volume, and cover stamped in ink instead of ink and gold." Folder 217, McClurg Records.

137. *The Plimpton Press Year Book* (Norwood, MA: Plimpton Press, 1911), v.

138. Ibid., 62.

139. Cutter, "Sui Sin Far's Letters," 271.

140. Sarah Pike Conger, *Letters from China* (Chicago: A. C. McClurg & Co., 1909), 375.

141. Ibid.

142. Sui Sin Far, *Mrs. Spring Fragrance*, 47.

143. Ibid., 52.

144. Mary Chapman has written about the story as a criticism of the suffrage movement and of predominantly white U.S. reform politics; Mary Chapman, "A 'Revolution in Ink': Sui Sin Far and Chinese Reform Discourse," *American Quarterly* 60, no. 4 (December 2008): 975–1001, quote on 988.

145. Sui Sin Far, *Mrs. Spring Fragrance*, 57.

146. Ibid.

147. Indeed, many of the book's characters take on autobiographical elements. Like Edith Eaton, Alice Winthrop worked in an office setting from a young age. At the same time, however, it is worth noting the similarity between the names of Ethel Evebrook and Edith Eaton. In a sense, Sui Sin Far aligns herself with both of Will Carman's love interests. In a later story in the collection, "The Wisdom of the New," Adah Charlton's name similarly resonates with Edith Eaton's. And then, in "The Chinese Lily," a character that is actually named Sui Sin Far sacrifices her own life for a disabled friend, Mermei.

148. Sui Sin Far, *Mrs. Spring Fragrance*, 58.

149. Ibid., 57.

150. Ibid.

151. Ibid., 58.

152. Box 21, Record Book 2, McClurg Records.

153. Ibid.

154. "News of Books," *New York Times*, August 31, 1913, BR456.

155. "Browne & Howell Co. File Petition in Bankruptcy," *Publishers Weekly* (January 30, 1915): 308.

156. Joseph King Goodrich, *Our Neighbors: The Chinese* (Chicago: Browne & Howell Co., 1913), 2–3.

157. F. G. Browne, "A Big Job to Put a Novel on the Market," *Chicago Tribune*, March 30, 1913, E2.

158. "News of Books," *New York Times*, August 31, 1913, BR456.

EPILOGUE: THE FUTURE AMERICAN

1. W. E. B. Du Bois, *The Souls of Black Folk* (Millwood, NY: Kraus-Thomson, 1973), 6.

2. Charles W. Chesnutt, "The Future American," *Charles W. Chesnutt: Essays and*

Speeches, ed. Joseph R. McElrath, Jr., Robert C. Leitz III, and Jesse S. Crisler (Stanford: Stanford University Press, 1999), 121–36.

3. Ibid., 134.

4. "Sui Sin Far, the Half Chinese Writer, Tells of Her Career," *Boston Globe*, May 5, 1912, SM6.

5. In the acknowledgements section of *Mrs. Spring Fragrance*, Sui Sin Far repeats this idea that writing is an act of motherhood. She thanks various magazines and periodicals "who were kind enough to care for my children when I sent them out into the world."

6. Sui Sin Far, *Mrs. Spring Fragrance*, ed. Hsuan L. Hsu (Ontario: Broadview Press, 2011), 226.

7. Wai Chee Dimock, *Through Other Continents: American Literature across Deep Time* (Princeton: Princeton University Press, 2006), 4.

8. Du Bois, *Souls of Black Folk*, 74.

INDEX

A. C. McClurg and Company: business records, 122–23, 146–48; history of, 118–23, 155–56; *Mrs. Spring Fragrance* and, 112–13, 147–49, 152; national influence of, 4, 9, 23–24, 113, 156, 157; *The Souls of Black Folk* and, 10, 111–17, 123–26, 128, 135–36; Sui Sin Far and, 139, 146–47, 153–54

Adams, Thomas R., 21

Adventures of Huckleberry Finn, The (Twain), 87

advertising: campaigns, 48, 63, 67–70, 73, 82, 128–30, 143; catalogs, 38, 40, 56–57, 59, 171n35; costs, 33, 39, 67, 72; exoticism and, 2, 13; fliers, 55–59, 62, 67–69; influence on interpretation, 20, 23, 51, 53, 55–59, 64–65; related titles, 25, 72; revenue, 101–2

African American print culture: novelists, 47, 82, 173n11; periodicals, 15, 66; readers, 19, 21, 116, 131; scholarship on, 8–9, 46–47, 63, 69, 117, 166n22, 173n15; white publishers and, 46–47, 116–17

afterlives, of books, 24, 136–37, 161–62

Aiiieeeee!: An Anthology of Asian American Writers, 142

Alemán, Jesse, 27, 42, 170n17

Alexander's Magazine, 21

ambiguity: in advertising 2, 59, 70; to attract readers, 12, 23, 53, 110; realism and, 59–60, 62, 71, 100; reception of, 19, 23, 61–62, 81, 107–8, 143; stereotypes and, 20, 64–65, 106, 165n13; as subversive, 4, 5–7, 19, 93, 96–97

American Indian Stories (Zitkala-Ša), 1

Ammons, Elizabeth, 5, 146

Andrews, William L., 47, 50, 75

Anglo-African Review, 4

anonymity, 12, 13, 25–26, 43–44, 92, 144

Aptheker, Herbert, 116, 123, 124, 131–32

Aranda, José F., Jr., 29, 32

Argonaut, 70

Arte Público Press, 27, 31

assimilation: coerced, 1, 12, 19, 84; into the middle class, 88–89, 98, 144; resistance to, 2, 5, 60

Atlanta Conferences, 111–12, 123

Atlantic Monthly: Chesnutt and, 10, 12, 22, 51, 61, 62, 65, 73, 78; Du Bois and, 111–12, 125–26, 143; "The Irish in American Life," 86; national influence of, 4, 51, 101; Zitkala-Ša and, 1–3, 5, 11, 13, 16, 18–19

Atlantic Monthly Advertiser, 69

author portraits: of Chesnutt, 55–56, 58, 62, 63, 159; of Dunne, 87; ethnicity and, 7, 46, 172n3; of Sui Sin Far, 143

authorial personae: ethnic identity and, 12–13, 62, 63, 69, 110, 126, 140–45, 170n16; impact on interpretation, 51, 107, 144–45, 158; manipulations of, 7, 17, 65, 139; passing as white, 56–57, 59, 141

Autobiography of an Ex-Colored Man, The (J. W. Johnson), 21